Globalization and Children

Exploring Potentials for Enhancing Opportunities in the Lives of Children and Youth

Globalization and Children
Exploring Potentials for Enhancing Opportunities in the Lives of Children and Youth

Natalie Hevener Kaufman
University of South Carolina
Columbia, South Carolina

and

Irene Rizzini
Universidade Santa Ursula
Rio de Janeiro, Brazil

Kluwer Academic/Plenum Publishers
New York, Boston, Dordrecht, London, Moscow

ISBN 0-306-47368-2

©2002 Kluwer Academic / Plenum Publishers, New York
233 Spring Street, New York, New York 10013

http://www.wkap.nl/

10 9 8 7 6 5 4 3 2 1

A C.I.P. record for this book is available from the Library of Congress

Printed in the United States of America

For Sharon Stephens and for our children:
Nafisa Rizzini Ansari, Moniza Rizzini Ansari, Carrollee Kaufman Hevener, and Athey Whiteman Kaufman

Contributors

Arlene Bowers Andrews is Professor of Social Work and Director of the Institute for Families in Society at the University of South Carolina. The Institute she currently directs is comprised of scholars and students from multiple academic disciplines who study the strengths, needs, and functions of families in changing societies within the southern U.S. and other parts of the world. Dr. Andrews is the author of *Victimization and Survivor Services*, co-editor of *The UN Convention on the Rights of the Child: Implementing the Right to an Adequate Standard of Living* and *Measuring and Monitoring Child Well-Being* and author of several articles and book chapters regarding family violence prevention and community systems development.

Gary Barker is Director of Instituto PROMUNDO, a Brazilian NGO that works on research, advocacy, policy analysis and training in the area of child and youth policy. He has worked for more than 15 years in the area of child and youth development, most of that time living in Latin America. He has served as consultant to the World Bank, UNICEF, the World Health Organization and UNAIDS, among others.

Malcolm Bush is president of Woodstock Institute, a 28 year-old research and policy nonprofit based in Chicago that works local, nationally and internationally to promote financial reinvestment and economic development in lower-income and minority communities. Prior to joining Woodstock, he was a regular faculty member at the University of Chicago writing about children and family policy including the book *Families in Distress: Public, Private, and Civic Responses*. His Ph.D. is from Northwestern University and his B.A. from Oxford University.

Louise Chawla is an Associate Professor in Whitney Young College, an interdisciplinary honors program at Kentucky State University in the United States, and Associate Faculty in the Doctoral Program in Environmental Studies at Antioch New England Graduate School. She has published widely on the topics of the development of environmental concern and responsibility, cultural

viii   Contributors

interpretations of nature and home, and children's environmental experience, including the books *In the First Country of Places: Nature, Poetry and Childhood Memory* and *Growing Up in an Urbanising World.*

Allison James is Reader in Applied Anthropology at the University of Hull and Director of the Centre for the Social Study of Childhood. She has worked in the sociology/anthropology of childhood since the late 1970s and has helped pioneer the theoretical and methodological approaches to research with children which are central to the new childhood studies. She is author or co-author of numerous articles and books on childhood including *Growing Up and Growing Old: Childhood Identities*; and *Theorising Childhood: Research with Children.* She has two co-authored books forthcoming: *Social Identities Across the Life Course* and *Childhood: Theory, Policy and Practice.*

Natalie Hevener Kaufman is Louise Fry Scudder Professor at the University of South Carolina and Faculty Associate at the Institute on Family and Neighborhood Life at Clemson University. Her books include: *Human Rights Treaties and the Senate: A History of Opposition*; *The Participation Rights of the Child* (with Malfrid Flekkoy); *The Implementation of the UN Convention on the Rights of the Child* (with Arlene Bowers Andrews); and *Measuring and Monitoring Children's Well-Being* (with Ben-Arieh et al.). Her articles have appeared in *Human Rights quarterly, International and Comparative Law quarterly*, the *Journal of Children's Rights,* and *Harvard Women's Law Journal.*

Elaine C. Lacy is an Associate Professor of History at the University of South Carolina Aiken. Her training in both the history of Latin America and in international business contribute to an ongoing scholarly interest in Latin America's economic situation. She has published a number of papers, articles, and chapters on politics and culture in Mexico, and is presently working on a book about Mexican cultural politics in the early 1920s.

Susan Limber is Director of the Center on Youth Participation and Human Rights and Associate Director of the Institute on Family and Neighborhood Life at Clemson University. She is also Associate Professor of Psychology at Clemson. Dr. Limber is a developmental psychologist, who received her doctorate in psychology and Masters of Legal Studies from the University of Nebraska-Lincoln. Her research and writing have focused on children's rights, youth participation, youth violence, and child protection. In 1997, Dr. Limber received the Saleem Shah Award for early career excellence in psychology–law policy, awarded by the American Psychology–Law Society of the American Psychological Association and the American Academy of Forensic Psychiatry.

Gary B. Melton is professor of psychology and director of the Institute on Family and Neighborhood Life at Clemson University. He is president of Childwatch International and a past president of the American Psychology–Law

Society and the American Psychological Association Division of Child, Youth, and Family Services. The author of more than 275 publications and a lecturer or consultant in more than 25 countries, Prof. Melton has concentrated his scholarly work in recent years on the application of international human rights law to child and family issues. He has received awards for distinguished public service from the American Psychological Association (twice), the American Psychological Foundation, Psi Chi, and Prevent Child Abuse America.

Per Miljeteig is Director of Childwatch International Research Network. He has served as Consultant to the World Bank Child Labor program, technical advisor to the Norwegian Ministry of Foreign Affairs, and leader of the Norwegian Forum for the Convention on the Rights of the Child. He has written papers and published articles on child labor, children's social networks, child–parent relations and policies for a better childhood, the history of day-care for children in Norway, and the history and the implementation of the Convention on the Rights of the Child.

Virginia Murphy-Berman received her Ph.D. in personality/social psychology from Northwestern University in Chicago Illinois. She currently holds the position of Professor of Psychology in the Psychology Department of Skidmore College. Dr. Murphy-Berman has published numerous articles in the areas of cross-cultural psychology and social policy evaluation and analysis. Dr. Murphy-Berman's current research interests include study of cross-cultural differences in ideas of fairness, social justice and in perceptions of children's rights.

Irene Rizzini is a Professor and a researcher at the Catholic University of Rio de Janeiro (PUC) and at Universidade Santa Ursula and Director of The Center for Research on Childhood; Rio de Janeiro, Brazil. Professor Rizzini serves as Vice-President of the Advisory Board of Childwatch International Research Network. She is the author of several books, among which are: *The Art of Governing Children: The History of Social Policies, Legislation and Child Welfare in Brazil; Disinherited from Society: Street Children in Latin America; The Lost Century: The Historical Roots of Public Policies on Children in Brazil; Images of the Child in Brazil: 19th and 20th centuries; Children and the Law in Brazil: Revisiting the History (1822–2000).*

Ross A. Thompson is Carl A. Happold Distinguished Professor of Psychology at the University of Nebraska. He also served on the Committee on Integrating the Science of Early Childhood Development of the National Research Council, which produced the report *From Neurons to Neighborhoods: The Science of Early Childhood Development.* He is Director of the Developmental Psychology Program, and a core faculty member of the Law–Psychology Program at the University of Nebraska. His books include *Preventing Child Maltreatment through Social Support: Critical Analysis; Early Brain Development, the Media, and Public Policy;* and (edited with Paul Amato) *The Postdivorce Family: Children, Families, and Society.* He also edited *Socioemotional Development,* and is co-author of *Infant–Mother Attachment.*

Brian Wilcox is Director of the Center on Children, Families, and the Law and Professor of Psychology at the University of Nebraska—Lincoln, where he is affiliated with the Law-Psychology and Developmental Psychology programs. He has published in a number of areas related to child, youth, and family policy, including adolescent sexual behavior and risk-taking, child maltreatment, welfare reform, and children and media. He is a co-author of *Big World, Small Screen: The Role of Television in American Society* and served as chair of the American Psychological Association's Task Force on Advertising and Children.

Sian Williams is Projects Technical Director at Caribbean Child Development Centre (CCDC), University of the West Indies, with responsibility for assistance to Caribbean Governments in early childhood policy and program development (funded by UNICEF Caribbean Area Office), consultation, and policy development regarding sexual exploitation and violence against children (funded by UNICEF Jamaica Office and the International Labour Organisation) and the Profiles Project to develop indicators and monitoring systems for the status of children and their learning environments on entry to primary school (funded by the InterAmerican Development Bank). She has worked in the Caribbean Region since 1993.

Kathleen K. Wilson is Professor of Community Development and Director of the Center of Neighborhood Development within the Institute on Family and Neighborhood Life, Clemson University. She has been involved in numerous rural community development projects around the world over the past 30 years. She is known best for her work at founding and nurturing community-based organizations that enhance positive outcomes in children, youth, and families. She has authored 27 books and numerous *What Works* reports useful in guiding the directions of community improvements.

Acknowledgments

This book is based on work from two seminars organized by Childwatch International: one in Cape Town, South Africa and the other in Kiawah Island, South Carolina, USA. We would like to thank the Directors of Childwatch International, Per Miljeteig and Randi Waerdahl for all their help with the organization and funding of that work. We would also like to thank Shelli Charles of the Institute on Family and Neighborhood Life at Clemson University for her invaluable help and thoughtful patience in the challenging tasks of organizing two international conferences. We are grateful to Rose September of the University of the Western Cape, Capetown, South Africa, for all her research, energy and dedication in helping to plan and organize the meeting in South Africa. We are especially grateful to Gary Melton for his vision and for his personal and professional support.

We are indebted to Carrollee Kaufman Hevener for her long hours editing and helping to prepare this manuscript for publication. We would also like to thank Sally Hansen, Julie Loggins, Delphine Ettinger, and Amy Lantz for their help and support in finalizing the manuscript. We want to thank William Myers and Andrew Dawes for their helpful comments on the Framework chapter.

Throughout our work we are grateful for the understanding and encouragement of our family and friends. Lee Jane would like to thank her partner, David Whiteman, and her other family members—Carrollee Kaufman Hevener, Athey Whiteman Kaufman, Susan Kaufman, Peter Waldron, Jacob and Miranda Kaufman–Waldron, Helene, John, and Jessie Rosenberg, Ted, Lynne, and Meg Kaufman, Murry Pierce and Kelly Lance. She would also like to thank her friends Robyn Newkumet, Eileen Newman, Angela and Alfred Nordmann, Elaine Lacy, Mike Scardaville, Martin Donougho, and Ellen Todd. Irene would like to thank all her team at the Center for Research on Childhood at the University of Santa Ursula and her colleagues at Pontificia Universidade Catolica (PUC), Rio de Janeiro, Brazil. She is also grateful to Gary Barker and colleagues at the Instituto Promundo for their partnership on projects designed to realize the ideas of this work in the everyday lives of children. We would both like to thank Malcolm Bush for his advice, his insights, and his enthusiastic support of the book.

Finally, this book was inspired by an idea of Sharon Stephens. Sharon was more than a friend to us; she was a great partner and an inspiring soul. The light that radiated from Sharon will accompany us in our pursuit of a better world for all children. Sharon will never leave us. Her compassionate heart, her beautiful energy and her open shining smile will always inspire us. Sharon's spirit was with us throughout this project and we dedicate this book to her.

Foreword

ALLISON JAMES

Globalization seems to be the word on everyone's lips, with politicians as much as academics extolling its benefits as well as its contradictions. For some, globalization means, in practice, that whether in Bangkok or Boston, in London or Rio, as travelers from wealthy countries they can be sure to find the beer, the pizzas, and the jeans that they can at home; they can be both at home and away simultaneously. For others, though, globalization has had rather different, often less beneficial, consequences. In their everyday lives people have come to find themselves tied in, albeit in often unseen ways, into larger economic and political systems over which they have no control; yet these systems cause radical changes—often for the worse rather than the better—in the pattern of their daily lives. And it is those who have least voice whose lives are usually affected the most.

In this book attention is drawn systematically—really for the first time—to a consideration of how processes of globalization variously impact upon the lives of children. Such an approach is not only most welcome in the field of childhood studies, but also long overdue. It will, at last, enable us to begin to contextualize in a broader framework some of the many issues to do with children's rights and participation which have long been discussed as separate and discrete issues within childhood studies.

For example, debates around child work and labor have been central within childhood studies and are frequently discussed alongside the difficulties involved in implementing, on a global stage, the UN Convention on the Rights of the Child (1989). The debate centers around the extent to which particular forms of child work might be held to contravene human rights or what might be the effect of a ban on forms of child labor in any particular local context. And yet often such economic/rights-based discussions are not extended beyond these arenas of debate and linked to considerations of children's broader political participation as citizens in an increasingly global world. In this book, at last, we find this lack being addressed in a comprehensive and meaningful way.

At the heart of this book, then, lies first the question of what a globalized world looks like and how is it experienced by children globally. Second, it asks how might children be encouraged to be participants in this globalized world,

rather than simply passive pawns at the mercy of the march of the globalization process. These are significant and important questions raised at a time
when, although questions of citizenship are very much to the fore in terms of
raising public awareness about children's rights, children's everyday lives are,
at the same time, at risk of being increasingly controlled and constrained under
the banner of "children's best interests." Central to the discussion which this
book pushes forward then is how those interests are being defined, by whom
and for whom on a global scale. If childhood studies have now come of age
then this book will help bring a greater maturity to this important and exciting
area of research.

Preface

PER MILJETEIG

This book is one result of a global trend that is not so much in the forefront when "globalization" is being discussed: the movement for children's rights. Its roots date back almost a century, when the British pioneer Eglantyne Jebb in the early 1920s started the Save the Children movement. She also convinced the League of Nations that children's rights should be on the agenda for international cooperation and spelled out in legal terms. This seed lay dormant for many decades, and sprang to full bloom with the International Year of the Child in 1979 and the drafting of the new Convention on the Rights of the Child (CRC). The prospect of a new international human rights treaty addressing children's human rights was controversial among governments, but it set in motion an engagement among non-governmental organizations (NGOs) worldwide. News about the negotiations in UN conference rooms spread quickly to interested groups around the world, and more importantly, these groups scrutinized the drafts and gave their feedback to the drafters. Some governments, such as the Brazilian, started drafting their own national legislation inspired by the budding CRC.

In the years since the CRC was adopted, we have seen an unprecedented early entry into force of this treaty. If skeptical in the outset, governments finally realized its importance. NGOs, both at local and international levels, started using it as guidance for their own work. At the same time they advocated strongly vis-à-vis governments to adhere to its principles, and vis-à-vis the public to make it widely known. Other groups were then inspired to take an interest in children's rights. One such group consists of academics and researchers, particularly from the social, medical, and legal sciences. They observed that CRC posed two main challenges to them: (1) To help interpret the spirit and principles of CRC—both in general and in relation to specific local settings, and thus help the implementation of it; (2) To develop a research approach whose results could benefit children. They meant research **for** children, rather than just research **on** children. This research approach required an inter-disciplinary approach not commonly seen before. It also was very conducive to international collaboration. The establishment of Childwatch International Research Network and the Scientific Committee on the Sociology of Childhood of the International Sociological Association are two examples of initiatives that are at the same time both the result of and contributors to this development.

Despite the very global nature of this new research approach, it was not very concerned with the effects of global trends on children and their daily lives. It has focused on certain issues of world-wide concern, such as child labor, street children, abuse and neglect, and children's participation to mention a few. Only in the last few years have we seen initiatives to gain understanding of how children are affected by global developments in general. What do the often dramatic changes in political and economic structures mean for children? How do they impact their lives and their understanding of their own situation? How do the less dramatic but quite influential developments in communication structures, such as e-mail and Internet, change the world for children and their access to information? Against this backdrop, a series of workshops was organized by Childwatch International and some of its member institutions. Scholars from various parts of the world were invited to share their views and discuss papers they were asked to prepare. This process also included people from disciplines previously not commonly associated with child research, such as political science and economics. They were invited to help introduce the necessary macro perspective and thus help expand our own perspectives. The organizers also had a "hidden agenda" which was to challenge people from these disciplines to take an interest in children's issues.

It is to be hoped that this book is just the beginning of a long series of efforts to look into global trends as they influence the lives of children, and seen from their perspectives. By being one of the first of its type, I also hope that it could help set the agenda for expanded international research collaboration.

Contents

Globalization and Children

Exploring Potentials for
Enhancing Opportunities in the
Lives of Children and Youth

PART I

The Global Perspective
Centering Children in the Globalization Debate

CHAPTER 1

The Impact of Global Economic, Political, and Social Transformations on the Lives of Children

A Framework for Analysis

Natalie Hevener Kaufman, Irene Rizzini,
Kathleen Wilson and Malcolm Bush

INTRODUCTION

Massive social, economic, and cultural changes, whenever they occur, are bound to affect the lives of children. Those changes might well affect children directly as in the case of war, migration, or rapid urbanization, or indirectly as their parents cope with new economic realities.

Although globalization today seems quantitatively different in scope from changing relationships between communities and countries in the past, the phenomenon of waves of settlement, conquest, or trade opening up a culture to other cultures is as old as the history of human settlements.[1] The contemporary patterns of interaction between countries are called globalization, partly because some phenomena affect so many countries and partly as a convenient short hand. There are many definitions of globalization because of the huge variety of types of contacts between societies.

The root *"global"* suggests change promoted by forces outside a particular society. For some observers, the growing influence of outside forces is the key

---

[1] Massively changing relationships between societies in the past were probably experienced as being as dramatic for the participants as any changes occurring today. Conquest, being sold into slavery, or emigrating to a new continent, affected the individuals involved as much as contemporary changes.

to the phenomenon. National governments and non-governmental local elites have less power or ability to exercise control over a full range of activities within nation states—economic activity, the flow of information, group formation and action, values transmission, and even the use of force. Rosenau (1997) has proposed that globalization includes "any development that facilitates the expansion of authority, policies and interests beyond existing socially constructed territorial boundaries" (pp. 360–361).

The effects of globalization can, of course, be as varied as are its constituent characteristics. Rapid industrialization may steadily increase living standards for many or few. In some countries rising gross domestic product (GDP) has brought better health care and education for children. Mortality rates have increased in some countries. New demands for increased job skills have made it harder for youth to connect to job markets (Sen, 1999). Speedy international communications via the Internet have mushroomed and can expose children with access to a computer literally to the world. This exposure brings new information and opportunities. At the same time these new influences might well undermine traditional values and ways of life. The transparency of a world covered by CNN can spotlight harms inflicted locally on children that might earlier have escaped attention. It can change the course of major events for good or ill.

Despite many legitimately different definitions of globalization we can construct a working definition that allows us to focus on some major impacts of global change on children. Globalization is a process that opens nation states to many influences that originate beyond their borders. These changes are likely to decrease the primacy of national economic, political, and social institutions, thereby affecting the everyday context in which children grow up and interact with the rest of society. Some of the impacts of globalization on children are therefore normative. Efforts to assess the effects on groups of children must be culturally sensitive. Research about the effects on children (and children's active and passive responses) is urgently needed if policies and programs that respond to children's needs locally, nationally, and internationally, are to be designed and implemented in a manner most likely to foster children's well being. Such policies are likely to be more effective if children participate in the debate about the nature of the challenges and opportunities facing them.

It should be apparent from the preceding paragraphs that global change can have positive or negative effects on children. But there is a concern that globalization has created significant inequalities. While the expansion of world trade has raised GDP in many countries and the absolute number of children living below the poverty line may have decreased, there is growing income inequality both within many countries and between northern and southern tier countries. The price of entry into some internationally competitive industries is beyond many countries. When young people are not able to enter competitive industries, there are enormous consequences for the work and wage opportunities. The development of global communications gives a competitive cultural advantage to those few countries with highly developed communications industries and hence heavily affects the influences to which children will be exposed. At its most stark, this phenomenon has been described as giving permanent competitive advantage to a few wealthy countries (Amir, 2000).

We have chosen to discuss global transformations along three dimensions: economic, political, and social. We are well aware that the processes of change and transformation are interactive so that some striking events may have local as well as international roots. In selecting some examples of change among a large number of trends, we focused on those that are likely to have a significant impact on the everyday lives of children.

ECONOMIC AND FINANCIAL TRANSFORMATION

The Major Forces of Transformation

Changes in national and international economies can be summarized in a variety of ways reflecting very different schools of thought. A progressive critique of the key changes sees the key overall change as a shift from the value of collective well-being and achievement to the value of individual opportunity (Teune, 1998). The major elements of this shift are: (a) liberating free enterprise or private enterprise from government regulation; (b) promoting international trade and investment; (c) reducing wages by de-unionizing workers and eliminating or reducing workers' rights; (d) eliminating price controls; (e) allowing the free movement of capital, goods and services; (f) reducing public expenditures on social and other public services by "privatization"; and (g) selling state-owned enterprises and goods and services to private investors.

Neo-liberals are likely to reply that the main purpose of these changes is to increase trade and production and that those increases will eventually redound to everyone's advantage—that a rising tide will lift all boats.

What is certain is that the scale of global trade and financial activity is immense. Foreign exchange trading exceeds a trillion dollars a day, though much of that total is speculative trading (Held, 1997). Multinational corporations (MNCs) are growing in size and influence. "MNCs account for a quarter to a third of world output, 70% of world trade, and 80% of direct international investment" (Held, 1997, p. 256). In 1990 there were over 35,000 multinational corporations with 150,000 foreign subsidiaries (Scholte, 1993).

The impacts of these changes are hotly debated. Some analyses suggest that average workers in the U.S. have lost out as a direct result of trade treaties. The North American Free Trade Agreement (NAFTA), for example, between the United States, Mexico, and Canada has been said to largely fail working families in each of the three countries. One analysis suggests that NAFTA has destroyed 800,000 actual and potential factory jobs in the United States, putting downward pressure on wages as workers move into the lower-paying service sector (Scott, 2001). This analyst continues, "Mexico has fared even worse. Imports have continued to outpace exports, leading to a global trade deficit in Mexico. The effect on workers has been stark—skyrocketing poverty, sinking real wages, fewer salaried jobs, and as in Canada, growing income inequality" (p. 1).

While many mainstream economists might reply that long-term, increased trade will produce higher living standards for everyone, that is little comfort to families facing massive short-term declines in living standards. Furthermore, some mainstream economists are pointing to disturbing short-term effects of a standard tool of development in southern tier countries. Some analyses suggest that the policy of the IMF (backed by the U.S. Treasury Department) of encouraging developing economies to open their capital markets to free flows of short-term foreign investments in the early 1990s led to the currency crises that dominated the rest of the decade (Blecher, 1999). The opening up of formerly closed economies led to massive private investment in export industries accompanied by freer trade and fewer restrictions on capital flows. Because these investments are built on foreign debt, the projects are very susceptible to currency crises. If a country is forced to devalue its currency, the foreign debt of the domestic firms will increase, and as more firms get into trouble, capital will flow from the country increasing both private and public sector crises. Such crises hit Thailand, South Korea, Malaysia, and Indonesia in 1997, and while South Korea and Malaysia recovered rapidly, the recovery in Thailand was slower, and Indonesia is still feeling massive political, economic, and social repercussions (Krugman, 2000).

Another vehicle for opening up the economies of southern countries has been loans from international agencies. New democracies that borrow from the International Monetary Fund or the World Bank can lose significant power over their national budgets. Sometimes conditions attached to loans have a direct impact on children. Loans from the IMF have sometimes led to cutbacks in health and education programs as countries struggle to meet debt repayment schedules. Debt repayment can account for a large share of domestic spending. For example, in Nigeria, where life expectancy is only 47 years, the government spent more on debt payment than on health and education combined in 1997. Under heavy pressure from non-profits and religious groups in 1999 the G7 group of countries dramatically expanded the Heavily Indebted Poor Countries (HIPC) initiative, and at the end of his term in office, U.S. President Bill Clinton signed legislation that provided $453 million in debt relief. While Oxfam, among other groups, argues that the HIPC countries will receive much less relief than the headlines suggest, the relief represents real progress. But some measure of debt relief is merely the first step in helping poorer countries ("Can Debt," 2000).

The complexities of current economic trends can be seen in the debate about child labor. By the standards of North America and Europe, child labor in some southern-tier countries is a massive problem. (It should be noted that there is evidence that child labor has been steadily declining for about a century, though it is rising in some countries.) According to the International Labor Organization (ILO), there are 250 million child laborers in the world,

30 million of whom live in Latin America and the Caribbean. Some research shows that labor has a negative effect on children's development as a whole. In Guatemala, for example, approximately one fourth of the children who belong to the economically active population do not attend school, and work is their main reason for dropping out of school when they reach the sixth grade. In some countries child labor takes extremely destructive forms. For example, again in Latin America, there is trafficking in children, which takes such forms as illegal adoptions, abduction of babies, forcing children and adolescents into prostitution networks, and trafficking of children by the military (Rizzini, Rizzini, & Borges, 1998). In its last meeting, the Working Group on Contemporary Forms of Slavery recommended urging states to strengthen the monitoring, prosecution, and punishment of police and government officials who are responsible for complicity in trafficking and prostitution.

In the case of child labor, the complexities of cause and effect come under two headings. The first is whether, in the light of the general decline of child labor, globalization has encouraged it in some countries; and the second is whether the response of the global community has done more harm than good. In this introductory chapter we will sketch out some of the arguments about the second question.

Just as the growth of international trade and international corporations create new global connections, so too does the growth of public and non-profit international organizations. We take up this subject in more detail in the section on political transformations. The topic of child labor has long been a focus of the ILO.

Some analyses of the impact of ILO Recommendations and other international standards about child labor argue that initially international standards did more harm than good because they did not recognize important cultural and economic differences among countries (Myers, 2001; Boyden & Myers, 1995). These analyses argue that Northern views of child labor, arising in part from nineteenth century British legislation, sought to ban child labor completely for children under a certain age. In Southern countries child labor can be seen as an important part of children's learning and development particularly when it is valued as such by parents and the community. However, because Northern views of children and work dominated international debate, international standards tended to reflect Northern views. Moreover, the implementation of inflexible standards could actually harm children. Boyden (1997) cites a well documented case in which thousands of children working in a Bangladesh garment factory were summarily dismissed from those jobs when the U.S. Congress considered legislation prohibiting the importation of products made with the involvement of workers under 15. The fired child workers ended up not going back to school but to more dangerous jobs.

More recent international discussions have recognized these issues and have tended to lay down principles rather than precise standards. The UN Convention on the Rights of Children (1989) gets around the problems caused by specific age limits with more general statements of objectives and principles. The newer standards are, however, sometimes specific about the worst harms caused by child labor. The ILO in its Worst Forms of Child Labor Convention (No. 182) produced Recommendation 190. Adopted in 1999, Recommendation 190 commits all ratifying members to "take immediate and effective measures to secure the prohibition and elimination of the worst forms of child labor as a matter of urgency" (Myers, 2001, p. 51).

The recognition of the value of children's work in some cultures does not, however, solve the problem that children who work to the exclusion of going to school will generally be condemned to the lowest paying sectors of their countries' economies for the rest of their lives. Not only do children need to be protected as they work, but also they need to attend school at the same time. We should also recognize that children who do not work may be harmed by the demands changing economies make on their parents. Non-working children may suffer from the effects of relocation as their parents move from rural to urban areas. They may be geographically separated from extended family and separated from their parents for much of the day as family members work longer hours or additional jobs to meet basic economic needs. Even in the urban centers of highly developed countries, children may have relatively little contact with parents who are working long hours outside the home.

A similarly balanced solution can be proposed in the debate about sweatshops that employ children's parents as well as children themselves. Many economists argue that the sweatshops of developing countries can be an improvement over the absolute poverty of the villages that new urban dwellers came from, and that those sweatshops are a route into a cash economy. Others argue that it is possible to keep the economic benefits of the new factories and press for greater safeguards. William Greider, a progressive economic journalist in the U.S., lists such safeguards as: (a) insisting that international corporations provide basic data about safety, hours, and wages to first world buyers; (b) setting standards first voluntarily and then incorporating them into trade agreements; and (c) attempting to exploit the laws in developed countries that apply to the host corporations to sue in their courts on behalf of workers who are maltreated in developing countries (Greider, 2000).

No introduction to the economic effects of global change can ignore the stark reality of growing inequality and its effects on children. Globalization is probably widening income inequality around the world (Zakaria, 2001). The degree of that inequality depends on how inequality is measured, but it seems that inequality is increasing, for example, between the top ten richest and lowest ten poorest nations. While poverty is falling, inequality is still rising. Thus, the poor are getting richer but the rich are getting richer at a faster rate.

The effects of poverty can be seen on gross measures of children's and parents' well-being. The World Bank reports a number of striking examples. Life expectancy in Sub-Saharan Africa is 50 years, and in Japan it is almost 80. Mortality among children under five in South Asia exceeds 170 deaths per thousand, while in Sweden it is below 10 per thousand. Over 110 million children in low-wealth nations lack access to primary education, while almost universal enrollment is the norm in industrialized countries (World Bank, 1990). Poverty in many countries is replacing or joining race and ethnicity as leading segregating stigma for children, and economic segregation clearly has political, psychological, and social repercussions. Gender interacts with poverty to cause particular harms to young girls. Among poorer countries or parts of poorer countries, the population ratios of women to men vary substantially. In the Indian state of Kerala, for example, there is a high ratio of women to men, whereas in China the ratio is low. The main reason seems to be the comparative neglect of female health and nutrition especially, but not exclusively, during childhood, and selective abortion is increasing in China (Sen, 1999). Gender also plays a role in reducing educational and social opportunities for young girls. They are frequently responsible for all the housework and care of younger siblings while their parents are working long hours (Rizzini, Rizzini, & Borges, 1998).

While it may seem obvious that income inequality is directly related to other important inequalities, a recent book suggests that income is often a flawed measure of general development (Sen, 1999). Poverty relief, Sen argues, is not a sufficient condition for permitting people full lives. If the goal of promoting development is for poor children and their families to achieve basic human freedoms, then we should concentrate on that central objective and not just the usual proxies for successful development, such as increases in gross national product or per capita income. (For a review of Sen, see Bush, 2001.) Both can, in fact, be inadequate and indeed misleading proxies for other indicators of well-being. "For example, the citizens of Gabon, or South Africa or Namibia or Brazil may be much richer in terms of per capita income than the citizens of Sri Lanka or China or the state of Kerala in India, but the latter have very substantially higher life expectancies than do the former" (Sen, 1999, pp. 5–6). The well-being of children depends on direct investments in their health and education as well as increases in their families' incomes.

The East Asian success stories, financial crises apart, point to the promise of modernizing economies. The big question is whether and how countries with less developed economies can take the same route. Is there a limit to the number of countries that can follow the export-driven model before an overproduction of goods and services results in a massive deflationary cycle at least in the short term as William Greider argues in his book *One World Ready or Not* (Greider, 1999)? Another problem is whether some countries lag so far behind in the resources needed to compete internationally that they cannot get to the starting line. One argument suggests that the economically powerful countries have crucial monopolies over, for example, technology, financial control of world markets, and access to natural resources to a degree that industries in the developing economies will be condemned to the role of subcontractors (Amir, 2000).

If it is true that some countries can no longer get to the starting line, children in those countries face the choice of migration or permanent impoverishment.

POLITICAL TRANSFORMATIONS

One of the most significant political transformations of the last several decades is the increase in the number of countries with at least nominally democratic forms of government. There has been a very significant drop in the number of authoritarian states: from two-thirds of all states in the mid-1970s to less than one-third by 1997. "Democracy has become the fundamental standard of political legitimacy in the current era" (Held, 1997, p. 251). By the early 1990s, 110 states had constitutional provisions that were "legally committed to open, multiparty, secret-ballot elections with a universal franchise" (Franck, 1992, pp. 47–48).

One extensive study of democratization describes the world as experiencing a fourth wave of democratization which began in Portugal in 1974 (Schmitter, 1996). This wave is distinctive in being more global, having a stronger regional impact, and less frequently interrupted with regressions to autocracy.

Latin America provides an important regional example. In 1975, only two countries in South America had elected presidents, while in Central America only Costa Rica had an elected government. Today there are elected governments throughout Latin America. These changes do not mean that full democratic rule has been consolidated throughout the region, but that democracy has been launched nearly universally (Dominguez & Lowenthal, 1996).

The relationship between democratization and globalization is not straightforward, but in some cases one of the conditions for new economic opportunities is some measure of democratic transformation. The price of entry into the European Community includes democratization, and the recent decision to provide international economic aid to what is left of Yugoslavia was clearly tied to that government's surrender of Slobodan Milosovic to the International Court of Justice at The Hague.

In theory, the growth of democratic regimes should improve the condition of children if only because a free press and free elections permit new debates about how to improve the condition of children. In practice, this improvement often occurs. Sen (1999) musters a number of reasons why democracy should be seen as a condition of development rather than a prize to be claimed after a country's economy has improved. There is no evidence, he argues, that freedom is inimicable to economic improvement, and many elements of that improvement, e.g. land reform, would seem to be helped by a population with basic freedoms. Famines, he insists, have never occurred in a country that is independent, that goes to the polls regularly, and that has opposition parties and independent newspapers. The reason is that famines very often have less to do with an absolute shortage of food than a mal-distribution of food and the poverty of a sub-population that makes food too expensive to buy in crisis situations. Lastly, he suggests that the public discussion that is permitted in a democracy is one key tool in reducing the high rates of fertility in developing economies.

During the transition to democracy, however, or in an imperfect democracy, children's concerns can still be ignored or the consequences of prior events can still exert harmful effect on children. In a country with docile opposition parties, widespread illiteracy and child malnourishment can still flourish (Sen, 1999). In Brazil, after the restoration of democracy in 1985, children and youth were still gunned down on the streets by the police or with the connivance of the police in Sao Paulo and Rio de Janeiro. In South Africa after the end of Apartheid, the newly elected democratic government was faced with the enormous problem of educating a generation of young people who had spent their formative years, not in school, but fighting against the white supremacist government. These young people were ill-equipped either to join the regular economy or catch up with their schooling.

The co-existence of democracy and economic change is not inevitable. One counter-example is Singapore where over the last 30 years economic transformation has been accompanied by the tightening control of an authoritarian "granny" state. China, with one-sixth of the world's population has pushed economic change while maintaining authoritarian control.

Paradoxically, even as more countries are adopting democratic rule, with citizens claiming more power to govern themselves, there are signs of decline in the power of national states. National decision making is challenged by the decisions of multinational corporations, the economic policies of the most powerful states and regional and global organizations. National boundaries become more porous to new ideas, people, and products, and to the problems of disease and pollution.

But as national governments lose some control over their social and political agendas, groups are organizing transnationally to take on the same issues. The organizations are varied: public and private, governmental and non-governmental, profit and non-profit, regional and global, addressing interests in many areas of society. These organizations create new forms of political participation that can affect even the strongest countries. Cathryn Thorpe has observed:

> Increasingly, this transformation of civic participation is redefining the terms of governance in North America, not only in the commercial arena but also on issues such as the environment, human rights, and immigration. Nongovernmental organizations, particularly grassroots groups, located throughout these societies are playing a growing role in setting the parameters of the North American agenda, limiting the ability of public officials to manage their relationships on strict government-to-government basis, and setting the stage for a much more complex process of interaction. (as quoted in Rosenau, 1995, p. 30)

Some of the new international civic activity has focused on the lives of children. The United Nations has fostered the development of international policy and law on topics not previously afforded serious international consideration, for example, the Cairo Conference on Population Control and the Convention on the Rights of the Child (CRC). The International Labor Organization has played an important role in advancing understanding and promoting action on child labor. The Defense of Children International has also played an active role. Research networks, such as the International Education Association, Childwatch International, and Save the Children contribute to improving the implementation of children's rights and providing the research needed to develop strong programs and the national and international monitoring of children's well-being.

Just as local activity can provide for an international debate, so international action can enliven local efforts. One good example comes from the work of UNICEF, which has direct connections with national governments and also influences policy through networks with local organizations. Non-governmental organizations (NGOs) have been involved in interpreting the everyday meaning of the rights expounded in the CRC. Governments are required to report to the Committee on the Rights of the Child, established by CRC, the ways in which they are implementing the treaty's provisions. In many countries, grass roots organizations have worked with international NGOs to produce "shadow" reports that sometimes contradict official reports and point to further reforms in policies and programs.

Brazil provides a good example of the interaction of local, national and international forces promoting the concern for the rights and well-being of low-income children. Brazil's Children's Act (1990) was born out of a national movement of NGOs, university based researchers, child advocates, and grassroots movements, including some linked to the Catholic Church. One of the results of this advocacy and social mobilization movement on behalf of poor children was a sub-debate about children in the context of the broader debate during the writing of the Federal Constitution, approved in 1988. This *rewriting* of the federal constitution included for the first time in Brazilian history, an article specifically pertaining to children's rights. Inspired in part by the CRC, the Statute of the Child and the Adolescent went through numerous revisions during the 1980s. With constant organization, advocacy, and public debate by broad segments of Brazilian society, it eventually became law in its current form in 1990. This statute, in terms of the level and detail, the scope of its protection and promotion of children's rights and participation, and the decentralized *method of implementation*, is considered one of the most progressive laws about children in the region (Rizzini, Barker, & Cassaniga, 2000).

Regional governmental organizations have developed their own policies supportive of children. The European Union, with its expanding programs, policies, and membership is an example of the potential growth and influence of regional organizations. The European Convention on Human Rights and Fundamental Freedoms, and the Court created under its jurisdiction, are affecting national law and political debate on such children's issues as corporal punishment, child custody, and adoption, among others.

The growth of national and international organizations about children and the resulting international, regional and domestic conventions and laws have certainly changed the language of the debate about children's conditions. The question remains about the particular impact on the actual condition of children and the possibilities for implementing provisions that remain unenforced. Another question that remains is the role children and young people should or could have in defining their condition and solutions to their problems and acting upon those solutions. In China, young people were at the center of the democracy movement that climaxed in 1989 in the forceful repression in Tianamen Square. Young people were part of the long and successful struggle for democracy in South Africa, though at great cost to themselves. Certainly the increase in global communication gives children the potential to have their voices heard in different ways. The national movement of street boys and girls in Brazil played an important part in including children's rights in the Brazilian Constitution. And at the global level, youth have participated at international conferences presenting their own perspectives on child labor, not as victims but as workers, and emphasizing the need for improving health and working conditions rather than abolishing child labor (Miljeteig, 2000).

SOCIAL TRANSFORMATION

The rapid social transformations of the twentieth century are as dramatic as in any century. Some are directly global in the sense that they involve different relationships between the inhabitants of different countries. Others, like rapid urbanization, are responses to domestic and international opportunities. We will briefly sketch just two examples and raise some questions about their impact on children. The first example is about the movement of people among countries (migration) and the second the huge increase in ideas and information within and between countries through electronic and other forms of communication.

Since the formation of human societies, there have been periods of massive migration, local and international. The second half of the twentieth century has been one such period. Some of those migrations have been voluntary but still dramatic. The U.S. 2000 Census, for example, shows some metropolitan areas gaining population for the first time in thirty years mainly because of immigration. As the gap between rich and poor countries continues to grow, mobility has become a major solution to the prospect of long-term poverty. People have always seen temporary or permanent migration as one way to improve their lives, and in late twentieth century, technology has made knowledge of attractive work options and the means of traveling to them more accessible. Families sometimes move their children within and across national borders to spend time, often on a regular, though temporary, basis with extended family members. These trips may be planned to reinstall bonds of language and culture, as well as familial relationships.

Some migrations are responses to harsher circumstances than poor economic opportunity and stem from natural disasters, and civil and international conflicts. The latter also create staggering numbers of refugees. A major organized response to a series of refugee crises was the establishment at the United Nations of the Office of the High Commissioner on Refugees. In 1997, 27.4 million people depended on that office for assistance and protection including refugees, returnees, internally displaced persons, and the victims of continuing conflicts.

Migrations bring different opportunities for different family members. It is a commonplace that older family members find adjustment to a new language and culture most difficult, but children can experience migration in different ways. Some adopt easily and cope with the tensions between parental values and the values of the new society by finding a path that acknowledges both. In some migrations, for example immigration to the U.S. from Mexico, families maintain close ties with both cultures, and children can gain from the richness of that dual experience. A study of inner city Los Angeles reveals that a large number of immigrant families are transnational, with children moving back and forth between their homes in the United States and the cities and towns of their parents' home country. That pattern suggests a mobility that could enlarge a child's life, but sometimes the effect is the opposite as fears about public life in the new country lead parents and children themselves to restrict their movement outside the home (Thorne, 1998). In the Dominican Republic poor families often send children to extended family members for care, frequently to distant locations within the country or to the United States, so that both parents can work.

The experience of migration can, of course, be mixed for any individual child. A reporter on a recent psychotherapy conference in London on "Lost Childhood and the Language of Exile" pointed out that the participants, all exiles themselves, did not see themselves as victims but as "lucky survivors of unlucky circumstances [who had] after all, ... overcome some of their pain and had transformed it to succeed in what we call the real world .... We even spoke of the advantages one gains when multilingual, of the expanded understanding that comes instinctively when crossing from one language to another. As children we could not know that, and felt only the hurts, the humiliations and embarrassments, experienced as outsiders" (Kurzweil, 2001, p. 481).

This quotation points to perhaps a universal feature of migration for children who leave home after acquiring their native language and a sense of their original culture. However, the particular circumstances of migration and arrival will create different experiences for children. What difference does it make, for example, when an immigrant family settles in a community with few other immigrants, compared to the experience of a child attending a Chicago public school where English as a Foreign Language is taught to children in over 50 different languages?

Migration physically moves a child to vastly new experiences. The explosion in electronic communication brings those experiences to children whose families stay in their home countries. Technical advancement in, and the global spread of, communications have caused a profound set of social transformations. These changes have made the world smaller by allowing instantaneous connection with geographically distant people and places. Computer technology including the Internet, satellite broadcasting, and telephone services contribute to the concept of the global village. Media conglomerates like Murdoch, Disney, and Time Warner are creating webs of global power for the transmission of news, opinions, and culture. These electronic connections promote and reinforce increased physical connections. Cheaper and more widely available travel, especially by air, has contributed to massive increases in tourism. In 1960 there were 70 million international tourists; a number that grew to 500 million by 1995 (Held, 1997).

As multi-national corporations threaten the economic autonomy of the nation state, these communication networks challenge the control of information by the state. In spite of efforts to restrict access to various media sources, national boundaries are becoming increasingly porous to international communications. Autocracies might still be able to control the physical movement of items and people, but they seem to have lost their capacity to control the flow of information across their borders. Satellite television, free radio, video cameras, computer networks, facsimile and Xerox machines, and cellular telephones all seem to have ways of getting around national (or imperial) barriers (Schmitter, 1996).

Some have suggested that the internationalization of technology may result in an equalization of the influence or cultural power between core and periphery states. Klak (1998) on the other hand, has argued that media influences are more unidirectional and are becoming increasingly so. The dominant role of U.S. corporate media interests is reflected, for example, in the media of St. Lucia in the Caribbean, where 95% of the television programming comes from the United States, and where the most widely read newspaper is the *Miami Herald*. On the other hand, the U.S. has seen a huge increase in Spanish and Chinese language television programming to serve those immigrant populations.

Technological changes have an important impact on children now that Internet communications are part of their world and an important instrument of socialization. In wealthy countries, children have computers in their own homes. In some southern countries, such as India, young people, even in remote villages, explore the Internet and participate in chat rooms in cyber cafes. The Gates Foundation in the United States announced in January 2001 that the Crownpoint Chapter of the Navajo Nation had become the 51st chapter to receive a new, public computing station through the Foundation. Four new computers were installed in the chapter house to give all 34,000 residents access to the Internet.

This example exemplifies the uneven distribution of access to global communications. A large disparity exists even in wealthy countries. The Gates Foundation quoted a National Telecommunications Information Administration report from 1998 that in rural areas, only 9% of American Indians had Internet access at home, compared to 18% for rural Caucasian homes. A more recent study conducted by the Kennedy School of Government at Harvard found that 57% of whites under the age of 60 had Internet or email access at home compared with 38% of black families. For households with annual incomes less than $30,000 a year those figures by race were 34% and 19%, respectively (*New York Times*, 2000).

Some people argue that the disparities in access are not solely a function of income. One academic commentator said, "The big question is why African Americans [in the United States] are not adopting this technology. It is not just price, because they are buying cable and satellite systems in large numbers. So we have to look deeper to cultural and social factors. I think there is still a question of 'what's in it for me?' " (Hoffman, 1999).

The vital question about access aside, some scholars debate the impact of computer and television use on children's development. Healy (1998) has suggested that the rush to technology by parents and schools might actually constitute a disservice to children. Healy cites work by David Elkind that suggests that school readiness, for example, has more to do with the ability to listen and express oneself, to complete a task, and to work with other children, than with skill on computers. Massachusetts Institute of Technology's Joseph Weizenbaum concurred; he expressed the view that children's interaction with human beings and the natural world are preferable to intensive time with technology. As with television, the greatest argument for limiting children's use of computers may be the question of time use and the diminishing of the time children, at least in wealthy countries, spend with adults and with their peers in a wide variety of activities. (See Chapter Eight below.)

CONCLUSIONS

This brief survey of the effects of the current wave of globalization on children shows just how large are the transformations in so many critical parts of ordinary life. On the other hand, it is possible to overstate the importance of these trends on a particular family in a particular place and to underestimate the strength of local culture that must adapt to but may also transform global trends in a local way. "Localizing dynamics derive from people's need for psychic comforts of close-at-hand, reliable support—for the family and neighborhood, for local cultural practices, for a sense of 'us' that is distinguished from 'them'" (Rosenau, 1997, p. 363). Those of us who are concerned about the well-being of children are very aware that many of their primary needs and concerns, like those of adults, are found close to home.

The entanglements of local, national, and international phenomena, however, suggest that the slogan of the environmental movement "think globally, act locally" is at best an incomplete strategy for the problems facing children, particularly in poorer countries. When the conditions under which a child works are determined not just by a factory owner but also regional and international trade treaties and conventions, local action on its own may well be insufficient to improve conditions. By the same token, no international convention will have an effect without a link to local action and power.

The differences in local reaction to international trends should not blind us to the broad facts of growing economic inequality. The fact that those inequalities are manifest to the poorest inhabitants of the poorest village via the Internet exacerbates their impact. There are also inequalities of other conditions that result, for example, from war, famine, natural disasters, and the worst child labor practices that are a challenge to all of us who say we are concerned about the condition of children.

The complexity of unraveling the impact on children of so many powerful changes in so many different circumstances is a challenge to our collective imagination and skills. But we should not embark on that task without the help of children themselves. Children are, after all, the prime actors who determine how they will respond to rapid changes, and many times they adapt much more readily than their parents and other elders. They are also the best informants about how they are reacting, not unbiased or all-seeing, but the actors with the "inside" information on how they experience the changing world (Bush & Gordon, 1982). The data collected from children can also be verified. "Clients' accounts of events are authentic, revisable and subject to empirical criticism just like other accounts" (Harre & Secord, 1972). Children also transform the world as they experience it, sometimes dramatically as in Tianamen Square, and sometimes more quietly as they chose among what is offered to them on the Internet. In so doing, they may help to shape markets, guide local political choices, and contribute to cultural change. Our efforts will be richer for their insights and help.

REFERENCES

Amir, S. (2000). *Capitalism in the age of globalization: The management of contemporary society.* London & New York: Zed Books. Second impression.

Blecher, R.A. (1999, April). Taming global finance: A better architecture for growth and equity. In executive summary of the book of the same title, The Economic Policy Institute website.

Boyden, J. (1997). Children and the policymakers: A comparative perspective on the globalization of childhood. In A. James & A. Prout (Eds.), *Constructing and reconstructing childhood: contemporary issues in the sociological study of childhood.* London: Falmer Press.

Boyden, Jo & Myers, W. (1995). Exploring alternative approaches to combating child labour: case studies from developing countries. *Innocanti Occasional Papers,* CRS 8, Florence: UNICEF International Child Development Centre.

Bush, M. Book review of *Development as Freedom,* Armatya Sen, New York, Alfred A. Knopf, 1999. In *Social Service Review,* 75, 1, September 2001, 514–517.

Bush, M. & Gordon, A. (1982). The case for involving children in child welfare decisions. *Social Work,* July 1982, 27, 4, 309–314.

Bush, M. & Gordon, A. (1978). The Advantages of Client Involvement in Evaluation Research. In T.D. Cook (Ed.), *Evaluation Studies Review Annual III.* Beverly Hills, California: Sage Publications.

Can Debt Relief Make a Difference? (2000, November 16). *The Economist.* In Global Policy Forum (2000). (December 4, 2000); global policy@globalpolicy.org.

Dominguez, J. & Lowenthal, A. (1996). *Constructing democratic governance: Latin America and the Caribbean in the 1990s.* Baltimore: Johns Hopkins University Press.

Franck, T. (1992). The emerging right to democratic governance. *American Journal of International Law,* 86, 46–49, 90–91.

Gates Foundation (2001). (January 25, 2001); www.gatesfoundation.org/press room/release.

Greider, W. (1999). *One world ready or not: The manic logic of global capitalism.* New York: Simon & Schuster.

Greider, W. (2000, January 31). Global agenda. *The Nation,* 11–16.

Harre, R. & Secord, P.F. (1972). *The Explanation of social behavior.* Oxford: Basil Blackwell.

Healy, J.M. (1998). *Failure to connect: How computers affect our children's minds—for better or worse.* New York: Simon & Schuster.

Held, D. (1997). Democracy and globalization. *Global Governance,* 3, 251–368.

Hoffman, D. (1999, July 19). Big racial disparity persists in Internet use. *New York Times* on the Web.

Klak, T. (1998). *Globalization and neoliberalism*. New York: Rowman & Littlefield.

Krugman, P. (2000, May 24–26). Crises: The price of globalization, Paper delivered at a symposium sponsored by the Federal Reserve Bank of Kansas City. Jackson Hole, Wyoming.

Kurzweil, E. (2001). Spanish scholars and London therapists. *Partisan Review*, 3, 475–482.

Miljeteig, P. (2000). *Creating partnerships with working children and youth*, unpublished report to the World Bank, Washington, DC.

Myers, W. (2001, May). The right rights? Child labor in a globalizing world. *The Annals of the American Academy of Political and Social Science*, 575. London: Sage Publications, 38–55.

New York Times. (2000, March 5). On the web.

Rizzini, I., Rizzini, I., & Borges, F. (1998). Children's strength is not in their work. In Salazar, Glasinovich, & Alarcon (Eds.), *Child work and education: Five cases from Latin America* (pp. 20–38). Florence, Haly: UNICEF.

Rizzini, I., Barker, G., & Cassaniga, N. (1998). *From street children to all children: Improving the opportunities of low-income urban children and youth in Brazil*. Amsterdam: Jacobs Foundation.

Rizzini, I., Barker, G., & Cassaniga, N. (2000). *Crianca nao e risco, e oportunidade: Fortalecendo as bases de apoio familiars e communitarias para criancas e* adolescents. Rio de Janeiro: USU Ed. Universitaria/CESPI/USU/Instituto Promundo.

Rosenau, J. (1995). Governance in the twenty-first century. *Global Governance*, 1, 13–43.

Rosenau, J. (1997, November). The complexities and contradictions of globalization. *Current History*, 360–364.

Ruiz, Z. (1998). *The impact of democratization in Dominican children's lives*. Paper presented at the Childwatch International symposium on the effects of political and economic transformation on children, Isle of Palms, SC.

Schmitter, P. (1996). The influence of the international context upon the choice of national institutions and policies in neo-democracies. In L. Whitehead (Ed.), *The international dimensions of democratization* (pp. 26–54). Oxford, England: Oxford University Press.

Scholte, J. (1993). *International relations of change*. Philadelphia: Open University Press.

Scott, R. (2001). U.S. workers must have fair trade. *Viewpoints*, Washington, DC: Economic Policy Institute.

Sen, A. (1999). *Development as freedom*. New York: Alfred A. Knopf.

Teune, H. (1998, July). *Concepts of globalization*. Roundtable presented at the meeting of the International Sociological Association, Montreal, Quebec.

Thorne, B. (1998, December). *Global economic restructuring and social relations among children*. Paper presented at the childwatch international symposium on the effects of political and economic transformation on children, Isle of Palms, SC.

Zakaria, Fareed. Some real street smarts: The protesters deserve credit for highlighting the problem. Pity they hate the solution. *Newsweek*, July 30, 2001, 25.

CHAPTER 2

Globalization in Cross-Cultural Perspective

VIRGINIA MURPHY-BERMAN AND NATALIE HEVENER KAUFMAN

INTRODUCTION

Globalization is defined in different ways by different disciplines but generally focuses on the decreasing importance of national borders in social, political, economic, and cultural processes and institutions (McLuhan, 1989). As a result of globalization, powerful new types of linkages among people and nations will be facilitated through the marketplace, the media, law, and technology. Movement of commodities, capital, information, and images across national and local boundaries will also be increased.

Although many potentially positive influences of globalization have been discussed, such as the opportunities it brings with it for increased flow of resources and knowledge around the world, these opportunities may not always come without significant costs. For instance, globalization processes have contributed to increasing income gaps between rich and poor nations, to the displacement of people and communities, and to loss of cultural identity among some nations and ethnic groups (Crafts, 2000; Schiller, 1996).

Scholars and the popular media in the West have tended to spend less time discussing the social influences of globalization and concentrated more on its economic implications. In this chapter we describe a cultural framework for considering the potential impact of globalization on the everyday lives of children and their families. We suggest that such a framework is helpful for facilitating the design of research that will assist policy makers operating in an ever connected world to enhance the well-being of children, their families, and communities.

CULTURAL DIFFERENCES IN FAMILY VALUES AND ROLES

Many definitions have been used to define the term "culture" (Shweder & LeVine, 1984; Smith & Bond, 1999). For example, culture has been conceptualized as a common way of construing or bringing meaning to events or a shared way of looking at the world (D'Andrade, 1987). It can also be identified as a system of perceived restraints that impose limits on the behavioral repertoire available for cultural group members (Poortinga, 1992). Culture can further be examined in terms of concrete behavior and shared values and behavioral assumptions (Stewart, Danielian, & Foster, 1998). Values in this sense define commonly endorsed cultural "oughts" or normative prescriptions for behavior. Assumptions, conversely, define shared beliefs about the nature of the world or an understanding of "what is".

Considerable differences exist across cultures in behaviors, values, and assumptions that pertain to children and families. For example, cultural variations exist in: (1) how authority within the family is viewed; (2) what is seen as the proper scope and timeframe for different types of commitments to family members; and (3) how loyalties and obligations to the self, the family, and the community are defined and balanced (Kagitcibasi, 1989). The settings in which children live and the types of connections individuals have with each other also show great cultural variability as well as customs and practices of behavior, societal "ethnotheories" about the nature of childhood, beliefs about the needs of children, and ideas about what constitutes effective child rearing (LeVine, 1974; Quinn & Holland, 1987; Miller & Goodnow, 1995; Whiting, 1980; Super & Harkness, 1997). An important question is how these cultural variations regarding the role, value, and function of children and families in society will mediate and/or be influenced by globalization forces.

INFLUENCE OF GLOBALIZATION ON CULTURAL VARIATIONS IN THE FAMILY

Some suggest that cultural variations in the family will become reduced and traditional collectivist structures will be replaced by more individualistic forms as the global marketplace enlarges. Some assume that this reduction will occur because individualistic patterns are seen as being more compatible with so-called "modernity" and the forces of economic capitalism (see Inkeles & Smith, 1974; Hofstede, 1980; Triandis, 1989; Giddens, 1990). In this view, families across the world are expected to become increasingly autonomous and smaller with less emphasis placed on large extended interdependent networks. Convergence to Western individualist forms, according to some, will also be hastened by the social and media dominance of Western cultures (Moghaddam, 1997). For instance, the global influence of CNN, Disney, and IBM cannot be denied.

Another view suggests that globalization and the breakdown of communication barriers may lead not to increased homogeneity, but rather to greater diversity in cultural values and beliefs (Jones, 1997; Canclini, 1995). Pieterse (1995) writes of cultural hybridization occurring through the formation of new global subcultures and the transformation of existing cultural practices into increasingly divergent forms. In this view, the impact of globalization will result not in a one-way flow from West to East, but rather will consist of multidirectional influences. Pieterse gives examples of a boy of Asian heritage in London playing football and a child of Native American background adding his or her own special flavor to a Mardi Gras celebration in New Orleans. Increased contact through telecommunications may also lead to formation of communities not tied to geographic boundaries but rather linked by commonalities of interest or experience. Thus, the very meaning of the word community and culture may undergo change.

Fukuyama (1992) presents a third view. He asserts that the push via globalization towards convergence and divergence may not be incompatible, and that we may see increased convergence at some levels and increased divergence at others. Fukuyama suggests that greater convergence may occur across nations in basic economic and political ideologies, with trends accelerating toward increased economic capitalism and democratization. However, he states that this type of convergence may take place within a framework that affirms cultural distinctiveness. For example, in Chinese culture very hierarchical and multi-generational extended family structures are valued. While China has shown increased use of capitalistic economic systems, they have at the same time maintained traditional values by utilizing more family-centric models of business operations. Thus, core values may be maintained at some levels while change occurs at others.

CULTURE AND CHANGE

Globalization influences may well hasten cultural change at multiple levels. New linkages among nations offer opportunities for people to explore cultural identities in previously uncharted ways. Through increased communication and contact, individuals may be nudged out of unreflective and automatic thinking about their cultural traditions and moved toward constructing alternative ways of viewing the world. Culture will provide a context from which change via globalization will be mediated and framed.

One cultural context dimension that has been much studied is so-called individualism/collectivism (see Kim, 1994 for discussion of individualism/collectivism). In stereotypic conceptions of individualism/collectivism, very different ideas concerning the socialization of children by parents and others to become productive members of society are also posited. Within these different conceptions, however, we see increasing examples of patterns in which seemingly disparate cultural values and assumptions have been combined. Furthermore, economic capitalistic influences have also been assimilated into individualistic and collectivistic societies in an interesting variety of ways.

Several examples of assimilative patterns are presented below to highlight the range of challenges that are present for the growth and development of families and children within different types of cultural contexts. These examples are also given to illustrate how globalization might work to facilitate the emergence of new cultural forms in which old dichotomies between the collectivistic and individualistic structures are less meaningful.

THE CHALLENGES OF INDIVIDUALISM:
A DIVERSITY OF PATTERNS

Economic capitalism, as stated, has often been assumed to be most compatible with individualistic, small nuclear family structures. In the stereotypic view of individualistic cultures, or what Kagitcibasi (1989) labels cultures of separation, a launching type model of parenting is endorsed. Here a main goal of child rearing is to prepare children for an adulthood in which they will leave the family and live self-sufficiently in a competitive, consumer-driven society (Smith & Bond, 1999). In this model, traits such as independence and assertiveness, which facilitate children's ability to ultimately separate from the family and function well on their own, are valued. The adult child's decisions concerning choice of career, decisions about when and whom to marry and selection of a community in which to live are preferably guided by personal goals, not the expectations of others (Triandis, 1989). Thus, another function of childhood socialization is to raise children in such a way that they develop a clearly articulated sense of themselves and their own values, beliefs, and interests. In-group boundaries are rather loose and permeable and the child and the eventual adult are expected to be able to easily form relationships with a broad range of individuals over the course of her or his life. This flexibility also allows individuals to move easily with changing market and employment needs. Caring obligations in individualistic cultures tend to be fairly restricted (e.g., the parent is obligated to care for the child, but adult children are not strictly obligated to care for their parents or for others in their extended family) and guided by personal choices, not imposed duty (Miller, Bersoff, & Harwood, 1990). Emphasis is on freedom and rights expression and development of one's own "voice" (Tyler, 1989). The family unit is separated from the broader extended family both functionally and emotionally.

In these so-called cultures of separation, too much stress on freedom and independence without balancing emphasis on responsibility and duty has been criticized as leading to loneliness, alienation, narcissism and the breakdown of the social order and commitment to others (Sampson, 1977; Bellah, Madsen, Sullivan, Swidler, & Tipton, 1985). Such cultures also express concern that rights may be overemphasized without concomitant consideration of the importance of societal obligations and cooperation. These concerns become especially urgent if one assumes that this independent type structure will be increasingly imposed on other cultures via pressures stemming from global capitalization. Some, for example, Greenfield (1994), suggest that there may not just be one type of independent family structure, and that through globalization compatible with economic capitalism, a range of forms may emerge. The work of Schwartz and Bilsky (1990) provides interesting data on how autonomy and social cooperation and commitment can be balanced in different ways among different types of individualistic societies. Schwartz and Bilsky have conducted major studies of the value patterns of a large variety of cultures and have identified several key dimensions on which these cultures appear to reliably vary. Three of these dimensions (mastery, intellectual autonomy, and affective autonomy) have often been associated with cultural individualism. Their findings suggest that these various elements of individualism may be quite different and may not always covary. For instance, according to Schwartz, the United States is a culture which is high on mastery and affective autonomy, but not particularly high on intellectual autonomy. Thus, in the United States culture, values that emphasize self-assertion, having control over one's environment, being competitive, and getting ahead of others and acting on the basis of personal desires and interests to achieve happiness are stressed more than values that relate to independence of thought and flexibility. The United States was also not as high as some other Western cultural groups on what Schwartz labeled egalitarian or voluntary social commitment to the welfare of others.

In contrast, Schwartz identified a Western European pattern in which emphasis on intellectual autonomy is combined with priority given to a sense of egalitarian sharing of resources with others. Additionally, in the Nordic cultures, a somewhat similar pattern of what might be called cooperative self-reliance was revealed in which value is placed both on the promotion of individual self-sufficiency and commitment to the welfare of others in society. Thus, children are socialized both to assert their own individuality and to connect to the larger community.

These alternative patterns of individualism suggest that the promotion of economic market capitalism may be facilitated in a variety of ways. Further, developing a sense of autonomy in children may not necessarily be incompatible with facilitating a sense of social cooperation and civic commitment.

THE CHALLENGES OF RELATEDNESS: DIFFERENT IDEAS OF ACHIEVEMENT AND COMPETENCE

In so-called cultures of relatedness, different challenges are present for adapting to social and economic changes presented by an increasingly interconnected world and global economic structures. In such cultures, children ideally should be raised so they will remain loyal and connected to the family over their lifetime (Kagitcibasi, 1994; Triandis, 1989). It is expected that during this period, interdependencies among family members will shift with the parents caring for the child when the child is young and the adult child caring for the parents when the parents are old. These caring duties are firm obligations, not personal choices. Thus, childrearing traits that facilitate the development of loyalty such as obedience and ability to be self-sacrificing are strongly endorsed. Ideally, the adult child's choices concerning whom to marry, where to live, and what career to pursue are at least partially governed by family expectations, as opposed to personal desires. Emphasis in child development is on cooperation and responsibility rather than self-assertion and independence. In-group boundaries are rather rigid and tight, and one is expected to form only a few intense relationships with a fairly small range of individuals over one's lifetime. The ideal family unit is the interconnected extended family.

There has been concern that too much emphasis on collectivist values may be seen as being stifling to children and as hampering the child's potential for inventiveness, individual achievement, and opportunity for creative participation in society. Heavy emphasis on in-group loyalties has also been believed by some to diminish individuals' commitment to the larger community and to the broader social good (see Triandis, 1995). The homogenization view would suggest that these potential costs of collectivist type values will be lessened as more interdependent cultural structures are replaced by more independent Western value frameworks. Those more in support of a diversity model, such as Marsella and Choi (1994) see modernization leading not to the obliteration of collectivist values, but to the emergence of new forms that are compatible both with economic growth and traditional values of relatedness. Marsella and Choi discuss, for instance, what they label Easternization effects to provide some examples of how collectivist values at the local family level can be successfully integrated with international development and opportunities for individual growth and achievement. Easternization refers to a process of social and economic development that involves alternative pathways and value systems than those that characterize Western societies. Although Eastern value structures are diverse, common characteristics across many Asian cultural groups involve emphasis on: (a) family reputation and social stability over personal achievement; (b) collective identification, particularly the belief that the family not the individual is the basic social unit; and (c) obedience, filial piety, and hierarchical power structures. Combined with this interdependent orientation is an emphasis on competitive achievement, although the form of achievement that is endorsed is quite different from the more individualistic Western model.

Similarly, Yang (1981) discussed the concept of social achievement orientation. This type of achievement motivation can be described as the tendency to strive toward standards of excellence that are externally determined and socially chosen. Achievement here is not seen as an individual experience, but rather as a means of bringing honor and glory to one's group. Children here are taught to realize the "self" through achieving and contributing to the goals of their family and extended in-group, not through independent accomplishment.

This emphasis on different patterns of autonomy and relatedness in childhood socialization practices has been echoed in work done by Kagitcibasi (1989; 1994) in Turkey. Kagitcibasi has identified the emergence of what she labels the autonomous relational self. In this pattern, unlike either the individualistic model of separation or the traditional collectivistic model of embeddedness, relatedness and autonomy are combined. Specifically, material independence of adult children from parents is combined with emphasis on lifelong emotional interdependence of families. Thus, separation is emphasized only in the economic sphere and continued emotional connectedness and embeddedness among family members is not negatively sanctioned but rather is promoted.

These examples suggest that children can be raised in ways that both support the development of autonomy and encourage a strong sense of relatedness with others. Emphasis on achieving and fulfilling one's duty may also not be incompatible and may be combined in a variety of ways that do not conform to the typical Western pattern. Through globalization influences these new types of collectivist structures may continue to emerge.

THE INFLUENCE OF LAW

Another vehicle through which new cultural forms may be reified is through international law. To the extent that globalization has contributed to the emergence of globally shared values, including universal principles of human rights and social justice, these values and principles are most clearly explicated in the international legal agreements which have been drafted and ratified since the end of World War II. Examination of many of these legal documents reveals similar tensions as have been discussed between the need to protect and assert the rights of the individual and the need to support and strengthen the bonds of the community.

Law and Values

Law reflects shared values and also functions to socialize citizens about desired and appropriate behavior. This socialization process is one formal means of maintaining and promoting cultural values (Melton & Saks, 1985). In a globalizing world, international law would play a formal role in the development of globally shared norms and values. Although there are some benefits to shared norms and values such as ease of economic exchange and ease of communication, there are as well dangers to universalizing norms and values, especially to the extent that the process is not consensual but dominated by a particular culture.

As we have seen, there are a variety of cultural perspectives and strategies for adapting to the changes which a globalizing world implies. No one of these perspectives or strategies need be considered universally superior or even ideal. International law, like constitutional law, rarely attempts to lay out rigidly defined detailed rules of behavior. Rather it reflects general principles and guidelines and describes constraints on allowable variations in the process of interpretation which is inevitably required in order for any law to be implemented.

International Human Rights Laws

One political reality of the late twentieth century is that the preponderance of control over economic, military, and communication resources lies with the West. The resultant power to influence the construction of global norms and values is undeniable. If we look carefully at international human rights law as one reflection of global norms, we find a preponderance of Western political, social, and economic values. Clearly, the approach taken to children reflected in international agreements places an emphasis on the individual as the holder of rights, a Western concept that goes hand in hand with economic individualism. What is crucial to be cautious about in the process of developing global norms is that we not allow a single world view to become dominant. We are arguing here that it is essential that the process of norm development continues to be one which recognizes, legitimizes, and encourages a full range of cultural strategies for achieving agreed upon goals. The daunting task facing the international community is to forge, in the most creative manner possible, a set of universal standards reflecting global respect for human dignity and the value of individual lives, as well as the value of group identity, while simultaneously supporting local interpretations and local strategies of implementation. This task will engage us all in a series of challenges—developing informed and sensitive ways to deal with the tensions and conflicts which arise from personal power struggles, on the one hand, and sincerely held value differences on the other. Such struggles are inevitable with any attempt to implement global agreements within diverse frameworks.

FACILITATION OF DIVERGENT MODELS OF CHILD DEVELOPMENT

International legal agreements and the systems of monitoring they have established allow for culturally diverse models of child development. This diverse development will occur, however, only if such agreements remain open to broad participation and interpretation, and remain sensitive to the desirability of culturally relevant strategies of implementation. Participation by groups who have previously been excluded from political power is essential if meaningful development, interpretation and implementation of globally shared norms is to occur. Tradition alone should not be a basis for setting aside widely accepted human rights norms. Often those who are the primary victims of human rights abuses have by these same traditions been without voice or power. To use a painful example from the southern part of the United States, many slave owners claimed that slavery was an important "southern tradition"; the application of "outside" legal and moral standards were necessary to challenge the "tradition" on behalf of the slaves who were allowed no voice. Infant betrothal, infanticide, rape and other ritualized mistreatment of children should not be removed from the application of international standards on the grounds that they are traditional.

In stark contrast, however, to traditional and exploitative practices which violate the very notion that children are human beings who are entitled to dignity, traditions and practices exist that promote the welfare of children and recognize their dignity, but do so in a manner that diverges from Western norms and expectations. As with all law, international agreements must be interpreted and applied in order to be endowed with social and cultural meaning. Even universal principles take on meaning only in local contexts.

THE INTERFACE OF LAW AND CULTURE: A NEED FOR RESEARCH

The interface of law and cultural values should be examined further. The cultural analysis outlined in this paper provides one framework for helping to generate types of research questions that could be looked at in such an examination. For instance, research conducted in the West suggests that children need experience with participation in decisions that affect them if they are to feel the world is fair and to feel efficacious (Tyler, 1989). Building on this idea, many international children's rights documents encourage attention to developing children's capacities for participation in their environments. Questions that cross-cultural researchers might examine include how the idea of efficacy is defined in various types of contexts and to what extent participation in decision-making increases feelings of efficacy across cultures. In individualistic cultures, for instance, attainment of one's unique "voice" seems to facilitate development of a positive sense of self. Western values also promote learning as an active process, requiring multiple opportunities for direct participation and performance by the learner (Bennett, 1988). In some less individualistic cultures, by contrast, optimal learning is assumed to be a more passive process, and status hierarchies more firmly dictate decision-making participatory opportunities. Optimal participation in such cultures, then, would be more restrained and more bound by role norms (Triandis, 1989). Different definitions also exist of what it means to achieve, to be competent as a child or an adult, to be committed to one's family, and to fulfill one's obligation to one's community. These differences need to be more fully investigated and understood if we are to develop culturally sensitive family policies.

We also need to more fully examine areas of apparent consensus brought about by the forces of globalization. For instance, trends toward democratization may facilitate increased concern with basic requirements for human dignity world-wide. An important question is the extent to which the elements of dignity are universal across cultures. For instance, in the West, dignity may be enhanced by achievement of personal fulfillment and individual recognition (see Markus & Kitayama, 1991). Within less Western contexts, by contrast, dignity may be more tied to adherence to cultural normative guidelines and fulfillments of obligations.

New cultural mixes have already emerged and will continue to do so through globalization influences. These mixes offer unique opportunities to reexamine old dichotomies and to revisit assumptions about what is in the "best interest" of the child. Cross-cultural research can be used to more fully explicate how change through both formal and informal means can be most positively structured across a variety of contexts to enhance the lives of children and families.

REFERENCES

Bellah, R.N., Madsen, R., Sullivan, W.M., Swidler, A. & Tipton, S.M. (1985). *Habits of the heart: Individualism and commitment in American life.* Berkeley: University of California Press.

Bennet, M. (Ed.) (1988). *Basic concepts of intercultural communication.* Yarmouth, Maine: Intercultural Press.

Canclini, N.G. (1995). *Hybrid cultures: Strategies for entering and leaving modernity.* Minneapolis: University of Minnesota Press.

Crafts, N. (2000). Globalization and growth in the twentieth century. *IMF Working Paper 0044,* Washington, DC.

D'Andrade, R.G. (1987). A folk model of the mind. In D. Holland & N. Quinn (Eds.), *Cultural models in language and thought* (pp. 112–148). New York: Cambridge University Press.

Kaufman, N.H. (1990). *Human rights treaties and the senate: A history of opposition.* Chapel Hill: University of North Carolina Press.

Fukuyama, F. (1992). *The end of history and the last man.* New York: Free Press.

Giddens, A. (1990). *The consequences of modernity.* Stanford, CA: Stanford University Press.

Greenfield, P. (1994). Culture as process: Empirical methods for cultural psychology. In J.W. Berry, P.H. Poortinga & J. Pandey (Eds.), *Handbook of cross-cultural psychology* (pp. 301–347). Boston: Allyn & Bacon.

Hofstede, G. (1980). *Culture's consequences: International differences in work related values.* Beverly Hills, CA: Sage.

Inkeles, A. & Smith, D.H. (1974). *Becoming modern: Individual changes in six developing countries.* Cambridge: Harvard University Press.

Jones, S. (1997). *Virtual culture: Identity and communication in cyberspace.* Thousand Oaks, CA: Sage.

Kagitcibasi, C. (1989). Family and socialization in cross-cultural perspectives: A model of change. In J. Berman (Ed.), *Nebraska Symposium on Motivation* (pp. 135–201). Lincoln: University of Nebraska Press.

Kagitcibasi, C. (1994). A critical appraisal of individualism and collectivism: Toward a new formulation. In U. Kim, H. Triandis, C. Kagitcibasi, S.C. Choi & G. Yoon (Eds.), *Individualism and collectivism: Theory, method and application* (pp. 52–65). London: Sage.

Kim, U. (1994). Individualism and collectivism: Conceptual clarification and elaboration. In U. Kim, H.C. Triandis, C. Kagitcibasi, S.C. Choi & G. Yoon (Eds.), *Individualism and collectivism: Theory, method and application* (pp. 19–41). London: Sage.

LeVine, R.A. (1974). Parental goals: A cross-cultural view. *Teachers College Record,* 76, 226–239.

Markus, H. & Kitayama, S. (1991). Culture and the self: Implications for cognition, emotion and motivation. *Psychological Review,* 98, 224–253.

Marsella, A. & Choi, S. (1994). Psychological aspects of economic development and modernization in East Asian countries: some issues and thoughts. *Psychologia: An International Journal of Psychology in the Orient,* 32, 201–213.

McLuhan, M. (1989). *The global village: Transformation in world life and media in the 21st century.* New York: Oxford Press.

Melton, G.B. & Saks, M.J. (1985). The law as an instrument of socialization and social structure. In G.B. Melton (Ed.), *Nebraska Symposium on Motivation: Vol. 33. The law as a behavioral instrument* (pp. 235–277). Lincoln: University of Nebraska Press.

Miller, P.J. & Goodnow, J.J. (1995). Cultural practices: Toward an integration of culture and development. In J.J. Goodnow, P.J. Miller & F. Kessel (Eds.), *New Directions for Child Development,* vol. 67 (pp. 5–16). San Francisco: Jossey-Bass.

Miller, J., Bersoff, D.M. & Harwood, R.L. (1990). Perceptions of social responsibilities in India and the United States: Moral imperative or personal decision? *Journal of Personality and Social Psychology*, 58, 33–47.

Moghaddam, F. (1997). Training for developing world psychologists. In S. Carr & J. Schumaker (Eds.), *Psychology and the developing world* (pp. 49–59). Westport, CT: Praeger.

Pieterse, J.N. (1995). Globalization as hybridization. In M. Featherstone, S. Laash & R. Robertson (Eds.), *Global modernities* (pp. 45–68). London: Sage.

Poortinga, Y. (1992). Toward a conceptualization of cultures for psychology. In S. Iwawaki, Y. Kashima, & K. Leung (Eds.), *Innovations in cross-cultural psychology* (pp. 3–16). Lisse, Holland: Swets & Zeitlinger.

Quinn, N. & Holland, D. (1987). Culture and cognition. In D. Holland & N. Quinn (Eds.), *Cultural models in language and thought* (pp. 28–42). Cambridge: Cambridge University Press.

Sampson, E. (1977). Psychology and the American ideal. *Journal of Personality and Social Psychology*, 35, 767–782.

Sassen, S. (1991). *The global city: New York, London, Tokyo*. Princeton, NJ: Princeton University Press.

Schiller, H. (1996). *Information inequality*. New York: Routledge.

Schmitter, P. The influence of the international context upon the choice of institutions and policies in neo-democracies. In Whitehead (Ed.), *The International dimensions of democratization*.

Scholte, J. (1993). *International relations of social change*. Philadelphia: Open University Press.

Schwartz, S.H. & Bilsky, W. (1990). Toward a theory of the universal content and structure of values: Extensions and cross-cultural replications. *Journal of Personality and Social Psychology*, 58, 878–891.

Shewder, R.A. & LeVine, R.A. (1984). *Culture theory: Essays on mind, self and emotions*. New York: Cambridge University Press.

Smith, P. & Bond, M. (1999). *Social psychology across cultures*. Boston: Allyn & Bacon.

Stewart, E., Danielian, J., & Foster, R. (1998). Cultural assumptions and values. In M. Bennett (Ed.), *Basic concepts of intercultural communication* (pp. 157–173). Yarmouth, Maine: Intercultural Press.

Super, C. & Harkness, S. (1997). The cultural structuring of child development. In J. Berry, P. Dasen, & T.S. Saraswathi (Eds.), *Handbook of cross-cultural psychology: Basic processes and human development* (pp. 1–41). Boston, MA: Allyn & Bacon.

Triandis, H.C. (1989). The self and social behavior in differing world contexts. *Psychological Review*, 96, 506–520.

Triandis, H.C. (1995). *Individualism and collectivism: New directions in social psychology*. Boulder: Westview Press.

Tyler, T. (1989). The psychology of procedural justice: A test of the group value model. *Journal of Personality and Social Psychology*, 57, 830–838.

Van Bueren, G. (Ed.) (1993). *International documents on children*. London: Martinus Nijhoff.

Whitehead, L. (1996). Three international dimensions of democratization. In Whitehead (Ed.), *The International Dimensions of Democratization*. Oxford, England: Oxford University Press.

Whiting, B. (1980). Culture and social behavior: A model for the development of social behavior. *Ethos*, 8, 95–116.

Yang, K.S. (1981). Social orientation and individual modernity among Chinese students in Taiwan: Further empirical evidence. *Journal of Social Psychology*, 113, 159–170.

CHAPTER 3

The Status of Children in International Law

NATALIE HEVENER KAUFMAN

INTRODUCTION

One of the purposes of International law is to lay out the common ground of understanding between two or more states and formulate that understanding into an agreement. Over time such agreements have come to be treated as creating binding obligations. Readers who are only familiar with international law through instances like the dramatic treaty breaking of Hitler's forces or the Iranian government's approval of the taking of the United States embassy mistakenly associate international law with pie in the sky idealism or paper promises cast into a void.

But the fact remains that the representatives of sovereign states take international law seriously. They are very reluctant to enter into internationally binding agreements; they meticulously and painstakingly peruse each word and comma, struggling to limit the nature and extent of the serious obligations they are accepting on a paper which they know all too well they cannot cast aside without painful consequences. That some state leaders do, in fact, act contrary to the obligations they have voluntarily accepted in no way changes the seriousness of their obligation or the relative ease with which the rest of the world can then identify that the state has indeed committed a violation of law.

The fact that human rights treaties have been drafted and ratified in substantial numbers and with substantive content in an age when sovereignty and nationalism are thriving, is itself a phenomenon worth investigating. Not only do the treaties define serious substantive obligations, but most lay out as well, a system of monitoring and implementation and some form of dispute resolution. We are surprised by this international legal development because human rights have until the second half of the twentieth century been, for the most part, a subject of purely national consideration. Human rights issues appeared to the drafters of the United Nations Charter, towards the close of the first half of the century, to be perfect examples of the need for Article 2 paragraph 7, which retained to the member states the right to cite national law in order to limit the international organization's jurisdiction.

The Charter and Judgement at Nuremberg and the Universal Declaration of Human Rights signaled a fundamental change in the conceptualization of the legal status of the individual, but the seriousness with which states have enlarged and expanded the domain of human rights has also signaled a fundamental change in the conceptualization of the state. To take internationally defined human rights seriously is to acknowledge that the idea of national borders as sacrosanct delimiters of solely domestic jurisdiction is an anachronism.

This conceptual change suggests that a new set of global norms is emerging, the very existence of which challenges our thinking about national/international dichotomies. If a state cannot claim exclusive jurisdiction over its own citizens within its own borders, to what extent is the concept of sovereignty usefully descriptive? This very question constitutes one of the only valid challenges which the right wing within the United States has made to the international human rights movement. They are absolutely correct in their claims that ratifying human rights treaties will subject the United States to international scrutiny and lay groundwork which could in the future be used to criticize in legal terms the actions of the United States government against its own people. Even without ratification, some human rights treaties have been so widely ratified, so frequently cited in international conferences and in UN resolutions, and so generally included in unilateral and international statements of government officials, it can be reasonably argued that the United States is bound by their provisions on the basis of customary international law (Kaufman, 1990).

HOW GLOBAL IS INTERNATIONAL LAW?

If we consider the large number of human rights treaties and the extensive ratification of these treaties with relatively few limiting attachments or conditions, it is impossible to deny that the formal apparatus of the state system has embraced a set of fairly consistent obligations which represents a new level of consensus on moral and ethical norms. Along with these treaties, we find an even larger number of declarations from international conferences, United Nations resolutions, regional international organization resolutions, unilateral, supportive statements by official representatives of governments, and individual state constitutional and statutory action which testify to the global governmental acknowledgment of the obligatory nature of international human rights norms.

Even when representatives of states publicly agree to statements of norms which they may not intend to implement fully or speedily, they are giving added force to the legitimation of the norms they adopt. And although the International Court of Justice stands symbolically as the ultimate arbiter of international law, it is in the national courts, national legislatures, national administrations, and national public policy debates that the impact of these norms will be most strongly felt. Government officials, members of legislatures, and national judges often find themselves caught up in rhetoric about human rights standards; although initially accepted with a view to applying them to foreign strangers they have been forced to see their application to familiar constituents.

Some have argued (Kaufman, 1995) that since the validity of international law partially depends on overt or tacit consent to the obligations set forth in the law, a process of law making or ratification which excludes significant groups may not be globally valid. For example, women's voices are rarely included in the formal governmental delegations that draft international law and may be absent, as well, from the governmental level ratification process. Children, or those who can claim to speak on behalf of children, will also generally fall into this category. An important exception to the normal process, however, was the very active involvement of non-governmental organizations (NGOs) in the drafting of the children's convention, including the most important child advocacy groups. Hopefully this example and the involvement of these groups, as well, in the monitoring process, augurs well for future international law codification. In addition to the participation of particular organizations, since women and children are not monolithic groups, it is especially important to seek diverse input into the interpretation and implementation of human rights treaties if they are to achieve the level of consent that would give them maximum validity.

Human rights treaties have also been challenged on the grounds that they often reflect western law and values and neglect the rich legal and cultural traditions of non-western societies. Although there is some merit in this accusation, it is important to note that multilateral human rights treaties were drafted by representatives of all the governments of the world and large numbers of non-governmental organizations. The normal drafting process allows as well for numerous opportunities for input from those not in attendance at the drafting conferences. Following adoption of the treaty there is, of course, a national process of ratification, which is in the minds of each delegation during the drafting process. Finally, most countries have a process of national legislation, which they use to incorporate the treaty provisions into their domestic constitutional system. Thus, a careful analysis of the drafting process of most human rights treaties reveals a very thoughtful and necessarily slow deliberation about each word and phrase primarily because the drafters aim for universality with respect for flexibility within maximally perceived allowable limits.

THE STATUS OF CHILDREN

What are the obligations vis à vis the child that states have taken on in the major domains of globalization?

The global recognition of human rights is one of the most significant dimensions of an emerging system of globally shared values. The extension of human rights regimes to encompass the least powerful citizens—ethnic, racial, and religious minorities, women and children—means that even the most vulnerable are now entitled to equal protection of the law. The creation of a High Commissioner for Human Rights is a more recent development which highlights the importance nations are attaching to the monitoring and implementation in this one area of global values consensus.

The underlying assumption of most law on human rights is the dignity of the individual. Individuals are posited to have rights because they are human aside from their membership in any particular national group. When we speak of inalienable rights, we are acknowledging an understanding that rights are not coterminous with nationality. One indication that this belief is fundamental is that when governments historically have deprived whole groups of people of their rights, they first deny their humanity and next deny them citizenship in the state. (For example, Jews in Germany under the Third Reich and African slaves in the United States prior to 1860.)

Thus, one of the hurdles for the group we call children is the presumption in many cultures that children are less than fully human; children can be denied fundamental rights until they reach an age of maturity. The rejection of the notion that children lack human rights has been developing throughout the century most notably since the Declaration of the Rights of the Child in 1924. The 1989 Convention on the Rights of the Child (CRC) lays aside any lingering idea that children are not entitled to human rights. (The Convention was preceded by the non-binding United Nations Declaration on the Rights of the Child, 1959.) The CRC covers the largest scope of any single human rights treaty and states take on extensive obligations for the survival, development, protection, and participation of children. The language includes all children and is in the form of binding obligations. "States shall respect and ensure the rights set forth in the present Convention to each child within their jurisdiction without discrimination of any kind, irrespective of the child's or his or her parent's or legal guardian's race, colour, sex, language, religion, political or other opinion, national, ethnic or social origin, property, disability, birth or other status" (Article 2, paragraph 1).

There are a number of regional rights documents that reinforce the international claim that children have legal rights. The European Convention on Human Rights and Fundamental Freedoms (1950) uses "everyone" in Article 5 (liberty and security of person) and Article 8 (respect for privacy, family life, home and correspondence) so one might presume that children are included. The European Social Charter (1961) most specifically in Article 7 (protection of children and young people at work), Article 10 (right to vocational education), and Article 17 (social and economic protection for mothers and children) specifically include children as those having rights.

In the American Convention on Human Rights (1969) Article 16 is devoted entirely to the "Rights of children," which protects children's status as minors, states their right to be with their parents, and their right to free education. And under Article 19 the child is entitled to protection by the family, society and the state. The child's education rights are elaborated in Article 13 of a protocol to this convention focusing on economic, social and cultural rights (1988).

Africa is the only region that has a separate regional agreement on children's rights, the African Charter on the Rights and Welfare of the Child (1990) (ACRWC). This document covers the same rights domains as the CRC and has specific articles devoted to regional concerns such as Article 26 on protection against apartheid and discrimination and Article 30 on children of imprisoned mothers. The Charter also sets up a regional committee to monitor the rights of the child as set forth in the treaty.

There are numerous other international legal agreements with one or more references to children's rights. Some will be discussed below as relevant to the domain of globalization.

To exemplify the globalization of human rights norms for children, we can look briefly at the concept of the dignity of the person which is essential to the very definition of what it means to have rights, and finds a central place in the CRC. One example of a norm that has been newly developed in the second half of this century is that of the right of the child to protection from abuse. Here is an issue which is still controversial within states, basically in tension with the right of the family to privacy, and in line with longstanding attitudes that the child is the property of the parents. As Van Bueren (1995) has pointed out, the lack of reservations to the CRC articles on abuse and neglect are a positive sign that states are willing to entertain the idea that children have the right to live in families without being subject to emotional or physical abuse (Article 19, paragraph 1).

Also related to respect for the dignity of the child is the even more controversial emergent norm prohibiting corporal punishment as degrading and humiliating. The Riyadh Guidelines aimed at the prevention of juvenile delinquency, for example, recommend "the avoidance of harsh disciplinary measures, particularly corporal punishment" (Section IV, paragraph 21 (h)). An example of this changing norm is an effort in Scandinavia to prohibit parental corporal punishment. The European Commission on Human Rights upheld a Swedish law prohibiting parental corporal punishment when it was challenged by Swedish parents, on the grounds of the vulnerability of children. The decision means that states that have ratified the European Convention are not required to abolish parental corporal punishment, but that if they choose to do so, they are not violating the rights of parents. One may hope that as research on the damage of corporal punishment and its conflict with the dignity of the child is more widely promulgated, a potential limitation on parental abuse may gain international status.

Although the CRC does not specifically prohibit parental corporal punishment, it is increasingly difficult to reconcile such practice with the convention's emphasis on the dignity of the child. The convention does provide a basis for eliminating corporal punishment in schools in one of the articles on education. Article 28, paragraph 2 requires states to "ensure that school discipline is administered in a manner consistent with the child's human dignity...." For children in the juvenile justice system, an especially vulnerable population, the United Nations Standard Minimum Rules for the Administration of Juvenile

Justice (The Beijing Rules) (1985) clearly states that "juveniles shall not be subject to corporal punishment" (Article 17.3).

GLOBAL DEMOCRATIZATION

Among the globally shared values are the prohibition on colonization, a
structural pillar of nineteenth century European foreign and economic policy,
and the right of self-determination. The international legal instruments which
affirm these values link the implementation of human rights to democratic
rule. Those who drafted the post World War II human rights treaties believed
that human rights were essential to democracy and that the international
protection of human rights was a method of preventing any future fascist
war making. Human rights are integral to our current understanding of what
democratization means.

With the increase in the number of democratic states has come a concomitant drop in the number of authoritarian states: from two-thirds of all
states in the mid-70's to less than one third by 1997. By the early 1990's 110
states had constitutional provisions that they were "legally committed to open
multiparty, secret-ballot elections with a universal franchise" (Franck, 1992,
pp. 47–48).

Although we are not yet entirely clear on the link between globalization
and democratization, there appears to be substantial analysis suggesting that
democracy is "contagious."

> ... [S]tudents of democratization have tended to concentrate on the internal dynamics
> of institution-building and mutual accommodation, regarding the international com-
> ponent of the generation of consent as generally secondary in importance .... Although
> there will always be some purely domestic and some exclusively international factors
> involved, most of the analysis will contain a tangle of both elements. In the contem-
> porary world there is no such thing as democratization in one country, and perhaps
> there never was. (Whitehead, 1996, pp. 23–24. Also see Klak)

These observations are not meant to indicate that democratic rule with all its
full ramifications has been consolidated or that it is inevitable, but that in an
impressive number of previously authoritarian states, democracy has been
launched. It is difficult to imagine a definition of democracy that does not rest
on fundamental civil and political rights. The CRC guarantees rights to freedom of speech (Article 12, ACRWC Article 7), assembly and association (Article
15, ACRWC Article 11). Also, children have the right to privacy and the right to
be protected by law from any interference with their privacy (Articles 16, 40,
ACRWC Article 10). The legal system spells out basic legal protections for children. These protections include the presumption of innocence, the right to be
informed of charges, to not be forced to testify against oneself, to legal assistance, to an interpreter, and to a hearing by an independent and impartial
authority (Article 40; ACRWC Article 40).

The Beijing Rules also provide extensive protections including "presumption of innocence, the right to be notified of the charges, the rights to remain

silent, the right to counsel, ... the right to confront and cross-examine witnesses and the right to appeal to a higher authority shall be guaranteed at all stages of proceedings" (Article 7, paragraph 1). Yet the most crucial link between human rights and democracy is the prevention of unjust exercises of authority by participation in the life of one's society.

GLOBALIZATION OF PARTICIPATION IN CIVIC LIFE

The nature of civic life is changing in the late twentieth century. With increased democratization, more people than ever before are eligible to participate in the public life of their countries. Also, as barriers to participation such as gender, minority group membership, property ownership, and age, among others, are eliminated, formerly disenfranchised groups not only have access to voting and holding public office, but also to more active participation throughout public life, in their communities, and in national policy debates.

Some have argued that the strength of a democracy is best measured by how well it treats its weakest members. Children's awareness of democratic processes and their participation in them are required on the basis of the dignity of the child and the experience of childhood as a stage in itself. But it is, of course, also necessary for the growth of a healthy democratic future for the society. Therefore, we are not surprised that human rights instruments place a heavy emphasis on the participation of the child in decision making, not only in public life, but also in private life.

The CRC lays down strong bases for the child's participation in public life. First, children have the right to the knowledge about the system and information for decision making that are the prerequisites to meaningful participation. In defining the right to education, the CRC emphasizes the development of the child's personality, respect for human rights, and the preparation of the child for "responsible life in a free society" (Article 29). Similar language appears in the ACRWC in Article 11 and in the Additional Protocol to the American Convention on Human Rights in the area of Economic, Social and Cultural Rights (1988) in Article 13.

As important, research indicates that children need the experience with participation in decisions affecting them if they are to feel efficacious as participants during their childhood and also as adults. In fact, in some ways, children's rights documents present a model for participation that might be instructional for enhancing adult participation. The CRC encourages attention to the child's environment in promoting the child's developing capacities for participation.

A good example of this approach is found in the United Nations Standard Minimum Rules for the Administration of Juvenile Justice (The Beijing Rules). In setting forth the "Fundamental perspectives," Article 1.2 calls upon states to "endeavor to develop conditions that will ensure for the juvenile a meaningful life in the community, which during that period in life when she or he is most susceptible to deviant behavior, will foster a process of personal development and education that is as free from crime and delinquency as possible." And Article 1.3 asks that states focus on positive measures that mobilize family, community groups, and schools to promote the young person's well-being.

Creating an environment conducive to the child's well being would require increasing opportunities and incentives for child participation. For example, the environmental approach to participation is clearly elaborated in the UNESCO Recommendation on Education (1974), which devotes an entire section (V) to civic education. These provisions call for civic education which appeals to children's "creative imagination" in helping them to learn about their rights and how to actively exercise their rights and freedoms (paragraph 12). Furthermore, the recommendation promotes "active civic training" aimed at helping young people to learn about how public institutions operate, and programs that "increasingly link education and action to solve problems at the local, national, and international levels" (paragraph 13).

The Riyadh Guidelines (1990) recommend a similar approach, emphasizing the importance of developing active rather than passive roles for children. One of the Fundamental Principles in the Guidelines is that "young people should have an active role and partnership within society and should not be considered as mere objects of socialization or control" (1.3).

GLOBALIZATION OF WAR AND CIVIL CONFLICT

Children are heavily involved in armed conflicts as participants as well as victims—fighting and supplying forces in and out of uniform. Protocol No. 1 to the 1949 Geneva Conventions for the first time makes illegal the participation of children in hostilities (Article 77, paragraph 2). The CRC limits children's participation to those above the age of 15. (Article 38, paragraph 2) Also after much debate and pressure from NGOs (to raise the age), the drafters of the CRC also set the age of recruitment at 15 adding an admonition to select the oldest first. The African Charter, by not setting any lower age, effectively raises the age of soldiering to 18 since it obligates states "to ensure that no child shall take a direct part in hostilities and refrain in particular, from recruiting any child" (Article 22, paragraph 2).

Larger and larger numbers of war casualties are civilians and a large percentage of these are children. Since 1949 there is clear international law protecting children who are civilians in wartime (Geneva Convention No. 4 Relative to the Protection of Civilian Persons in Time of War, 1949). Intergovernmental organizations have established zones of peace during conflict, which allow children to be brought out and immunized as well as given special medical care.

Regionally, the ACRWC requires states to apply the protective humanitarian law of armed conflicts to all children (Article 22). But the African Charter and the CRC do not maintain the standard set by the Geneva Conventions Protocol. Both treaties use the much weaker "all feasible measures" when referring to the level of help required for civilian children in time of hostilities, although during the drafting "all necessary measures" was suggested (CRC Article 38, paragraph 4; African Charter Article 22, paragraph 3). None the less, taken as a whole, the current international law, although not nearly strong enough, does point to a high level of protection for non combatant children. In addition, the United Nations in 1993 established a Special Rapporteur on the Protection of Children in Armed Conflict (UNDoc A/Res/48/157 Dec. 20, 1993).

GLOBAL MIGRATION

The twentieth century has seen large scale movements of people across national borders for a variety of reasons. Some are voluntary, people in search of better jobs or living conditions; others are involuntary, most often resulting from internal and external conflicts. The Office of the United Nations High Commissioner for Refugees in 1997 oversaw the welfare of 27.4 million people: 14.4 million refugees; 4 million returnees; 5.4 million internally displaced persons; 3.5 million victims of continuing conflicts. One half of these refugees are children (UNHCR Guidelines). The Guidelines on Refugee Children (1988) promulgated by the UNHCR is a statement of emergent customary law norms, in some instances, codified in provisions of the CRC.

The CRC in Article 22 provides for the rights of the child refugee. Such children are entitled, when traveling with or without their parents, to all "appropriate" protection and humanitarian assistance, including all the rights in the Convention as well as rights covered in other humanitarian agreements. States also take on the obligation to work with the UN, other intergovernmental and non-governmental organizations to help refugee children to be reunited with their families. The African Charter reiterates almost the same language in the provision on refugee children (Article 23) and adds that the provisions apply "to internally displaced children whether through natural disaster, internal armed conflicts, civil strife, breakdown of economic and social order or howsoever caused" (paragraph 4).

GLOBAL COOPERATION

Just as global transportation and communication has made it easier for individuals and groups to commit violations of national and international law, so too, these advances have made it easier to bring about cooperative ventures to collectively address these violations. There are many treaties aimed at closing gaps between and among national systems in both law and implementation that are exploited by violators of children's rights. One example is traffic in children.

Governments for over a century have joined together to address the international dimensions of slavery. One dimension of the problem is that of traffic in children. Although there have for decades been agreements outlawing traffic in women, and later children, the CRC contains the most universally ratified and broadly defined treaty provision outlawing this crime. States have accepted an obligation to "take all appropriate national, bilateral and multilateral measures to prevent the abduction of, the sale of or traffic in children for any purpose or in any form" (Article 35). Clearly in matters of this kind it is essential to maximize the number of cooperating states, since national laws are ineffective for preventing and punishing criminals if violators are free to move without penalty across state borders.

The African Children's Charter also prohibits traffic in children (Article 29) and prohibits, as well, the use of children in begging. And the Committee on the Rights of the Child has plans for a protocol to the CRC focused on traffic in children.

Unfortunately, individuals also take children across state borders when they are unhappy with custody arrangements. Again, multilateral agreements are necessary to provide for prevention as well as effective and safe return of children. States are obligated under the CRC to help prevent the illegal removal of children from the state and to enter into agreements including already existing ones aimed at ending such activity (Article 11). The Convention on the Civil Aspects of International Child Abduction (1980) states as its purpose ensuring "that right of custody and of access under the law of one Contracting States are effectively respected in the other Contracting States" (Article 1).

Several regional treaties were specifically drafted for the purpose of promoting international cooperation for the return of children illegally taken across national borders. The European Convention on Recognition and Enforcement of Decisions Concerning Custody of Children and on Restoration of Custody of Children (1980) lays out legal and technical arrangements aimed at uniformly and systematically applying one another's custody agreements within Europe. And the Inter-American Convention on the International Return of Children (1989) makes similar arrangements for the Americas.

Another subject which is the focus of a series of international legal arrangements is that of international adoption and foster care. The seriousness and scope of this attention is apparent from the documents, including the: Convention Concerning the Powers of Authorities and the Law Applicable in Respect of the Protection of Infants, 1961; Convention on Jurisdiction, Applicable Law and Recognition of Decrees Relating to Adoptions, 1965; European Charter on the Adoption of Children, 1967; Resolution on Placement of Children, 1977 (of the Council of Europe); Recommendation of the Committee of Ministers to Member States on Foster Families, 1987 (Council of Europe); Inter-American Convention on Conflict of Laws Concerning the Adoption of Minors, 1984; Declaration on Social and Legal Principles relating to the Protection and Welfare of Children, with Special Reference to Foster Placement and Adoption Nationally and Internationally, 1986 (UN General Assembly resolution). There are also relevant provisions in the CRC (Article 21) and the ACRWC (Article 24).

GLOBAL TECHNOLOGIES AND COMMUNICATIONS TRANSFORMATIONS

New communications technologies challenge the monopoly of information by the state. In spite of efforts to restrict access to various media sources, transnational and national group efforts as well as foreign governmental activity make such restrictions increasingly ineffective. Schmitter (1996) links these developments directly to democratization. "Autocracies might still be able to control the physical movement of items and people, but they seem to have lost the capacity to control the flow of information across their borders. Satellite television, free radio, video cameras, computer networks, facsimile and Xerox machines, and cellular telephones all seem to have ways of getting around national (or imperial) barriers" (p. 34). One might add that anti-democratic groups outside of government with agendas of control face similar problems.

Some have suggested that the internationalization of technology has resulted in an equalization of the influence or cultural power between core and periphery states. Klak (1998), on the other hand, persuasively argues that the media influences, at least, are more unidirectional and are becoming increasingly so. He provides the example of St. Lucia in the Caribbean where 95% of the television programming comes from the United States and where although there are numerous small newspapers, the most widely read is *The Miami Herald*. "The mass media presents Caribbean people with more information about the United States than about their own societies, and what is shown about the Caribbean itself is often filtered through the priority system of the corporate-controlled U.S. mass media" (pp. 10–11).

The impact of these transformations on children is legion. Controversies rage over whether and to what extent computer technology is beneficial or damaging to young children and debates continue over the philosophical or commercial potential of children's television programming. The CRC drafters devoted an entire article to mass media, indicating their awareness of the actual and potential significance of media in the lives of children. States are obligated to "ensure that the child has access to information and material from a diversity of national and international sources, especially those aimed at his or her social, spiritual and moral well-being and physical and mental health" (Article 17). The article contains provisions referring, among others, to the cultural and linguistic needs of the child, especially those in minorities, the importance of children's books, and the need for guidelines to protect children from damaging effects of various media.

The Riyadh Guidelines also outline specific provisions related to the mass media, based on the assumption that the media has social responsibilities *vis à vis* children. For example, the mass media "should be encouraged to portray the positive contributions of young people to society" (Article 41). The Guidelines are specific: "The mass media generally, and the television and film media in particular, should be encouraged to minimize the level of pornography, drugs and violence portrayed and to display violence and exploitation disfavourably, as well as to avoid demeaning and degrading presentations, especially of children, women and interpersonal relations, and to promote egalitarian principles and roles" (Article 43). The American Convention on Human Rights, with a nod towards the potential damage the media can do children, allows for the state to engage in censorship "for the sole purpose of regulating access to [public entertainments] for the moral protection of childhood

and adolescence" (Article 13, paragraph 4). The European states have produced resolutions and treaty provisions focused on the potential damage of
advertising, on and off television, aimed at and employing children.

ECONOMIC GLOBALIZATION

For some observers, globalization is focused on economics. They point to
a number of economic transformations which indicate the decreasing importance of national borders in the international economic system. Even without
government spending, trade as a part of national economic activity has been
expanding. Although trade is concentrated within the regions of Europe, North
America, and Pacific Asia, trade between regions has been growing as well.
More states are involved in bilateral trading and larger populations are affected
by new multilateral arrangements.

World financial expansion has been even more dramatic. Foreign
exchange turnover is more than a trillion dollars a day. For every $55 traded in
foreign exchange, there is $1 in real trade (Held, 1997). A very large part of the
foreign exchange market is speculative, fluctuating widely over time. The
liberalization of the market since the early 1980's has produced a more integrated international financial system. The resulting financial system means
that national markets are very sensitive to changes elsewhere in the world and
independent national monetary policies are hard to plan and implement.

In addition, multinational corporations (MNCs) are growing in size and
influence. "MNCs account for a quarter to a third of world output, 70 per cent
of world trade, and 80 per cent of direct international investment" (Held, 1997,
p. 256). In 1990 there were over 35,000 transnational corporations with
150,000 foreign subsidiaries. (Scholte, 1993). MNCs frequently have economic
resources, and concomitant political influence, greater than the national governments of the states in which they operate.

All these trends have important political consequences for national economies, for national governments, and for democratic governance. One group
of scholars who fears the substitution of market forces for formerly governmental and political forces argues that important social and distributive
justice problems will be exacerbated. Rather than applaud the diminishing
power of the state, they rue this trend, arguing that the state, in the absence of
global government, holds responsibility for overseeing the needs of the politically powerless and the economically disadvantaged. If poverty is, in fact, even
in part a result of the adoption of the capitalist free market economic model,
then conditions for the poor can only deteriorate in the face of the globalization of such a model. (For well articulated, more fully developed presentations
of this argument, see: Judt relevant to Europe and Kothari for a perspective on
the developing world.)

The CRC reveals the drafters' serious concern about child labor and
exploitation. There is proactive language that states recognize the child's right
to "rest and leisure," to time for play and recreation (Article 31, paragraph 1).

There is also prohibition on the economic exploitation of the child and affirmation of a prohibition on children performing work which is hazardous to the child's health, would interfere with the child's education, or be harmful to the child's "physical, mental, spiritual, moral or social development" (Article 32, paragraph 1). Provision is made for minimum age for employment, regulation of hours and working conditions, and enforcement sanctions for child labor matters (Article 32, paragraph 2).

The regional treaties also address issues of child labor and exploitation. The ACRWC covers the same ground as the CRC (Article 15). The drafters of the European Social Charter devoted an article to "The right of children and young persons to protection," which covers, among other concerns: a minimum age for work, with special attention to the potential hazards to the young person in setting the age; the need to ensure that work not interfere with education; the number of working hours; and the right to fair wages and fair benefits (Article 9). The International Labour Organization has also overseen the development of a number of treaties on child labor, including the Convention Concerning Minimum Age for Admission to Employment, 1973; Medical Examination of Young Persons (Industry) Convention, 1946; and a treaty that supplements the slave trade convention and bans practices in which children are bound over for labor when they reach maturity.

Treaty provisions may also reflect an understanding of the impact of the economics of the family environment on the child. The CRC obligates states to assist families in providing a standard of living adequate for the physical, mental, spiritual, moral and social development of the child, thus linking economic conditions to child development (Article 27). Awareness also exists of the potential negative impact instability and unpredictability of family economic situations may have on children's lives. The Riyadh Guidelines, in discussing Socialization Processes (Section IV), draw attention to the need for special attention to "children of families affected by problems brought about by rapid and uneven economic, social and cultural change" (Article 15).

OVERVIEW: WHITHER GLOBALIZATION

It is easy to overstate the importance of globalization by positing the disappearance of the nation state system; the eclipse of nationalism and ethnic, religious, racial, and cultural attachments; the decline of the distinction between core and periphery; or the insignificance of local organizations, family life, or personal action.

To do so is to undervalue countervailing forces of fragmentation and localization. As discussed in Chapter One, there are always some interests, needs and concerns that will most likely always be best addressed close to home. Of course, the combination of local and global forces can, in fact, be accommodated. The reasons lie primarily in the reality of multiple loyalties and multiple interests. Not only will these loyalties and interests emerge and change with internal and external change, but also since no single group will be monolithic or dominant, the groups will balance one another. Rosenau (1997) suggests that the single "highest" loyalty concept so long identified with the nation state is itself an outmoded concept. But since states can no longer perform many of the functions they were previously believed to perform, especially the guarantee of security, and if territoriality itself is on the wane, then multiple loyalties will become the norm. "For the reality is that human affairs are organized at all these levels for good reasons; people have needs that can only be filled by close-at-hand organizations and other needs that are best served by distant entities at the national or transnational level" (p. 364). Perhaps these "close-at-hand" needs are most apparent when contemplating the every day lives of children since we expect that they will have many needs met by parents, extended family, guardians, friends, teachers, health care workers, and a myriad of others who are very close by. Even as we consider these people we are immediately conscious of the many ways in which they and the children to whom they are close are receivers of and participants in the globalization process.

As with any contemplation of globalization, considering the impact on the lives of children can lead to totally unsatisfying generalizations—"there's some good, some bad." Complex phenomenon and competing opinions of experts can result in generalizations which appear to be the very truisms one would have constructed without the benefit of research. Can we construct globally valid observations that could guide our research, to better understand and improve the well being of children where they live?

Certainly, for the most part, globalization forces, to whatever extent they are under the control of human decision makers, are being planned and implemented with little attention to the everyday lives and even futures of children. That does not mean that there are not significant and even powerful groups attempting to introduce into these deliberations some attention to childhood and children's lives. Similarly, children and child advocates are themselves part of the process of globalization even in ways not captured in the notion of human control. Probably most of us, at least some of the time, feel like children in the sense of wonder and helplessness that the world is changing in ways that seriously affect us but offer us minimal opportunities for participation. These are times in which thinking globally and acting locally invites personal strategizing for ourselves and with "our" children. The international legal arrangements which have been forged by representatives of governmental and non-governmental organizations offer a child-centered philosophy, practical steps for action, legitimacy for our undertakings, and reason to hope that we may even succeed.

REFERENCES

Dominguez, J. & Lowenthal, A. (eds). (1996). *Constructing Democratic Governance: Latin America and the Caribbean in the 1990's*. Baltimore: The Johns Hopkins University Press.
Franck, T.M. (1992). The emerging right to democratic governance. *American Journal of International Law*, 86, 46–91.

Held, D. (1997, Sept/Dec). Democracy and globalization. *Global Governance*, 251–268.

Judt, T. (1997, Sept/Oct). The social question redivivus. *Foreign Affairs*, 95–117.

Kaufman, N.H. (1995). Critiquing gender-neutral treaty language: The convention on the elimination of all forms of discrimination against women. In Peters & Wolper (Eds.), *Women's rights: Human rights*. New York: Routledge.

Kaufman, N.H. (1990). *Human rights treaties and the senate: A history of opposition*. Chapel Hill, NC: University of North Carolina Press.

Klak, T. (1998). *Globalization and neoliberalism*. New York: Rowman & Littlefield Publishers, Inc.

Kothari, R. (1997). Growing amnesia: An essay on poverty and human consciousness. In B. Weston, R. Falk, & H. Charlesworth (Eds.), *International law and world order* (pp. 1338–1348). St. Paul, MN: West.

Ohmae, K. (1993, Spring). The rise of the region state. *Foreign Affairs*, 78–92.

Rosenau, J. (1997, November). The complexities and contradictions of globalization. *Current History*, 360–364.

Sassen, S. (1991). *The global city: New York, London, Tokyo*. Princeton: Princeton University Press.

Schmitter, P. (1996). The influence of the international context upon the choice of national institutions and policies in neo-democracies. In Whitehead (Ed.), *The international dimensions of democratization* (pp. 26–54). Oxford: Oxford University Press.

Scholte, J.A. (1993). *International relations of social change*. Philadelphia: Open University Press.

Van Bueren, G. (Ed.) (1993). *International documents on children*. London: Martinus Nijhoff Publishers.

Van Bueren, G. (1995). *The international law on the rights of the child*. London: Martinus Nijhoff Publishers.

Whitehead, L. (1996). Three international dimensions of democratization. In Whitehead (Ed.), *The international dimensions of democratization* (pp. 3–25). Oxford: Oxford University Press.

CHAPTER 4

Democratization and Children's Lives

GARY B. MELTON

We live in a peculiar time.

On the one hand, democracy[1] appears to be at an unprecedented point of acceptance in nearly every region of the globe (Karatnycky, 2000; Potter, Goldblatt, Kiloh, & Lewis, 1997). The dramatic disintegration of the Soviet empire and the long-awaited fall of apartheid in southern Africa have been paralleled by other significant changes that have achieved less media attention in the West. Where military dictatorships were prevalent a generation ago, democracies now predominate in Latin America and the Caribbean. Electoral democracies now are also the mode in sub-Saharan Africa and the Asia-Pacific region. Even in the Islamic world, where there has been greatest resistance to democratization, there are signs of democratic stirrings, with free elections having been held in 1999 in Indonesia and Nigeria.[2] Altogether, approximately 100 new multiparty democracies have been established in the past 20 years—a simply extraordinary level of political change (Olson, 2000). The global trend is especially remarkable when one considers that universal suffrage was not achieved until the 20th century—in some cases, well into the 20th century—even in the most advanced democracies (Dahl, 1998).[3]

---

[1] The sine qua non of democracy is political equality: equal opportunities for (a) participation in political debate, (b) voting, (c) learning about policy alternatives and their consequences, (d) control of the agenda, and, at least for adults, (e) inclusion in the class of people owed full rights (Dahl, 1998).

[2] According to the 1999 Freedom House survey (Karatnycky, 2000), only one of the 41 countries with a Muslim majority (Mali) is free, 14 are partly free, and 26 are not free. In 1999, however, two large Islamic countries (Indonesia and Nigeria) became electoral democracies; eight Islamic countries (none of them in the Arab world) are now so classified. Moreover, when one takes into account the Muslims living in countries in Europe, the Americas, and South Asia where they are in the minority, the majority of the world's Muslims live in electoral democracies. Furthermore, even in Iran, democratic movements have recently had some impact.

[3] Only New Zealand extended the vote in national elections to women before 1900 (Dahl, 1998). Belgium, France, and Switzerland did not do so until after World War II. Of course, the U.S. did

Of course, democracy still is not universal. With 37% of the world's governments classified by Freedom House as "not free" (i.e., lacking electoral democracy and respect for basic civil liberties), counterexamples are not difficult to find (Karatnycky, 2000). Most notably, the democratic aspirations of the substantial proportion of the world's population living in China continue to be largely unfulfilled. Restrictive theocracies and monarchies rule in much of the Persian Gulf region. Bloody civil wars in Liberia, Rwanda, and Sierra Leone tragically illustrate the fragility of democracy in Africa. Less dramatically but more extensively, the domination of governments in the developing world by the Washington Group[4] of lenders and donors illustrates the still minimal control that poor people have over their own fate in much of the world, even if the rudiments of democratic government are present (see, for example, Pantin, 1994, with regard to the situation in the Caribbean nations).

At least in the short term, the economic restructuring encouraged by the Washington Group may have undermined government-based economic and social supports for disadvantaged populations. For example, just two years after the first democratic elections in South Africa, the government rejected the long-standing social-democratic platform of the majority African National Congress party in favor of the Growth, Employment, and Redistribution (GEAR) macroeconomic strategy, which focuses on national debt reduction and relies primarily on private-sector growth (Lever & Krafchik, 1998). Reporting on the effects of similar developments in neighboring Zimbabwe, Sanders (1999) provided convincing evidence that economic structural adjustment increased income inequality and adversely affected nutrition, obstetric care, and primary and secondary school enrollment.

In large part, however, these instances are remarkable precisely because of their deviation from the prevailing trend. Democracy may rapidly be approaching the point that it is not only the gold standard but also the *only* form of government that the global community regards as legitimate (Franck, 1992). Although democracy remains far from universal, there is no longer a plausible competing ideology in world affairs. Indeed, even those who reject democratic principles feel the need to market their program as "democratic." It was common during the period of Communism's greatest strength to label decidedly undemocratic regimes as "Democratic Republic of...," illustrating the nearly universal appeal of democratic systems. Even in the last Communist holdouts, limits on civil and political rights may slowly be loosening as governments lacking a Soviet protector recognize the economic advantages—perhaps even

---

(*cont.*)

not meaningfully and consistently provide for suffrage for African Americans in some states until the enactment of the Voting Rights Act of 1965.

[4] The Washington Group refers to several international development organizations that are based in Washington, D.C., and that have pursued a policy of promoting free-market economic reforms in recipient nations. Key organizations usually considered to be a part of the Washington Group include the World bank, the International Monetary Fund, and the U.S. Agency for International Development.

the necessity—of support for at least a limited free market and thus for liberalization of choices available to the citizenry.

On the other hand, the strongest counter-trend to democracy's apparent triumph may rest in the established democracies themselves, not in the nations that have yet to embrace democratic tenets fully. Two recent treatises by Harvard political scientist Robert Putnam and his colleagues brilliantly illustrate this disturbing point. In the first of these volumes (Pharr & Putnam, 2000a; see also Pharr & Putnam, 2000b, and Pharr, Putnam, & Dalton, 2000), the contributors present evidence for a dramatic decline since 1970 in public confidence in political parties, government institutions, and political leaders across the established democracies of North America, Europe, and Japan. At the same time, however, public support for democratic values has continued or increased. In short, citizens in diverse cultures remain committed to democracy in concept, but they no longer trust governments and politicians to protect the interests of common people.[5] This cynicism is also present among South African (Finchilescu & Dawes, 1998) and Eastern European (Macek, Flanagan, Gallay, Kostron, Botcheva, & Csapo, 1998; Oswald, 1999; Patzeva, 1994; Samsonova, 1998) adolescents.

Similar findings have been observed in surveys of young people in the advanced democracies. Hahn (1998) summarized the low trust in government indicated in her study of secondary school students in Denmark, England, Germany, the Netherlands, and the United States: " 'Politics,' 'politicians,' and 'government' seem to be dirty words for many youth...." (pp. 31). Hahn also found declining and, in most cases, low levels of interest in political matters among the youth whom she surveyed.

Indeed, U.S. data suggest that citizens' sense of alienation, distrust of government and neighbors, and isolation from civic and political life are most pronounced among young people (Bennett, 1998; Putnam, 2000; Rahn & Transue, 1998). For example, the annual national survey of entering college freshmen (Sax, Astin, Korn, & Mahoney, 1999) shows marked and persistent trends toward increasing boredom, sense of being overwhelmed, oversleeping, and preoccupation with "being very well-off financially." At the same time, each cohort of new freshmen reports less political and religious interest, less motivation to make a difference in society, and less involvement in student organizations, studying, productive work in the home and community, and serious

---

[5] Analogous results have been obtained in newly emerging democracies. Initial euphoria about the establishment of democratic institutions has typically been followed by widespread disappointment in the performance of the new governments but continued confidence in democracy per se. For example, within two years after South Africa's first national elections, the proportion of the adult population indicating that their country is "heading in the right direction" dropped from 80% to 64% among Blacks, 73% to 49% among Coloreds (people of mixed race), 77% to 44% among Asians, and 70% to 31% among Whites (Harris, 1997). Increasingly smaller minorities have indicated satisfaction with "the way democracy works in South Africa," obtaining and discussing political news has sharply declined, and two thirds of adults polled have indicated their belief that the current government is at least as corrupt as the former apartheid regime (Mattes, Thiel, & Taylor, 1998).

conversations with teachers and peers. Strikingly, only 15% of entering freshmen plan to join *any* organization during their time in college.

When one considers that the sample is relatively privileged and successful and, therefore, probably more optimistic, trusting, and engaged than their more disadvantaged peers (Putnam, 2000), the findings of the survey of college freshmen are even more alarming. Disturbingly, analogous results have been found in time-sampling studies of junior and senior high students (Larson, 2000). Alienation—reflected in frequent boredom and low investment in productive activity—appears to be the modal experience for America's young people.

As these data indicate in regard to adolescents and young adults, the public malaise about democracy as a system of government has been paralleled by a sharp decline in the well-being of democracy as a way of life. Putnam (2000) persuasively demonstrates this point in his other recent book, an encyclopedic defense of an argument that he first made in an article (Putnam, 1995) that he published in a rather obscure academic journal five years earlier. That article attracted unusual attention from newspaper columnists as well as academicians.

In these works, Putnam presents vast data from diverse sources to make the point that, since about 1970, Americans have been increasingly "bowling alone." Not only have Americans been bowling alone more often (and markedly less often in bowling leagues), but they also have been increasingly absent from the voting booth, the newspaper stand, the civic club, the political campaign, the fraternal organization, the union hall, the church or synagogue, the volunteer project, the bridge club, the softball park, the picnic grounds, and the neighborhood tavern. These changes, which have been dramatic in their magnitude, add up to a marked and continuing decline in *social capital*, defined by Putnam (2000) as the "connections among individuals—social networks and the norms of reciprocity and trustworthiness that arise from them" (p. 19).[6]

This decline has personal consequences. It means that there are fewer venues in which people will notice when one has cause for celebration or despair. Increasingly, "natural" helping must be constructed if it is to occur (for examples, see Melton, Limber, & Teague, 1999; U.S. Advisory Board on Child Abuse and Neglect, 1993). People are increasingly alone when meeting life's challenges, both big and small, which may account in large part for the widespread perception that life is harried and that there is not enough time for family life (Mellman, Lazarus, & Rivlin, 1990). Few would debate the point that the quality of life is poorer when television viewing is up and interpersonal trust and almost every form of social interaction are down.

The decline in social capital also has social and political significance. Comparative research (for example, Putnam, 1993) shows that the strength of democratic institutions is directly related to the level of social capital in a society. By its nature, democracy requires (and stimulates) citizen participation. Voluntary associations make the exchange of information and ideas easier. By so doing, civic organizations also provide practice in exercising tolerance of

---

[6] A comprehensive presentation of research and theory on social capital can be found at http://www.worldbank.org/poverty/scapital/index.htm.

diverse points of view and identifying and considering the interests of a broader group, perhaps even the community as a whole. Furthermore, they offer opportunities for the kinds of experiences that convince people that, by their actions and words, they can make a difference. By joining together, people can increase the volume of their voices to a point that they are more likely to be heard. Social capital provides the fuel for collective action.

Such experiences build trust in government as well as one's neighbors. Indeed, it is likely that the declining confidence in government reflects the concurrent decline in social capital:

> Citizenries made up of people who are civically engaged are more likely to ask for and get good government—and the reverse is also true. Thus, breakdowns in civic engagement can translate into poor governmental performance. All citizens are adversely affected, inciting them to give their government low marks. (Pharr & Putnam, 2000b)

This phenomenon can be seen across the industrialized, democratic world. Its significance is especially grave for the United States, however, because it has historically been the outlier among nations in level of social capital. Indeed, the reliance on voluntary associations has been so great in our history that such activity may be a defining characteristic of American culture.

Early in the 19th century, Toqueville (1835/2000) found Americans' participation in community life to be without a parallel elsewhere:

> Americans of all ages, all conditions, and all minds constantly unite together. Not only do they have commercial and industrial associations in which all take part, but they also have a thousand other types: religious, moral, solemn, frivolous, very general and very particular, immense and very small. The Americans form associations in order to hold holiday celebrations, found seminaries, build hostels, erect churches, disseminate books, and send missionaries to the ends of the earth; in this manner they create hospitals, prisons, and schools. Finally, if it is a question of bringing a truth to light or developing a sentiment with the aid of a great example, they form associations....
>
> I have come across types of associations in America that I confess I did not even conceive of, and I have often admired the infinite art with which the inhabitants of the United States succeed in establishing a common goal for a great number of men and in making them march toward it voluntarily. (p. 211)

America would clearly suffer a great loss if we continued to experience a marked decline in social capital. Because of their monumental significance for both the nation and the world, the trends that Putnam and his colleagues identify need careful examination.

Putting the trends together shows that there is nearly universal support for democracy in concept, but that sustaining democracy is increasingly difficult. In that regard, the problem stems not so much from preserving the rudiments of democracy as a form of government as from maintaining democracy as a way of life. In Dewey's (1916/1997) terms, democracy "is primarily a mode of associated living, of conjoint communicated experience" (p. 87). To use Toqueville's (1835/2000) more literary phrasing, the strength of a democracy is found in the "habits of the heart" (p. 128) of its people.

By its nature, democracy requires that citizens tolerate expression of opposing even outrageous views and that they can and do participate in their own governance (Sullivan & Transue, 1999). The equality that is definitive of democracy demands that citizens make an honest effort to understand one another. Democracy thus brings expectations of personal openness, interpersonal trust, and expression of these values through engagement in civic life— matters that should be of great interest to behavioral scientists.

CHILD DEVELOPMENT IN DEMOCRACIES

An obvious critical need exists to better understand the paradox that global support for democracy is markedly increasing at the same time that faith in democratic institutions and participation in civic life appears to be rapidly declining. As a normative matter, democracy is fundamental to responsive governance. Through the provision of structures and norms for free expression and self-governance, democratic governments communicate respect for the humanity of all the citizens within them—a respect that should be expressed in societal transformations in everyday life. Thus, the growing disparity in many countries, including the United States, between the form and the experience of democracy is a matter of great concern.

So far I have focused, at least implicitly, on the intrinsic value of societal organization in a manner that consistently communicates personal respect and that, therefore, consistently creates self-respect. As a practical matter, a society that embraces democratic ideals is far along the way toward making the Golden Rule a norm for everyday social interaction.

In the remainder of this article, however, I take a more utilitarian approach. My principal thesis is that the strength of democratic institutions relates directly and causally to the well-being of children, in terms of both their current quality of life and their future capacity and motivation to participate in, and contribute to, society (see Qvortrup (1994, 1997) arguing for attention to children as *human beings* as well as *human becomings* and, therefore, for use of indicators of their current well-being as well as predictors of their future productivity). Therefore, for the sake of children and ultimately the society as a whole, we must recognize and respond not only to the opportunities posed by the growth of democracy but also the risks engendered by its increasing fragility (see Melton, 1993).

In what he regards as his most sweeping and controversial claim about the benefits of democracy, Robert Dahl, perhaps the most distinguished contemporary scholar on the subject, has posited that "[d]emocracy fosters human development more fully than any feasible alternative" (Dahl, 1998, p. 55, italics omitted). In essence, Dahl argues, only governments that secure their power by consent of the governed are likely to be sufficiently concerned about their citizens' well-being to keep those interests in the forefront:

> All other regimes reduce, often drastically, the scope within which adults can act to
> protect their own interests, consider the interests of others, take responsibility for

important decisions, and engage freely with others in a search for the best decision. A democratic government is not enough to insure that people develop these qualities, but it is essential. (p. 56)

Democracy (compared with other systems of government and political culture) benefits children in at least four broad ways. First, it *provides the foundation for a community of social networks* supportive of child development and family life. Specifically, democratic experiences bolster parents' confidence in themselves and their neighbors so that all are more likely to invest in their communities (U.S. Advisory Board on Child Abuse and Neglect, 1993). Adults outside the immediate family then share sufficient *collective efficacy* and become available as additional sources of information, models, emotional support, direct assistance (for example, emergency child care), and informal social control (see Cochran & Brassard, 1979; Sampson, Raundenbush, & Earls, 1997; Thompson, 1995). Children need a supportive environment as they begin to explore beyond the boundaries of the family (Earls & Carlson, 1993). Therefore, social capital, as defined by affiliation with a religious organization, perceived social support, and support within the neighborhood, affects children's well-being even in the preschool years (Runyan, Hunter, Socolar, Amaya-Jackson, English, Landsverk, Dubowitz, Browne, Bangdiwala, & Mathew, 1998). Across childhood and adolescence, neighborhoods in which families are connected to one another—in which, for example, adults know the names of the children in the home next door—have greater school readiness, educational achievement, and child mental health, and less adolescent sexual activity, juvenile delinquency, and child maltreatment (Leventhal & Brooks-Gunn, 2000).

When citizens have the power to govern themselves as equals, they must take each other seriously if they are to be effective. Therefore, "[o]nly a democratic government can provide a maximum opportunity for exercising moral responsibility" (Dahl, 1998, p. 55, italics omitted). A democratic community at its best is one in which people care about each other; the result is collective responsibility for the well-being of children.

Second, democracy *promotes cohesion and warmth in family relationships*. More than 150 years ago, Toqueville (1835/2000) observed that family relationships in democratic societies were warmer and more spontaneous and egalitarian than in societies with aristocratic or authoritarian social and political systems. Building from a similar view, the United Nations acted in the first months after the end of the Cold War to proclaim an International Year of the Family (held in 1994) focused on the theme of protecting "the smallest democracy at the heart of society."

Family relationships built on mutual respect rather than authority and role obligations do not only offer greater warmth—in effect, a more pleasant environment—for family members. Even for college students, perceptions of procedural fairness in family decision making—in effect, permitting everyone a say—affect young people's willingness to accept parental decisions, their judgments about the legitimacy of those decisions, and their trust of their parents (Tyler & Degogey, 1995).

Moreover, such experiences of shared personal control in the context of supportive relationships enable young people to become more competent and engaged. The substantial body of research on the relative merits of democratic and authoritarian child rearing shows that, when children are encouraged to participate in decisions, and rules are enforced flexibly, they are generally "more outgoing, spontaneous, and creative while children reared in authoritarian family environments are timid, conforming, and less curious" (Earls & Carlson, 1993, p. 101; see also Deković & Janssens, 1992). Children in democratic families are more likely to develop the civic virtues of "friendliness, loyalty, responsibility, honesty, and moral courage" (Earls & Carlson, 1993, p. 102). The family sense of social responsibility ultimately translates into youth civic engagement, such as community volunteer work (Flanagan, Bowes, Jonsson, Csapo, & Sheblanova, 1998).

Third, democracy *facilitates the economic security* necessary for expectable conditions of childhood and thus for basic security, happiness, and development of personal competence (Hartmann, 1939/1958). The United Nations Development Program has concluded that human rights and human development, including national economic and social development, are inextricably linked in a two-way causal relationship (Olson, 2000). As Nobel Laureate Amartya Sen (2000) has framed the relationship, freedom is both the means to and the endpoint of economic development.

Democracy builds on economic strength and the resulting need for educated workers. In an analysis of 75 countries during the second half of the 20th century, Feng and Zak (1999) found that transitions to democracy could be predicted from per capita income, the equality of distribution of wealth, educational level, and strength of democratic history. Similar analysis of Latin American history shows national democratization to be very highly correlated ($R^2 = .84$) with two variables, the per capita daily newspaper circulation and the number of tractors per hectare (Kelly, 1998). Stated differently, democracy tends to prosper when the political economy improves to a point that there is a free marketplace of ideas and a movement from feudal relationships in authority over, and use of, the land.

At the same time, democracy enables further economic development. Business is able to grow when there is predictability emerging from legal protection of property rights and enforcement of contracts and information needed for market assessment and product development flows freely (Dahl, 1998). Additionally, openness to ideas enables the development of an educated workforce.

This phenomenon has direct effects on child well-being. In particular, with provision for the education of girls, democratic nations at all income levels have much higher contraception rates, much smaller family sizes, and much lower infant mortality rates than do dictatorships (Bellamy, 1999; Zweifel & Navia, 2000).

Perhaps most important for child development, democracy consistently prevents economic and social catastrophes. Sen (2000) has pointed out that "no substantial famine has ever occurred in a democratic country—no matter how poor" (p. 51). With the motivation to keep electors reasonably satisfied, democratic leaders observe and act on dangerous conditions before famines and other preventable disasters occur.

Accordingly, democratic governments ensure that basic social and economic needs come before military aspirations in the allocation of societal resources (J. Grant, 1992, 1993). This phenomenon is based not only in the desire to please the electorate but also the diminished fear that accompanies free trade. In the same vein, modern representative governments never wage war against one another (Dahl, 1998). International trade requires a level of trustworthiness that avoids the catastrophe of armed conflict.

However, the relationship between a free market and a democratic society is not a simple one. "Because market capitalism inevitably creates inequalities, it limits the democratic potential of polyarchal democracy by generating inequalities in the distribution of political resources" (Dahl, 1998, p. 176, italics omitted). Fortunately, strong democratic institutions ensure that governments must attend to popular concern with such inequities. "In no democratic country does a market-capitalist economy exist (nor in all likelihood can it exist for long) without extensive government regulation and intervention to alter its harmful effects" (Dahl, 1998, p. 176). Moreover, sustained commercial exchanges require the development of codes of ethical conduct that mitigate the excesses of capitalism (Sen, 2000).[7]

Fourth, democracy *facilitates children's personal development* as individuals in society and, by so doing, facilitates societal development. Not accidentally, the nearly universal recognition in international law (Convention on the Rights of the Child (CRC), 1989) of the obligation to respect the dignity of children came after the end of the Cold War and the full ascendancy of democracy with its concern for the rights of all people. Such recognition logically results in a mandate to prepare children to be "fully prepared to live an individual life in society" (CRC, 1989, preamble).

Thus, the international community commits itself to enable every child to grow in *personality*. In the sense that international human rights law uses the term,[8] the meaning of *personality* is probably closer to *personhood* than the colloquial or psychological definition. The child's right to registration of his or her birth (CRC, 1989, Article 7) might be argued to be the most fundamental element of the right to development of the personality. Ultimately, however, to enable self-expression, the latter right is operationalized in a duty of the state to ensure the provision of education and foster other basic resources and tools for personal development. With a commitment to citizen involvement in

---

[7] The distortions of the market that have occurred in some countries formerly in the Soviet bloc, particularly Russia, can be traced to the absence or weakness of such institutions (Sen, 2000; Soros, 1997).

[8] The term *personality* is found in several key human rights instruments. Most broadly, the CRC (1989) states a principle, repeated in the African Charter on the Rights and Welfare of the Child (1990, preamble; as reprinted in Van Bueren, 1993), that "the child, for the full and harmonious development of his or her personality, should grow up in a family environment, in an atmosphere of happiness, love, and understanding."

governance, democracies are most likely to take these steps (Dahl, 1998). The need for development of the personality is emphasized particularly in regard to governments' responsibility for education. For example, the International Covenant on Economic, Social and Cultural Rights (1966) provides that "education shall be directed to the full development of the human personality and the sense of its dignity" (Article 13, § 1). The Basic Principles for the Treatment of Prisoners echoes this language (1990, § 6); see also the Convention Against Discrimination in Education (1960, Article 5, § 1(a); as reprinted in Van Bueren, 1993), providing for education "directed to the full development of the human personality and to the strengthening of respect for human rights and fundamental freedoms...." Similarly, the Convention on the Rights of the Child (1989) requires that "education...shall be directed to the development of the child's personality, talents and mental and physical abilities to their fullest potential" (Article 29, § 1(a))—language that also appears in the African Charter on the Rights and Welfare of the Child (1990, Article 11, § 2(a); as reprinted in Van Bueren, 1993) and the Riyadh Guidelines (United Nations Guidelines for the Prevention of Juvenile Delinquency, 1990, § 21(b)).

Democracy also creates conditions that promote children's social development. With values on equality and free expression, democracy stimulates diversity in peer relations and thus greater opportunities for moral, social, and cognitive development (Frønes, 1995). Further, the experience of civic engagement builds interpersonal trust (Brehm & Rahn, 1997).

Of course, not only do children gain from democracy, but democratic societies are dependent on the healthy growth and development of their children. Bross (1991) argues that children's rights are necessary for national development.[9] Recognition of such status enables the development of human capital and facilitates the basic trusting relationships needed for a democratic society.

IMPLICATIONS FOR POLICY AND PRACTICE

Support Capacity Building in Transitional Societies

The broad literature on the relationship between democracy and child development indicates the critical importance of support for democratic institutions.

---

[9] The Plan of Action for Implementing the World Declaration on the Survival, Protection, and Development of Children (1990, § 3; reprinted in Van Bueren, 1993) recognized the significance of child development in national development:

> Progress for children should be a key goal of overall national development.... As today's children are the citizens of tomorrow's world, their survival, protection and development is the prerequisite for the future development of humanity. Empowerment of the younger generation with knowledge and resources to meet their basic human needs and to grow to their full potential should be a primary goal of national development. As their individual development and social contribution will shape the future of the world, investment in children's health, nutrition and education is the foundation for national development.

Although democracy has emerged in many countries in recent years, it is often still fragile. Therefore, the established democracies have a duty to assist in the development and stabilization of the elements important in sustaining the changes that have occurred. (As the widespread disapproval of government and alienation of citizens demonstrates, a parallel, although less severe, need exists in the West.)

To a large extent, the task is to change the habits of the heart (Samsonova, 1998). In an address less than a month after assuming the presidency of the newly democratic Czech government in 1990, Vaclev Havel (as cited in Challenger, 1998) eloquently stated the challenge:

> The worst thing is that we live in a contaminated moral environment. We fell morally ill because we became used to saying something different from what we thought. We learned not to believe in anything, to ignore one another, to care only about ourselves. Concepts such as love, friendship, compassion, humility, or forgiveness lost their depth and dimension.... Let us not be mistaken: the best government in the world, the best parliament and the best president, cannot achieve much on their own. And it would be wrong to expect a general remedy from them alone. Freedom and democracy include participation and therefore responsibility from us all. (p. 53)

Unsurprisingly, civic engagement is especially weak in many transitional societies (see, for example, Mondak & Gearing, 1998, in regard to Romania). For example, political discussion is not yet a part of everyday life, and mass media have not developed as pluralistic forums for public debate. Even if there is superficial agreement about the importance of democracy, differences between East and West persist in work orientation and goals (Watts, 1994).

The former system had many lacunae that weakened family and community life and, that now present special challenges for social and political development. Most obviously, the historical use of informers and the value placed on passive acceptance of social mores and political values diminished identification with the community (Moodie, Marková, Farr, & Plichtová, 1997). When people are afraid to express themselves, their public reticence ultimately translates into private behavior that is cold and unresponsive, a powerful impediment to strong community and family ties.

Challenges also remain from more subtle influences of the former Communist regimes on child development and family life. For example, transitions to adolescence and adulthood occurred substantially earlier in the former German Democratic Republic (and other Central and Eastern European countries), relative to the Federal Republic of Germany (and other Western European nations), a difference that persists, although to a lesser degree (Silbereisen, Schwarz, & Rinker, 1995; Walper, 1995). This phenomenon apparently resulted in large part from housing policies of the former regimes. Specifically, given the housing shortage, the ticket to obtaining one's own apartment was having children. Therefore, although fertility rates in Eastern and Western Europe were comparable, the average age of first childbearing was much younger in the East (Melton, 1993, and citations therein; see also Kovaõík, 1998).

In several instances, formerly Communist regimes engaged in ethnic relocation policies designed to undermine national aspirations (see, for example,

Heidmets, 2000, in re the Russian minority in Estonia) or weaken minorities (see, for example, Mondak & Gearing, 1998, in re the Hungarian minority in Romania). These politically motivated and often forced migrations are at the root of many of the ethnic conflicts that have tragically emerged in post-Communist Central and Eastern Europe, with some disastrous results. Interestingly, however, children and youth are leading the way in resolving at least some of these disputes. For example, home and school exchanges are the principal bridges between Estonian- and Russian-speaking communities in Estonia (Heidmets, 2000).

Perhaps most generally, parents, teachers, and adult leaders of youth organizations are facing new problems in their attempts to guide young people in formerly Communist societies. In that regard, we must remind ourselves of the problems faced by the explosion of consumer choices in the West. As one commentator states, "what once felt like freedom now feels like a multiple-choice quiz that never ends" (Pitts, 1999, p. A11; see also Brinson, 1999). Surely this experience is heightened many times over in the former Soviet bloc. For example, parents who had very few choices to make when they were adolescents now have to develop strategies for monitoring and regulating the decisions that their teenaged children make. Thus, societal dilemmas become expressed at a micro-level in families' everyday lives.

Given all of these challenges, the need in emerging democracies for assistance in building civic institutions is obvious. Successfully meeting this need may also provide clues about effective strategies in reducing youth alienation and isolation in the West.

Improve and Increase Civic Education

There also are pronounced needs for education of young people in democracy in the West. Remarkably most countries give little systematic attention to education of young people in their roles as citizens (Hahn, 1998; Torney-Purta, Schwille, & Amadeo, 1999). Even in the United States, which emphasizes civic education more than most countries do (Frazer, 2000; Hahn, 1998; Torney-Purta et al., 1999), civics courses generally focus on the structure of government (for example, how a bill becomes law) rather than the process of citizen involvement or the principles of democracy (Niemi & Junn, 1998). Moreover, civics education in the United States typically does not follow a developmental sequence, and the modal point at which formal civics education occurs is 12th grade (Niemi & Junn, 1998).

This practice contrasts starkly with developmental knowledge about the nature and timing of political socialization. In particular, research is clear that fundamental ideologies typically are well established by middle childhood, that core concepts (e.g., freedom of expression) are substantially understood by that age, and that adults' level of political participation is highly predictable from their analogous behavior in early adolescence, such as wearing campaign buttons and running for student offices (see, for example, Helwig, 1997; Melton & Limber, 1992; Ruck, Abramovitch, & Keating, 1998).

Just as the content of civics education needs to be reformed to focus on how citizens can become involved in the political process and why they should, greater attention should be given to the political socialization that occurs through the hidden curriculum of everyday life in schools and other institutions of childhood (Tapp & Melton, 1983). UNICEF director Carol Bellamy (1999) made this point in her annual report on the state of the world's children:

> Article 12 [of the Convention on the Rights of the Child (1989)]…, which assures children the right to express their own views freely in matters that affect them [see Melton, 1999], requires major policy changes in the many schools that currently deny children the opportunity to question decisions or influence school policy.
>
> But the rewards are vast: Schools that encourage critical thinking and democratic participation contribute to fostering an understanding of the essence of human rights. And this, in turn, can make education an enabling force not just for individuals, but for society as a whole, bringing to life the entire range of human rights. (p. 11)

Overcoming both the relative inattention to civic education and the increasing disengagement of young people will be no mean feat. Nonetheless, it is an achievable goal. Movement in this direction does not require vast curricular changes, particularly in educational systems (like those in the United States) that are already relatively egalitarian. For example, simply promoting discussion about events of the day would be a step in the right direction: "School will never allow students to get a taste of the vitality of everyday conversation and the yeasty give and take of civic deliberation in the larger world until they enjoy frequent opportunities to talk to each other and their teachers" (Preskill, 1997, p. 317). Heavy reliance on discussion as a mode of instruction would promote democratic socialization by fostering an appreciation of diverse points of view, providing practice in collective deliberation, and instilling norms of civility and mutual respect in group discourse (R. Grant, 1996; Yankelovitch, 1999).

Research on civic education gives additional reason for optimism. Even though current efforts are typically neither systematic nor grounded in developmental research, exposure to conventional civic education does positively affect students' knowledge and attitudes (Niemi & Junn, 1998). Better planned approaches are likely to be even more effective. For example, a natural experiment in post-Communist Poland showed that 14- and 15-year-old students who participated in active "democratic games" and "market simulations" were more likely than students in traditional civics classes to adopt moderate views about political and economic system—in effect, to cast a critical eye at competing models and to incorporate diverse points of view (Slomczynski & Shabad, 1998).

Build a Norm of Child Participation

As implied in the preceding section, democratic socialization is most likely to occur when there are opportunities for children to engage in democratic processes. In some measure, democracy comes naturally when children are respected as people. By its focus on the child's right to be heard in "all matters affecting the child," the CRC (1989, Article 12) makes clear that respect for the dignity of children implies a norm of participation by children in the various settings of their everyday lives (Lücker-Babel, 1995).

Although participation is a natural result of respect for children's rights, it does not follow that such respect itself is "natural." Public policy should be reformed so that the various settings of which children are a part "demand" (in an environmental-psychological sense) their participation (Melton, 1999). For example, the standard of care for pediatric health professionals should be expanded to require that they have a conversation with their child patients about treatment alternatives, even if children do not have authority to make the resulting decisions on their own. Similarly, use of a learner's-permit model combined with a preference for shared decision making would enable children and youth to assume ever greater levels of autonomy and, in the process, to practice skills in negotiation and consideration of diverse perspectives.

Support the Development of Youth Organizations

In the same vein, policymakers and helping professionals who work with children need to support the development of structures to enable children's and adolescents' participation in the community. As Putnam's (1995, 2000) work makes clear, experience in voluntary associations is at the root of democratic life. Significantly, the one time when adolescents consistently report that they are both concentrating and intrinsically motivated is when they are participating in youth-led organizations (Larson, 2000).

For such engagement to occur, however, involvement must not be rote. The seeming anomaly in the anomic trends shown on the annual national survey of college freshmen is the increasing frequency with which the respondents report having been a community volunteer while in high school (Sax, Astin, Korn, & Mahoney, 1999). This finding is unsurprising, however, when one considers the large increase in the United States in school requirements for community service as a condition of passing a course or even of graduating. This kind of "volunteer" activity does not promote civic engagement. In fact, it trivializes citizen contributions, especially when the activity (e.g., picking up trash in a vacant lot) is neither self-initiated nor interactive. As a result, volunteering and social trust are *negatively* (although nonsignificantly) correlated among high school students in the past generation (Rahn & Transue, 1998).

Build a Norm of Parent Participation

Development of tolerance for others' views and of trust in political institutions is most likely to occur when democracy is a family matter. When children see meaningful participation by their parents in community affairs, especially those most salient to children themselves, there are opportunities for parents to model such involvement. Additionally, parents' involvement may increase opportunities for children's own participation.

Thus, an important step toward restoring faith in public institutions may be to build parent participation in the schools, which is currently minimal. On average, teachers do little to encourage parent participation (Eccles & Harold, 1996; Norman & Smith, 1997). When participation is sought, such requests are often perceived as punitive (Mannan & Blackwell, 1992) or meaningless (Hoover-Dempsey & Sandler, 1997), and parents accordingly feel unwelcome (Norman & Smith, 1997).

The good news, though, is that an increase in parent participation is relatively easy to accomplish. Contrary to conventional wisdom, parent participation is only weakly related to parent characteristics (Eccles & Harold, 1996). Instead, the attitudes of school staff are most important (Epstein, 1982; Epstein & Dauber, 1991). When teachers believe that parents have an important role to play in their children's education, regardless of the parents' education or wealth, then the school staff provides parents with opportunities for participation, and parents usually follow through.

Such activities are also consistent with recent public-private initiatives for community renewal (Johnson, 1995). As central institutions in neighborhood life, active efforts to make schools welcoming for parents are likely to increase their sense of collective efficacy. Schools potentially offer a venue around which to organize networks of reciprocal family support (Melton, Limber, & Teague, 1999). In short, schools are reservoirs of social capital waiting to be created.

Provide Settings Small Enough to "Demand" Participation

As such programs are developed, we must remember that small is better (at least if the goal is increased civic engagement). As research on schools (Gump, 1965/1978) and churches (Wicker, 1978) has long shown, the size of a setting is negatively related to the proportion of active participants, the frequency of participation, and the participants' sense of responsibility, competence and belonging (Melton, 1983). Ironically, bigger means less social diversity for the average student, because there are fewer opportunities for meaningful interaction with other students (Garbarino, 1980).

Study the Requisites for Meaningful Child Participation

As research on the relationship between setting size and the rate and meaningfulness of participation illustrates, careful pursuit of a relevant research program will facilitate the development of programs to build social capital and to strengthen children's democratic socialization. Arguing that participation in civil society should be an organizing construct for applied developmental science, Lerner and his colleagues (Lerner, Fisher, & Weinberg, 2000) contend that evaluation research should begin to focus on the five Cs (competence; connection, character, confidence, caring) and the clusters of attributes that they signify: "intellectual ability and social and behavioral skills; positive bonds with people and institutions; integrity and moral centeredness; positive self-regard, a sense of self-efficacy, and courage; and humane values, empathy, and a sense of social justice, respectively" (p. 17). Lerner et al. believe that these traits are illustrative of the ingredients required if children are to grow into active participants in their communities.

More generally, we need to learn about the factors affecting the perceptions of children of different ages and backgrounds about the nature of their place in political life. In particular, researchers should strive to increase our understanding of the circumstances under which children and youth regard their participation in various settings as meaningful (Melton, 1999). In both established and emerging democracies, such studies would illuminate the ways that programs and policies can be designed to build and sustain children's civic engagement and sense of collective efficacy.

LOOKING AHEAD

The most obvious message of the evidence discussed in this article is that, while democracy is attractive to peoples around the world, facilitative of children's development, and perhaps even morally required (Franck, 1992), its full implementation requires concerted, sustained effort. We have known for a long time that building respect for democratic values is difficult, even in established democracies. Strong support for tolerance of political and social minorities' full participation in civic life is found largely among elites who have the privilege of working in the marketplace of ideas (McClosky & Brill, 1983; Melton & Saks, 1985).

The events of the past decade have dramatically illustrated the principle that democracy does not just happen. Democracy may represent a universal striving for personal respect, but it is not an accidental creation. Noting, for example, the system of "robber capitalism" that has emerged in post-Communist Russia, international philanthropist George Soros (1997) has concluded with some chagrin:

> If there is any lesson to be learned, it is that the collapse of a repressive regime does not automatically lead to the establishment of an open society. An open society is not merely the absence of government intervention and oppression. It is a complicated, sophisticated structure, and deliberate effort is required to bring it into existence....
> ...Even if the concept of the open society were universally accepted, that would not be sufficient to ensure that freedom and prosperity would prevail. The open society merely provides a framework within which different views about social and political issues can be reconciled; it does not offer a firm view on social goals. If it did, it would not be an open society.... Only in a closed society does the concept of the open society provide a sufficient basis for political action.... (pp. 53, 58)

Thus, we have a need to fill in the content of democratic socialization. To build the necessary confidence that ordinary people can make a difference, an element that must be added is a political commitment to children's rights coupled with careful establishment of neighborhood institutions that invite and demand that all children become full participants in their communities—in effect, that no child is left on the outside. For our children and ourselves, we must resolve to end the age of alienation among our young people before we descend into a society without community, a society in which relationships no longer matter very much. Such a goal is formidable, but it is achievable. There are historical precedents for changes of such magnitude in social norms. Consider, for example, the change in racial attitudes that occurred in the southern United States. Between 1963 and 1966, there was a startling 37-point drop in the proportion of White Southerners who objected to racial integration of the public schools (Reed, 1986). In 1942, almost all White Southerners objected; by 1980, only 5% did. To use a more recent example, participation in the resistance to the attempted coup in the waning days of the Soviet Union was linked to commitment to democratic values, including political tolerance, and to recruitment by another person (Gibson, 1997). When the power of ideas is matched by even modest social support, individuals really can change the world. When such a change happens in the interest of children and youth, even on a small scale, the ingredients are present for sustainable inculcation of democratic norms.[10]

REFERENCES

Basic Principles for the Treatment of Prisoners, U.N. Doc. A/Res/45/111 (1990).

Bellamy, C. (1999). *The state of the world's children 1999: Education.* New York: UNICEF.

Bennett, S.E. (1998, September). Young Americans' indifference to media coverage of public affairs. *PSOnline*, pp. 535–541. (Available at www.apsanet.org)

Brehm, J., & Rahn, W. (1997). Individual-level evidence for the causes and consequences of social capital. *American Journal of Political Science, 41*, 999–1023.

Brinson, C.S. (1999, March 6). Conspicuous consumption has become a way of life. *The [Columbia, SC] State*, p. A10.

Bross, D.C. (1991). The rights of children and national development: Five models. *Child Abuse and Neglect, 15*(Supp. 1), 89–97.

Challenger, D.F. (1998, Spring). The positive potential in public life: Citizenship and civic education. *Kettering Review*, 49–58.

Cochran, M.M., & Brassard, J. (1979). Child development and personal social networks. *Child Development, 50*, 601–616.

Convention on the Rights of the Child, U.N. Doc. A/Res/44/25 (1989).

Dahl, R.A. (1998). *On democracy.* New Haven, CT: Yale University Press.

Dekoviö, M., & Janssens, J.M.A.M. (1992). Parents' child-rearing style and child's sociometric status. *Developmental Psychology, 28*, 925–932.

Dewey, J. (1997). *Democracy and education: An introduction to the philosophy of education.* New York: Free Press. (Original work published 1916.)

Earls, F., & Carlson, M. (1993, Winter). Towards sustainable development for American families. *Daedalus, 122*, 93–121.

Eccles, J.S., & Harold, R.D. (1996). Family involvement in children's and adolescents' schooling. In A. Booth & J.F. Dunn (Eds.), *Family-school links: How do they affect educational outcomes?* (pp. 3–34). Mahwah, NJ: Erlbaum.

---

[10] In individual schools (but in at least one instance, most of the schools in an entire country), a bullying prevention program has successfully inculcated the norm that no child will be left out (Olweus, 1993; Olweus & Limber, 1999).

Epstein, J.L. (1982). Teachers' reported practices of parent involvement: Problems and possibilities. *Elementary School Journal, 83*, 103–113.

Epstein, J.L., & Dauber, S.L. (1991). School programs and teacher practices of parent involvement in inner-city elementary and middle schools. *Elementary School Journal, 91*, 289–305.

Feng, Y., & Zak, P.J. (1999). The determinants of democratic transitions. *Journal of Conflict Resolution, 43*, 162–177.

Finchilescu, G., & Dawes, A. (1998). Catapulted into democracy: South African adolescents' sociopolitical orientations following rapid social change. *Journal of Social Issues, 54*(3), 563–583.

Flanagan, C.A., Bowes, J.A., Jonsson, B., Csapo, B., & Sheblanova, E. (1998). Ties that bind: Correlates of adolescents' civic commitments in seven countries. *Journal of Social Issues, 54*(3), 457–475.

Franck, T.M. (1992). The emerging right to democratic governance. *American Journal of International Law, 86*, 46–91.

Frazer, E. (2000). Citizenship education: Anti-political culture and political education in Britain. *Political Studies, 48*, 88–103.

Frønes, I. (1995). *Among peers: On the meaning of peers in the process of socialization.* Oslo: Scandinavian University Press.

Garbarino, J. (1980). Some thoughts on school size and its effects on adolescent development. *Journal of Youth and Adolescence, 9*, 19–31.

Gibson, J.L. (1997). Mass opposition to the Soviet Putsch of August 1991: Collective action, rational choice, and democratic values in the former Soviet Union. *American Political Science Review, 91*, 671–684.

Grant, J.P. (1992). *The state of the world's children 1992.* Oxford, England: Oxford University Press.

Grant, J.P. (1993). *The state of the world's children 1993.* Oxford, England: Oxford University Press.

Grant, R.W. (1996). The ethics of talk: Classroom conversation and democratic politics. *Teachers College Record, 97*, 470–482.

Gump, P.V. (1978). Big schools, small schools. In R. G. Barker & Associates (Eds.), *Habitats, environments, and human behavior: Studies in ecological psychology and eco-behavioral science from the Midwest Psychological Field Station, 1947–1972* (pp. 245–256). San Francisco: Jossey-Bass. (Originally published 1965.)

Hahn, C.L. (1998). *Becoming political: Comparative perspectives on citizenship education.* Albany: State University of New York Press.

Harris, M. (1997). Monitoring optimism in South Africa. *Social Indicators Research, 41*, 279–304.

Hartmann, H. (1958). *Ego psychology and the problem of adaptation.* New York: International Universities Press. (Originally published 1939.)

Heidmets, M. (2000, June). *Children's participation in social and political change: Estonia.* Paper presented at a symposium sponsored by Childwatch International and UNESCO on Children's Participation in Community Settings, Oslo.

Helwig, C.C. (1997). The role of agent and social context in judgments of freedom of speech and religion. *Child Development, 68*, 484–495.

Hoover-Dempsey, K.V., & Sandler, H.M. (1997). Why do parents become involved in their children's education? *Review of Educational Research, 67*, 3–42.

International Covenant on Economic, Social and Cultural Rights, U.N. Doc. A/Res/2200A (1966).

Johnson, C. (1995, July). Renewing community. *Governing, 9*, 51–58.

Karatnycky, A. (2000). The 1999 Freedom House survey: A century of progress. *Journal of Democracy, 11*(1), 187–200.

Kelly, P. (1998). Measuring democracy in Latin America: The Fitzgibbon index. In P. Kelly (Ed.), *Assessing democracy in Latin America: A tribute to Russell H. Fitzgibbon* (pp. 3–11). Boulder, CO: Westview.

Kovaõík, J. (1998). Czech families in the second half of the 20th century: Part 3. *Náhradní Rodinná Péõe, 2*, 57–60.

Larson, R.W. (2000). Toward a psychology of positive youth development. *American Psychologist, 55*, 170–183.

Lerner, R.M., Fisher, C.B., & Weinberg, R.A. (2000). Toward a science for and of the people: Promoting civil society through the application of developmental science. *Child Development, 71*, 11–20.

Leventhal, T., & Brooks-Gunn, J. (2000). The neighborhoods they live in: The effects of neighborhood residence on child and adolescent outcomes. *Psychological Bulletin, 126*, 309–337.

Lever, J., & Krafchik, W. (1998). Spending on socio-economic services. In W. James & M. Levy (Eds.), *Passages in democracy-building: Assessing South Africa's transition* (pp. 69–78). Cape Town, South Africa: Idasa.

Lücker-Babel, M.-F. (1995). The right of the child to express views and to be heard: An attempt to interpret Article 12 of the UN Convention on the Rights of the Child. *International Journal of Children's Rights, 3*, 391–404.

Macek, P., Flanagan, C., Gallay, L., Kostron, L., Botcheva, L., & Csapo, B. (1998). Postcommunist societies in times of transition: Perceptions of change among adolescents in Central and Eastern Europe. *Journal of Social Issues, 54*(3), 547–561.

Mannan, G., & Blackwell, J. (1992). Parent involvement: Barriers and opportunities. *Urban Review, 24*, 219–226.

Mattes, R., Thiel, H., & Taylor, H. (1998). Citizens' commitment to democracy. In W. James & M. Levy (Eds.), *Passages in democracy-building: Assessing South Africa's transition* (pp. 91–109). Cape Town, South Africa: Idasa.

McCloskey, H., & Brill, A. (1983). *Dimensions of tolerance: What Americans believe about civil liberties.* New York: Russell Sage Foundation.

Mellman, M., Lazarus, E., & Rivlin, A. (1990). Family time, family values. In D. Blankenhorn, S. Bayme, & J.B. Elshtain (Eds.), *Rebuilding the nest: A new commitment to the American family* (pp. 73–92). Milwaukee: Family Service America.

Melton, G.B. (1983). Ruralness as a psychological construct. In A. W. Childs & G. B. Melton (Eds.), *Rural psychology* (pp. 1–13). New York: Plenum.

Melton, G.B. (1993). Is there a place for children in the new world order? *Notre Dame Journal of Law, Ethics, and Public Policy, 7*, 491–532.

Melton, G.B. (1999). Parents and children: Legal reform to facilitate children's participation. *American Psychologist, 54*, 935–944.

Melton, G.B., & Limber, S.P. (1992). What children's rights mean to children: Children's own views. In M. Freeman & P. Veerman (Eds.), *The ideologies of children's rights* (pp. 167–187). Dordrecht, Netherlands: Martinus Nijhoff.

Melton, G.B., Limber, S.P., & Teague, T. (1999). Changing schools for changing families. In R.C. Pianta & M.J. Cox (Eds.), *The transition to kindergarten* (pp. 179–213). Baltimore: Paul H. Brookes.

Melton, G.B., & Saks, M.J. (1985). The law as an instrument of socialization and social structure. In G.B. Melton (Ed.), *Nebraska Symposium on Motivation: Vol. 33. The law as a behavioral instrument* (pp. 235–277). Lincoln: University of Nebraska Press.

Mondak, J.J., & Gearing, A.F. (1998). Civic engagement in a post-Communist state. *Political Psychology, 19*, 615–637.

Moodie, E., Marková, I., Farr, R., & Plichtová, J. (1997). The meanings of the community and of the individual in Slovakia and in Scotland. *Journal of Community and Applied Social Psychology, 7*, 19–37.

Niemi, R.G., & Junn, J. (1998). *Civic education: What makes students learn.* New Haven, CT: Yale University Press.

Norman, J.M., & Smith, E.P. (1997). Families and schools, islands unto themselves: Opportunities to construct bridges. *Family Futures, 1*(1), 5–7.

Olson, E. (2000, June 30). Rights and strong economies go hand-in-hand, UN study finds. *International Herald-Tribune*, p. 4.

Olweus, D. (1993). *Bullying at school: What we know and what we can do.* Cambridge, England: Blackwell.

Olweus, D., & Limber, S.P. (1999). *Blueprints for violence prevention: Book 9. Bullying prevention program*. Boulder, CO: University of Colorado, Center for the Study and Prevention of Violence.

Oswald, H. (1999). Political socialization in the new states of Germany. In M. Yates & J. Youniss (Eds.), *Roots of civic identity: International perspectives on community service and activism in youth* (pp. 97–113). Cambridge, England: Cambridge University Press.

Pantin, D. (1994). Techno-industrial policy in the restructuring of the Caribbean: The missing link in Caribbean economic policy. In H.A. Watson (Ed.), *The Caribbean in the global political economy* (pp. 49–64). Boulder, CO: Lynne Rienner.

Patzeva, M. (1994). The creation of new meaning in the process of democratization of Eastern Europe. *Journal of Russian and East European Psychology, 32,* 5–12.

Pharr, S.J., & Putnam, R.D. (Eds.). (2000a). *Disaffected democracies: What's troubling the Trilateral countries?* Princeton, NJ: Princeton University Press.

Pharr, S.J., & Putnam, R.D. (2000b, May 26). Why is democracy more popular than democracies? *Chronicle of Higher Education.* Retrieved May 26, 2000, from the World Wide Web: http://www.chronicle.com

Pharr, S.J., Putnam, R.D., & Dalton, R.J. (2000). A quarter-century of declining confidence. *Journal of Democracy, 11*(2), 5–25.

Pitts, L. (1999, March 6). Too many choices leave columnist all tuckered out. *The [Columbia, SC] State,* p. A11.

Potter, D., Goldblatt, D., Kiloh, M., & Lewis, P. (Eds.). (1997). *Democratization.* Cambridge, England: Polity Press.

Preskill, S. (1997). Discussion, schooling, and the struggle for democracy. *Theory and Research in Social Education, 25,* 316–345.

Putnam, R.D. (1993). *Making democracy work: Civic traditions in modern Italy.* Princeton, NJ: Princeton University Press.

Putnam, R.D. (1995). Bowling alone: America's declining social capital. *Journal of Democracy, 6*(1), 65–78.

Putnam, R.D. (2000). *Bowling alone: The collapse and revival of American community.* New York: Simon & Schuster.

Qvortrup, J. (1994). Childhood matters: An introduction. In J. Qvortrup, M. Brady, G. Sgritta, & H. Wintersberger (Eds.), *Childhood matters: Social theory, practice and politics* (pp. 1–23). Aldershot, England: Avebury.

Qvortrup, J. (1997). Indicators of children and the intergenerational dimension. In A. Ben-Arieh & H. Wintersberger (Eds.), *Monitoring and measuring the state of children: Beyond survival* (pp. 101–111). Vienna, Austria: European Centre for Social Welfare Policy and Research.

Rahn, W.M., & Transue, J.E. (1998). Social trust and value change: The decline of social capital in American youth, 1976–1995. *Political Psychology, 19,* 545–565.

Reed, J.S. (1986). *The enduring South: Subcultural persistence in mass society* (rev. ed.). Chapel Hill: University of North Carolina Press.

Ruck, M.D., Abramovitch, R., & Keating, D.P. (1998). Children's and adolescents' understanding of rights: Balancing nurturance and self-determination. *Child Development, 64,* 404–417.

Runyan, D.K., Hunter, W.M., Socolar, R.R.S., Amaya-Jackson, L., English, D., Landsverk, J., Dubowitz, H., Browne, D.H., Bangdiwala, S.I., & Mathew, R.M. (1998). Children who prosper in unfavorable environments: The relationship to social capital. *Pediatrics, 101,* 12–18.

Sampson, R.J., Raudenbush, S.W., & Earls, F. (1997). Neighborhoods and collective efficacy: A multilevel study of collective efficacy. *Science, 277,* 918–924.

Samsonova, T. (1998, November). Current shifts in Russian national mentality: The new versus the old. *International Psychology Reporter, 2,* 17–18.

Sanders, D. (1999). Lessons from Zimbabwe. In R. Barnes-September (Ed.), *Child research 2000: A call for action* (pp. 58–66). Cape Town, South Africa: University of Western Cape, Institute for Child and Family Development.

Sax, L.J., Astin, A.W., Korn, W.S., & Mahoney, K. (1999). *The American freshman: National norms for fall 1999.* Los Angeles: University of California, Los Angeles, Higher Education Research Institute.

Sen, A. (2000). *Development as freedom*. New York: Alfred A. Knopf.

Silbereisen, R.K., Schwarz, B., & Rinker, B. (1995). The timing of psychosocial transitions in adolescence: Commonalities and differences in unified Germany. In J. Youniss (Ed.), *After the Wall: Family adaptations in East and West Germany* (pp. 23–28). San Francisco: Jossey-Bass.

Slomczynski, K.M., & Shabad, G. (1998). Can support for democracy and the market be learned in school? A natural experiment in post-Communist Poland. *Political Psychology, 19*, 749–779.

Soros, G. (1997, February). The capitalist threat. *Atlantic Monthly, 279*, 45–58.

Sullivan, J.L., & Transue, J.E. (1999). The psychological underpinnings of democracy: A selective review of research on political tolerance, interpersonal trust, and social capital. *Annual Review of Psychology, 50*, 625–650.

Tapp, J.L., & Melton, G.B. (1983). Preparing children for decision making: Implications of legal socialization research. In G.B. Melton, G.P. Koocher, & M.J. Saks (Eds.), *Children's competence to consent* (pp. 215–233). New York: Plenum Press.

Thompson, R.A. (1995). *Preventing child maltreatment through social support: A critical analysis*. Thousand Oaks, CA: Sage.

Toqueville, A. (2000). *Democracy in America* (S. Kessler, Ed.; S.D.J. Grant, Trans.). Indianapolis: Hackett. (Original work published 1835)

Torney-Purta, J., Schwille, J., & Amadeo, J.-A. (Eds.). (1999). *Civic education across countries: Twenty-four national case studies from the IEA Civic Education Project*. Amsterdam, Netherlands: International Association for the Evaluation of Educational Achievement.

Tyler, T.R., & Degogey, P. (1995). Community, family, and the social good: The psychological dynamics of procedural justice and social identification. In G.B. Melton (Ed.), *Nebraska Symposium on Motivation: Vol. 42. The individual, the family, and social good: Personal fulfillment in times of change* (pp. 53–91). Lincoln: University of Nebraska Press.

United Nations Guidelines for the Prevention of Juvenile Delinquency, U.N. Doc. A/Res/45/112 (1990).

U.S. Advisory Board on Child Abuse and Neglect (1993). *Neighbors helping neighbors: A new national strategy for the protection of children*. Washington, DC: U.S. Government Printing Office.

Van Bueren, G. (Ed.). (1993). *International documents on children*. Dordrecht, Netherlands: Martinus Nijhoff.

Voting Rights Act of 1965, 42 U.S.C. § 1971.

Walper, S. (1995). Youth in a changing context: The role of the family in East and West. In J. Youniss (Ed.), *After the Wall: Family adaptations in East and West Germany* (pp. 3–21). San Francisco: Jossey-Bass.

Watts, M.W. (1994). Was there anything left of the "socialist personality"? Values of Eastern and Western German youth at the beginning of unification. *Political Psychology, 15*, 481–508.

Wicker, A.W. (1978). Importance of church size for new members. In R.G. Barker & Associates (Eds.), *Habitats, environments, and human behavior: Studies in ecological psychology and eco-behavioral science from the Midwest Psychological Field Station, 1947–1972* (pp. 257–264). San Francisco: Jossey-Bass.

Yankelovitch, D. (1999, Fall). Why dialogue is necessary. *Kettering Review, 17*, 6–13.

Zweifel, T.D., & Navia, P. (2000). Democracy, dictatorship, and infant mortality. *Journal of Democracy, 11*(2), 99–114.

PART II

Global Trends in Children's Lives

Enhancing the Understanding of Children in the Context of Global Change

CHAPTER 5

Children and Family Life

ARLENE BOWERS ANDREWS

In support of the International Year of the Family (IYF) (1994), the United Nations issued publications that observed:

> The family is universally recognized as the basic unit of society; All over the world, families are as different and diversified as they are alike;
>
> The family must be viewed as a living, evolving institution; In recent years, the ever-increasing concern for the fundamental rights and well-being of individuals has led to recognition of families as forming a crucial social net for individual well-being; A renewed interest in family has accelerated in different parts of the world as the result of harsh economic realities and sweeping socio-political changes and shifts in traditional values;
>
> The family faces what may be the most difficult challenge in the history of the human species; many societies are changing so rapidly that the speed of change alone is a major factor in family stress;
>
> The family has responded to these changes in ways ranging from adaptation to total breakdown;
>
> In most countries, as families have rapidly evolved; policies have lagged behind the changes, leading to failure to adequately support families in society;
>
> The struggle of families to respond successfully to change has been significant and deserves careful study.
>
> (United Nations, 1992)

What is most predictable about a child's family life today is that is it unpredictable. For the sake of brevity with regard to an enormous topic, this chapter will focus on the rapid pace and complexity of change as one of the most significant trends affecting families with children. Historically, political, economic, and social transitions were likely to occur over generations, perhaps decades. Recently, they are more likely to occur within years, perhaps weeks, even overnight. Historically, change from a child's perspective involved occasional innovations and crises within their own and neighboring communities. Recently, innovations are frequent and numerous, affected by the increasing connections among masses of people from distant and different places.

While the pace and complexity of life have accelerated, the fundamental requirements for human development in the earliest years have changed little. Families matter throughout life, but the early years are most crucial to human development. Throughout the world, children rely on families for healthy physical, mental, social, moral, and spiritual development. A strong family provides stability, affection, order, and essential economic and social resources (Bronfenbrenner, 1990). Families rely on their communities and states for support as they nurture their young. Reciprocally, healthy families socialize children to support society. The IYF motto, "Building the smallest democracy at the heart of society," recognizes that society sits on a foundation of common values, beliefs, and behavior that are learned in the family.

During the twentieth century, recognition of the value of family stimulated intentional efforts to strengthen and support families. For many children, these efforts are fruitful. Large numbers of children throughout the world are healthier, better educated, more liberated, and wealthier than ever before. In all socioeconomic groups, many parents and other family caregivers have carefully attended to optimal child development, positive family relations, and generous affection. Technological and political advances have enabled these changes.

Unfortunately, the gap between the enriched family life of these children and that of children with deprived family lives is growing. Children are increasingly likely to be abandoned or neglected; to live in households with instability, conflict, and violence; to be disconnected from their family members, particularly their fathers or grandparents; or to have parents with minimal social or community supports.

Children from enriched and deprived families and those in between have been exposed to comparable demographic trends in family, but the effects have been different. A key difference in the family's adaptation is in its ability to organize and mobilize resources essential for development.

FRAMEWORK

Association of Family and Household Characteristics with Child Well-Being

International trends in family life can best be interpreted through a framework that incorporates core factors that influence the association of family and household characteristics with child well-being. The factors in a child's immediate social environment include: (1) household: the domestic unit, or the people who live together in the same residence(s) (they may or may not be related); (2) family: people to whom the child is related by blood, marriage, legal connection, or social recognition (these persons may or may not live together in a household); and (3) social network: people familiar with any household or family member, adult or child (e.g. parent's intimate partner, friends, neighbors, teachers, schoolmates, congregation members, co-workers).

The child's household, family, and social network are nested in a broader social environment; together, they constitute the family environment of the child. The child's household, family, and social networks vary according to: (1) the structure/composition: e.g., the number of people in the group, their relation to one another, age, gender, race, and other structural characteristics; (2) the organization/processes: the way the group functions; e.g., communication, frequency and duration of interaction (time together), stability of relationships over time (commitment), norms and expectations regarding roles and responsibilities of members, caregiving style, degree of order and discipline, degree of conflict or chaos, typical activities (e.g. work, leisure, home management), cooperation, degree of sharing, crisis management; and (3) the resources: social, economic, and political assets available to the group; e.g., tangible resources such as money, housing, transportation; personal resources such as adults' educational level, caregiver time, physical and mental health of members; situational factors such as life stressors, coping resources, and opportunities to mobilize community resources.

The broad variability of these factors that affect and comprise the family environment account for the diversity in family composition and styles. A nurturing family environment for a child must be composed of adequate numbers and types of people who are organized for supporting child development and able to access necessary resources within their cultural environment. This family environment varies substantially from one culture to another and from one political/economic situation to another as the structure, organization, and resources undergo transition. When the structure is too small, composed of powerless people, or unbalanced relative to society (e.g. absent males), the processes are disorganized or conflicted, the resources inadequate, and the child suffers.

TRENDS IN FAMILY LIFE

The increasing pace and complexity of political and economic transformations have coincided with social transformations of direct relevance to family environments. Families are growing smaller, in part due to declining fertility rates (UN, 1997), smaller sibling groups and extended kin networks, and the increase in single parent families (Burns & Scott, 1994). They are also less socially stable, because parents are less likely to stay together after conception or stay committed to one another. Births to mothers without committed partners or husbands are increasing (Burns & Scott, 1994), and marriage is declining (due to postponement, never getting married, or cohabitation). Divorce, remarriage, and redivorce rates are high, and given high remarriage rates, children are more likely to be in blended family networks. Additionally, for a variety of reasons (e.g. abuse, no extended family caregivers, incarceration, war, and parental illness), children may be residing with neither biological parent.

Family environments are less geographically stable for many reasons, including an increase in migration (Lalonde & Topel, 1997; Parfit, 1998). Forced migration occurs due to war, civil conflict, and disasters (Parfit, 1998). Additionally, mobility often occurs as parents divorce or connect with new partners (Acock & Demo, 1994). Employment opportunities increasingly require family mobility, and migratory distances are increasing.

There is less cohesion within family environments due to age segregation, which keeps family members apart. Family members spend time in the community with agemates (e.g. parents at work sites, children at child care or schools for increasing extended periods, and grandparents living independently). Family members are also divided by their individual activities, which keep them disconnected (Galinsky, Bond, & Friedman, n.d.; Savord, 1995). For example, Women as well as men are likely to work outside the home, leaving no one to tend the nest. Work pulls parents away from home, and balancing work and home is becoming more stressful. Leisure time choices also pull family members into independent activities or peer groups rather than adult/child family interaction. Family members are increasingly unlikely to be familiar with one another's peers (i.e., with urbanization and increased rural mobility, the community is larger and less cohesive), and children are increasingly likely to care for themselves and siblings with few, if any, adults nearby.

We are also seeing more diverse family environments. Many communities show increasing support or tolerance for "nontraditional" families, such as those with gay and lesbian parents, single male parents, or grandparents raising their grandchildren without the child's parent. Families are more likely to include members blended by race, religion, or ethnicity. Due to technology, increasingly, families are able to care for members with severe disabilities or illnesses at home; people with disabilities are able to live longer and enjoy a higher quality of life if they have adequate family caregiving.

We also see much greater female influence in families. Although the division of labor varies, most cultures expect males and females to assume some responsibility for families. Increasingly, among vulnerable populations, women are assuming most family responsibilities (United Nations, 1997b). Historically, female-headed families were due to death of father or distance by migration. In just one generation, the rate of absent fathers by choice (their own, their partner's, or both) has increased dramatically across the world. When these fathers leave, unlike their ancestors who sent money and advice back home, the men tend to keep their resources for themselves (Burns & Scott, 1994). Mothers change partners, and children typically stay with their mothers. This phenomenon is beginning to extend across generations, so children thus have mothers and grandmothers as the most stable influences in their lives.

In spite of dramatic changes, extended families are more emotionally interdependent. Throughout history, in rural agrarian cultures, interdependence among generations has prevailed, with children being valued for their ability to contribute to the family economy and provide security to family members in old age (Kagitcibasi, 1996). As material interdependence across age has decreased (due to urbanization and education), emotional interdependencies have not changed. In nonwestern cultures, children are valued for their psychological contributions; thus, even in highly developed nonwestern countries (e.g. Japan) the interdependent model of extended family strength has persisted.

The western culture of individualism has promoted the value of the nuclear family, relatively separate from extended family members and separated by generation. Parenting tends to be more permissive to promote self-reliance of the child. While independence is highly valued, high levels of interaction between parent and child occur and the main reason for planned childbearing is emotional.

The structure and organization of families varies dramatically across cultures and within cultures. Yet these patterns of smaller size, shifting members of the family network, geographic mobility, separation of family members in daily life, increasing diversity, female influence, and emotional interdependence are emerging throughout the world.

INFLUENCE OF THE BROADER SOCIAL ENVIRONMENT

Forces in the broader social environment affect the trends in family life. These forces tend to occur around the world, manifesting in remarkably similar ways across cultures. They include gender issues, developmental expectations related to age, migration, war and civil conflict, and economic factors at the family level.

Gender Issues

The social status of a child's male and female relatives and caregivers can vary dramatically. Issues of violence, gender roles, and discrimination are directly relevant to child well-being. An unacceptable number of children start life in the context of violence; they are conceived through sexual assault and exploitation. These children are the result of predatory or seductive relationships involving higher status males and lower status females, such as: adult-child, master-slave, boss-employee, homeowner-domestic worker, and rich-poor (Males & Chewsky, 1996; Ooms, 1995). Far more children are exposed to brutality against their female caregivers (Carter, Weithorn, & Behrman, 1999). Sexual assault of female children begins at an early age. In developed and developing countries, over half of all murders occur in the family with most of the victims being women and female children (Weinhold & Weinhold, 1993).

Slowly but surely, gender roles are changing as women acquire political power by gaining suffrage, holding political office, and acquiring independent wealth (Sivard, 1995). Women are resisting the historic domination that men have exerted. For many, relations between men and women are fragile or conflicted (as evidenced by low relational commitment rates and high divorce). For others, caregiving and income-producing activities are becoming more balanced among men and women.

Discrimination based on gender continues. Women and girls are gaining educationally, but they still are less likely than males to be enrolled in school, to be literate, or to attain a high level of education (Sivard, 1995). The 1997 United Nations Human Development Report revealed that no society treats its women as well as its men, although the gender gap is broadest in the developing

countries (United Nations, 1997b). With more children raised by single mothers, the chances of a mother getting an adequate education are challenged.
Even though women are more able to get jobs and are increasingly likely to be
the main source of family financial support, they earn substantially less than
men for comparable jobs. The good news is that in the past two decades, their
rate of pay relative to men's is increasing (Sivard, 1995; UN, 1997a).

Many children have limited exposure to adult males. Males die or become
seriously disabled at younger ages than women, primarily because of exposure
to war, dangerous jobs, community violence, and risky situations. Males are
more likely than women to be imprisoned or to live away from their households due to military service, job search, or job requirements.

Age and Development

Societies have changed in ways that affect the expectations of people in
different age groups, particularly those making the transition from childhood
to adulthood. Improved health has dramatically improved life expectancies.
These factors have powerfully affected family life.

In developed areas, improved health and the need for prolonged adolescence to prepare for entry into complex jobs have created conflicting forces that
affect family formation and maintenance. Children are becoming sexually
mature at earlier ages but are less able to financially and socially support a family until older ages than in the past (for U.S. data, see Alan Guttmacher Institute,
1994). Thus childbirth often precedes committed mating relationships. Most
often, in these cases, the child is raised in the mother's family of origin.

Globally, men and women can expect to live longer than in the past (U.S.
National Institute on Aging, 1996). As they continue to develop, their attachments may change, they separate and find new partners, and the family structure
evolves. Also, as life expectancy increases, families include more generations.
Intergenerational transfers are changing in complex ways; within the family,
they continue to be bi-directional, with old supports to young and young to old
as circumstances change.

Migration

People are increasingly migrating within and across countries. Typically
they move voluntarily to pursue better paying jobs or healthier environments.
Internal migration is common in developed countries. In 1981, over 17% of the
population in Australia and the U.S. changed residence. The average number
of lifetime moves per person for a 1970 cohort was 12.9 moves in the U.S. and
7.35 moves in Japan (Greenwood, 1997). Migration is most common for young
adults, including parents of young children. Migration peaks slightly again at
about retirement age.

In developing countries, internal rural to urban migration has been well documented, but rural to rural migration, where data is available, seems to be even more common (Lucas, 1997). Young adults are most likely to migrate. Data on temporary compared with permanent migration is difficult to find. International voluntary migration is also primarily for reasons of employment. For example, in 1980, 21.8% of the Australian population was foreign-born; 6.8% of the U.S. population; and 1.2% of Spain's population. Average educational levels for immigrants to developed countries are quite high (Lalonde & Topel, 1997).

War and Civil Conflict

Political violence continues to kill many men and women of parenting age (Apfel & Simon, 1996). Each year thousands of children lose their homes, neighborhoods, and other property due to intentional destruction. Millions of children live in refugee status due to forced migration or displacement, and hundreds of thousands are unaccompanied by adult family members.

Family Economics

The world economy exerts influence on the local economy, which directly affects a child's family economic status. At the outset of the 21st century, children in certain areas of the world are living in the midst of economic prosperity never before experienced by such large numbers of families while others are faced with persistent poverty. In 1999 the United Nations concluded that "in a majority of countries, growth for the foreseeable future will fall far short of what is necessary to affect a substantial improvement in living standards and a reduction in the number of people living in poverty" (1999b, p. 3). Even among families that are financial stable, employment problems and work stress affect child well-being.

Malnutrition and nutritional diseases affecting mothers and their children continue to be the greatest threats to child development. Female-headed families are most likely to get stuck in poverty. Most of the world's poor children live in rural areas, in large families within agricultural economies (UN, 1997).

While many people are thriving in the new opportunities created by political and economic transformations, relatively uneducated or semi-skilled workers have been displaced from jobs by technology. This displacement has affected women and men, but psychologically seems to affect the man's traditional view of self as provider for the family. By being unable to provide, the man is more likely to pull away from family responsibilities (Wilson, 1996).

Unemployment rates have disproportionately affected young people (those under age 25), who are also the age group with young children (UN, 1997). Real income has declined in many areas; parents may work extraordinarily long hours or multiple jobs, leaving less time for childrearing. Labor unions have declined; people are more likely to be employed by corporations based in distant places rather than by people known to them within their communities or states. Thus, workers feel relatively less empowered.

Parents who are happy at work and feel a sense of personal control over their jobs tend to interact more with their children (National Research Council, 1994; Galinsky, Bond & Friedman, n.d.). Increasingly, people are creating their own jobs or demanding work environments that support their family lives. Unfortunately, many parents cannot influence their job situations. They must tolerate the conditions or starve. In particular, parents in transitional economies who have experienced job shifts are more likely to suffer health problems related to stress (UN, 1997).

Race/Ethnicity

Children in oppressed groups learn in their families to survive and cope with the prejudice and discrimination they face in the larger society. The family serves as a buffer against hostile societal forces. While some political reforms have created greater opportunities for historically oppressed groups, many political transformations and conflicts have exacerbated persistent discriminatory patterns against oppressed populations, such as the recent atrocities in Rwanda and Bosnia-Herzgovina. Political, socio-economic, and cultural discrimination against minorities is prevalent in many areas.

Conversely, children also learn hatred and intolerance in the family. As mobility brings increasingly diverse groups together, children are exposed to more people who are different from them. Increasing communication and mobility among various regions of the world have increased direct contact among people of diverse racial, ethnic, and religious backgrounds. Several countries have recently recognized multiple religious and linguistic groups within their borders and have begun to provide culturally relevant support.

Consumer Values

In a global economy marked by promotion of excessive use of consumer goods, children are taught values that place individual gratification and material possessions over social responsibility and spiritual values. Families are at risk of neglecting the promotion of child development in favor of immediate material gratification.

Technology

Mastery of technology begins at home. The technological revolution has created extraordinary opportunities for families but has also aggravated the disparities between rich and poor, generating what has become known as the "digital divide" (United Nations, 1999a). Technology has enabled children and adult family members with disabilities to live at home and manage life activities. Children have access to enhanced educational opportunities and technological advances offer their caregivers increased flexibility and freedom. On the other hand, compulsive attention to the Internet, television, or video games can erode family communication and/or increase family stress. Rapid technological change eliminates certain jobs while creating others (usually fewer) that require higher skill and education, contributing to the dislocation of many unskilled and semi-skilled workers. This dislocation causes higher unemployment or family disruption as parents migrate away from their families in search of work (United Nations, 1997a).

CONCLUSION

Many of the world's children have increased opportunities and more diverse support as a result of smaller, stronger family systems in more prosperous conditions. These children may benefit from the stimulation related to changing social networks and physical environments. The trends in family life and contextual societal forces pose risks, though, such that unless family caregivers and communities exert intentional effort to assure supports for children, a child is increasingly likely to be isolated, insecure about the future (due to transient relationships), and deprived of essential resources for development. Research is needed to better understand the implications for child development of rapid and complex changes in family life.

Across the world, states and communities are organizing to strengthen the social environments that surround children and their families. Policies and programs generally fall into these categories: (1) improved transfers from the state to strengthen family resources (economic and material support); (2) improved support from communities, particularly in strengthening woman-to-woman and man-to-man support in family processes (e.g. connections, stress relief, conflict management) and provision of child development resources (e.g. home visiting, preschool and after-school child care); and (3) education and support to promote resilience and healthy coping as family transitions occur (e.g. divorce, relocation, and family member illness).

The child of the twenty-first century is quite likely to grow up with different sets of adult caregivers at different stages; a constellation of siblings and cousins who include full, half, step, and foster or adoptive relations; and residences and family networks at several locations. The structure may change, but the need for consistent, nurturing processes and sufficient resources will remain the same. How families organize themselves and mobilize resources, with state and community support, will substantially affect child well-being.

REFERENCES

Acock, A.C. & Demo, D.H. (1994). *Family diversity and well-being.* Thousand Oaks, CA: Sage.

Alan Guttmacher Institute. (1994). *Facts in Brief: Teenage productive health in the United States.* NY: Author.

Apfel, R.J. & Simon, B. (Eds.) (1996). *Minefields in their hearts: The mental health of children in war and communal violence.* New Haven, CT: Yale University Press.

Bronfenbrenner, U. (1990). Discovering what families do. In D. Blankenhorn, S. Bayme, & J.B. Elstain (Eds.), *Rebuilding the nest: A new commitment to the American family* (pp. 27–38). Milwaukee: Family Service America.

Burns, A. & Scott, C. (1994). *Mother-headed families and why they have increased.* Hillsdale, NJ: Lawrence Erlbaum.

Carter, L.S., Weithorn, L.A., & Behrman, R.E. (Eds.). (1999). "Domestic violence and children" [Special issue]. *Future of Children* 9, 3.

Cochram, M. & Lamer, M. (1990). *Extending families: The social networks of parents and their children.* Cambridge: Cambridge University Press.

Ermisch, J. & Ogawa, N. (Eds.). (1994). *The family, the market and the state in ageing societies.* Oxford: Clarendon Press.

Galinsky, E., Bond, J.T., & Friedman, D.E: (n.d.). *The role of employers in addressing needs of employed parents.* NY: Work and Families Institute.

Greenwood, M.J. (1997). Internal migration in developed countries. In M.R. Rosenzweig & O. Stark (Eds.), *Handbook of population and family economics*, vol. 1B (pp. 648–720). Amsterdam: Elsevier.

Kagitcibasi, C. (1996). *Family and human development across culture: A view from the other side.* Mahwah, NJ: Lawrence Erlbaum.

LaLonde, R.J. & Topel, R.H. (1997). Economic impact of international migration and the economic performance of migrants. In M. R. Rosenzweig & O. Stark (Eds.), *Handbook of population and family economics*, vol. 1B (pp. 799–850). Amsterdam: Elsevier.

Lucas, R.E.B. (1997). Internal migration in developing countries. In M.R. Rosenzweig & O. Stark (Eds.), *Handbook of population and family economics*, vol. 1B (pp. 721–798). Amsterdam: Elsevier.

Males, M. & Chewsky, K.S.V. (1996). The ages of fathers in California adolescent births, 1993. *American Journal of Public Health*, 86, 565–568.

National Research Council. (1994). *America's fathers and public policy: Report of a workshop.* Washington, DC: National Academy Press.

Ooms, T., Cohen, E., & Hutchins, I. (1995). *Disconnected dads: Strategies for promoting responsible fatherhood.* Washington, DC: The Family Impact Seminar.

Parfit, Michael. (1998). Human migration. *National Geographic*, 4, 6–35.

Rosenzweig, Mark R. & Stark, Oded (Eds.). (1997). *Handbook of population and family economics.* Vols IA & IB. Amsterdam: Elsevier.

Sivard, R.L. (1995). *Women: A world survey.* Washington, DC: World Priorities.

United Nations. (1992). *Family matters. Occasional Papers Series*, No.1. Vienna: Author.

United Nations. (1997a). *1997 report on the world social situation.* NY: United Nations, Department for Economic and Social Information and Analysis, Microeconomic and Social Analysis Division.

United Nations. (1997b). *Human Development Report 1997.* Cary, NC: Oxford University Press.

United Nations, Population Division. (Feb. I, 1998) *World population projections to NY:* UN Secretariat, Dept. of Economic and Social Affairs, Population Division.

United Nations. (1999a). *Report of the UN workshop on technology and families, Dublin Ireland.* NY: United Nations, Division for Social Policy and Development.

United Nations. (1999b). *World economic and social survey*, 1999. NY: UN Secretariat, Dept. of Economic and Social Affairs.

U.S. National Institute on Aging. (Dec. 1996). *Global aging in the 21st century* Washington, DC: U.S. Bureau of the Census.

Weinhold, J.B. & Weinhold, B.K. (1993). Partnership families: Building the smallest democracy at the heart of society. *Occasional papers series, no.6.* Vienna: United Nations.

Wilson, W.I. (1996). *When work disappears: The world of the new urban poor.* NY: Knopf.

CHAPTER 6

Civic Participation by Children and Youth

SUSAN P. LIMBER AND NATALIE HEVENER KAUFMAN

Over the last generation, research has documented a disturbing trend toward increasing disengagement of Americans from civic life, whether in political involvement (e.g., voting), membership in voluntary associations, or a sense of collective efficacy (i.e., the belief that ordinary citizens can make a difference) (Putnam, 1995). Since the 1970s, membership has dropped significantly in civic, political, religious, educational, fraternal, and humanitarian organizations. As Melton and colleagues (Melton, Limber, & Teague, 1999) note, "whether the venue is the voting booth, the union hall, or the Parent-Teacher Association meeting, many fewer Americans are present than were in attendance a generation ago" (p. 180).

This disconnection and alienation appears to be particularly pronounced among youth. For example, data from an annual survey of 250,000 freshmen entering U.S. colleges and universities (Sax, Astin, Korn, & Mahoney, 1999) reveal a decline in students' commitment to civic engagement over the last 10–15 years. For example, although 75% of the 1999 freshman class reported that they had performed volunteer work during their last year in high school (a record high for the 34-year history of the survey), declining numbers of students reported an interest in leading or even participating in civic life. Such patterns do not appear to be unique to the United States. As Torney-Purta and colleagues (Torney-Purta, Schwille, & Amadeo, 1999b) observed,

> The absence of a sense of social cohesion or a sense of belonging to the civic culture has been noticed in many societies. The personal commitment by individuals to shared identities that transcend ethnic, linguistic or other group affiliations and which contribute to social cohesion has weakened in many areas of the world. Countries find themselves with increasing numbers of adolescents who are disengaged from the political system. (p. 14)

These trends point to a need to better understand the participation of youth in a civil society. Critical to this understanding is an analysis of key indicators of participation by children and youth in civic life.

INDICATORS OF YOUTH PARTICIPATION

Recent efforts to define and measure youth participation have identified several key indicators of youth participation in civic life (Ben-Arieh, Kaufman, Andrews, Goerge, Lee, & Aber (2001), including (a) civic and community awareness, (b) civic and community values, (c) civic and community activities, and (d) opportunities for civic and community activities. Each of these indicators will be explored briefly and relevant data from several recent studies will be reviewed.

Civic Awareness

In order to be an effective participant in civic affairs, a child must know about the questions of public importance and the mechanisms for expressing views and influencing decisions. Measures of civic awareness include youths' knowledge of democratic institutions and principles, youths' knowledge of current events and opportunities for civic involvement, their understanding of democratic processes, and their self-reports of concern for social problems.

To date, the most comprehensive cross-cultural examination of civic knowledge or awareness is the IEA (International Education Association) Civic Education Study, a study of nearly 90,000 14-year-olds in 28 countries who were surveyed on topics ranging from their knowledge of democratic principles, to their attitudes toward government, to their participation in civic activities (Torney-Purta et al., 2000). Results from the study suggest that 14-year-olds in most countries have an understanding of fundamental democratic institutions and values, but frequently this understanding is superficial. In nearly all countries, students who display more civic knowledge come from homes that have more books (a measure of the educational level of parents) and aspire to higher levels of education themselves. Moreover, schools that model democratic practices in classrooms (i.e., have an open climate for discussing issues) are the most effective in the promotion of civic knowledge among students.

Civic and Community Values

Democracy is premised on a citizenry that not only is educated about civic matters but that also is motivated to participate in civic affairs, both formally and informally. This motivation, in turn, requires that individuals perceive that participation of citizens is important and effective. Thus, measures of civic values among children and youth include beliefs in the importance of contributing to the community and society (e.g., community service, voting), and tolerance for expression of minority viewpoints.

As noted previously, the annual surveys of American college freshmen (Sax et al., 1999, 2001) provide one glimpse into the motivation of students to participate in community. Results from recent surveys reveal declining numbers of students who report an interest in taking part in civic activities. For example, in the 1999 survey (Sax et al., 1999) the percentage of freshmen who felt that it was very important or essential for them to "influence social values" fell to 36%, the lowest point in 13 years. Similarly, students' desires to "participate in community action programs" (21%), "help clean up the environment" (18%), and "help others who are in difficulty" all fell to their lowest points in a decade. The most recent survey of American freshmen (Sax, Lindholm, Astin, Korn, & Mahoney, 2001) revealed even higher rates of past volunteerism (78% had performed volunteer work in the last year, and 28% reported that their high schools had required community service for graduation), but students exhibited only marginally greater commitment to civic values or interest in participating in civic life than in the previous couple of years. For example, fewer than one-quarter felt that the chances were very good that they would participate in volunteer or community service work in the future, and only 23% believed it was very important to participate in community action programs (compared with 78% who felt that it was very important to be very well-off financially).

The IEA Civic Education Study (Torney-Purta et al., 2000) gives insight into the motivation of somewhat younger students to participate in their community. Findings suggest that with the exception of voting, 14-year-olds are unlikely to believe that conventional political participation is particularly important. For example, four of five students in all countries indicated that they do not plan to take part in conventional political activities as adults (i.e., join a political party, write letters to newspapers about social and political concerns, or be a candidate for a local or city office). However, 14-year-olds placed somewhat greater importance in non-conventional forms of civic and political engagement. For example, 59% reported that they expected to collect money for a social cause as an adult, 45% indicated that they would collect signatures for a petition, and 44% noted that they likely would participate in a non-violent protest. Respondents also were very likely to endorse the following activities as ways of demonstrating good citizenship: taking part in activities to promote human rights, activities to protect the environment, or activities to benefit people in the community. Finally, 14-year-olds displayed generally positive attitudes toward political and economic rights of women and immigrants, although boys exhibited less positive attitudes than did girls. For example, more than 55% of respondents strongly agreed (and an additional 30–35% agreed) that women should have the same rights as men and are entitled to equal pay for the same job. Ninety percent agreed that immigrants should have the right to equal educational opportunities, and more than three-quarters agreed that immigrants should have the right to retain their customs and their language and have the right to vote.

Civic and Community Activities

Another indicator of civic participation is the active participation by children and youth in the public lives of their communities and beyond.

Measures include the membership of youth in organizations (e.g., political organizations, community service organizations) within the school and other community settings, volunteering in community service activities, and political activity (e.g., wearing a political button, participating in a campaign).

Students in the IEA Civic Education Study (Torney-Purta et al., 2000) were asked to indicate whether they had participated in various civic-related organizations. Overall, a minority of students reported that they had participated in a student council or parliament (28%), a charity collecting money for a social cause (28%), volunteer activities to help the community (18%), an environmental organization (15%), a human rights organization (6%), or a youth organization affiliated with a political party or union (5%). There was considerable variability in students' responses by country, however. For example, 50% of American youth reported that they had volunteered in their communities, and 40% had participated in a charity collecting money for a social cause. By contrast, the percentage of peers in Poland who participated in these activities was 5% and 9% respectively.

Opportunities for Civic and Community Activities

In addition to examining the civic awareness, values, and activities of children and youth, it is critical to analyze the opportunities that communities and larger societies offer children to participate (Ben-Arieh et al., 2001). Measures of such participation include adults' and children's perceptions of opportunities for children's involvement in decision making in various contexts (e.g., their homes, schools, communities) and children's perceptions of adults' responsiveness to their participation in various contexts. For example, several questions from the IEA Civic Education Study (Torney-Purta et al., 2000) probed the openness of the classroom environment to active decision-making and participation by students. Results suggest that although an open and parliamentary classroom climate promotes civic knowledge and engagement, this approach is not the norm in most countries. For example, whereas 39% of participants reported that students often feel free to express opinions in class and 38% reported that students are often encouraged to make up their own minds about issues at school, nearly one-quarter felt that these occurrences happened rarely or never.

Several other studies have examined children and youths' beliefs about the responsiveness of adults to their participation within the community. A consistent theme that emerges is that youth frequently do not believe that they are taken seriously by adults (Ekman, 1999; Green, 1999; Hazenkamp, 1992; Riepl, 1999). For example, in a survey of 269 Austrian youths who had taken part in two municipal projects, a majority of youths expressed satisfaction with the results of the projects, but 56% indicated that their views were not taken seriously by adults, and 25% perceived at least partial misuse of the participation project by adults (Riepl, 1999).

At one level it would not be surprising if these perceptions of youth were indeed well founded. The very notion that children are entitled to rights is relatively new. In most societies, including the most developed Western industrialized nations, children and youth were formerly seen primarily as pre-adults, without rights and essentially the property of their parents, certainly lacking any public political significance. The mutually reinforcing social forces that began to change these attitudes include the increase in child development research, legislation aimed at education and protection of children, and the development of internationally defined human rights. Throughout the twentieth century there were efforts to increasingly legitimize rights for children and these efforts culminated in the Convention on the Rights of the Child (CRC), which today has been ratified by all but two states, the United States and Somalia (and the U.S. has signed the treaty).

This widespread acceptance of the CRC means that the treaty provides a useful statement of the global consensus on the nature and extent of partici-pation rights of children and youth. These include the right to freely express opinions and to have one's opinions taken into account in any matter or pro-cedure affecting the child (Articles 12, 13). The Convention also provides for the right of freedom of association (Article 15) and of thought, conscience and religion (Article 14). The Convention provides for children and youth to have the right to participation in activities of society and to take part in decision-making, in the family, in school, and in their communities. The governments of the world, on behalf of their states, have taken on the responsibility of pro-viding the conditions necessary for children and youth to exercise participa-tion rights, and the expression of these rights expands with the increasing maturity of the child.

THE IMPORTANCE OF PARTICIPATION BY CHILDREN AND YOUTH

Participation by youth is important for youth themselves, for their community, and for democratic societies at large.

Significance for Children

First, participation has significance for children's own lives. Encouraging children to express their opinions and feelings about their own lives and events in their world and to participate actively in the world around them sig-nals a respect for children as human beings (Weithorn, 1998). Communicating this respect to children will help them to develop a positive sense of self and self-respect. As Weithorn (1998) notes, "to enable children to stand up for themselves, for others, and to those who will try to influence them, we must help them develop their dignity and self worth" (p. 7). Participation also plays an important role in other aspects of children's social and personality development. Through participation, children learn ideas and values that are not easily understood if they are merely passive learners. For example, active

participation can give children valuable experience in making difficult decisions and working effectively within a group toward a common goal. For example, in a study of 13 to 17-year-old Austrian youth who participated in
municipal projects, three-quarters reported an enhancement of personal skills,
such as the ability to work in teams, 85% reported an improvement in their
abilities to adopt realistic perspectives and cope with problems, and 83%
reported that the projects fostered an attitude of solidarity (Riepl, 1999).

Participation can also help to promote a sense of mastery and control among
children and youth (Flanagan & Gallay, 1995; Weithorn, 1998). As Weithorn
(1998) suggests, "in general, age-appropriate participation in decisions that affect
children is likely to help them feel that they can positively influence their own
lives and those of their families and communities" (p. 7).

In an extreme example of the effects of political participation on youths'
sense of mastery and control, Barber (1999) found that those youth who participated in the Palestinian Intifada reported having grown in maturity, self-
confidence, and effectiveness.

Meaningful political participation by children and youth also may support
their developing sensitivity to the problems and needs of others (Damon, 1998;
Flanagan & Gallay, 1995; Green, 1999; Youniss et al., 1997). For example, in
their study of 5,600 12–19 year-olds in 7 countries, Flanagan and colleagues
(1999) observed that children who volunteered in their communities attached
a greater importance to working to improve their communities, helping the less
fortunate, and helping their country and society, than did non volunteers.
Although these findings are correlational and must be interpreted cautiously,
it is plausible that the voluntary activity helped to instill in children and youth
a sensitivity to the needs of individuals within their communities and society.
This increased sensitivity is likely to benefit community members as well as
the child him/herself. For example, helping children to develop senses of
themselves as altruistic may enhance their self-esteem, as they come to see
themselves as helpful and giving individuals (Weithorn, 1998).

Another potential benefit of civic and political participation by children
and youth is that it may increase their political understanding and reasoning,
their democratic beliefs, and their political and civic behavior (Flanagan &
Gallay, 1995; Green, 1999; Riepl, 1999; Youniss, Su, & Yates, 1999). As Torney
and colleagues (Torney, Oppenheim, & Farnen, 1975) recognized 25 years ago,
children do not acquire civic knowledge or democratic beliefs through rote
memorization, flag salutes, patriotic rituals, or other such forms of passive
learning. Rather, it is through meaningful participation in the political realm
that such abilities and beliefs develop most readily. For example, 85% of the
children and youth in Riepl's (1999) study of Austrian youth reported that their
democratic consciousness was strengthened as a result of having taken part in
one of two municipal participation projects. Similarly, in their study of high
school seniors in the United States, Younis and colleagues (1999) found that
the frequency of community service was positively related to a variety of "conventional" political behaviors (e.g., had they or were they likely to vote, work
on a political campaign, or contribute money to a political candidate) as well

as "unconventional" political behaviors (e.g., had they or would they in the future boycott an organization or participate in a public demonstration for a cause).

Significance for Future Civic Engagement

Participation by children and youth in civic activities also may set in motion a lifetime pattern of engagement in political and civic activity. For example, in a nationally representative, longitudinal study of high school seniors in the United States, Glanville (1999) found that participation in *instrumental* extra-curricular activities (such as the school newspaper, student, government or political clubs, and youth organizations in the community) during high school was related to high rates of increased early adult political participation (including voting, working for a political campaign, attending political rallies, or contributing money to a political campaign, net of potential selection factors. Participation in *expressive* activities (e.g., athletic teams, chorus, band, and honorary clubs), on the other hand, was unrelated to political participation as adults.

Similarly, a retrospective study of adults who had been members of 4-H as youth revealed that former 4-Hers, compared with former nonmembers, were more likely to be members of various groups within their communities as adults (Ladewig & Thomas, 1987, cited in Yates & Youniss, 1998). Former 4-Hers were nearly four times as likely to be a member of a political group and two times as likely to be part of a civic group or other community group. They were also more likely to be officers of such groups. Similar benefits were observed for participation in other types of groups such as scouts and YMCA for participation in civic (two times as likely), community (nearly two times as likely), and political groups (nearly four times as likely).

According to Youniss (1997), participation in organized groups during adolescence has a lasting impact because such participation introduces youth to the basic roles and processes required for civic involvement and helps youth incorporate civic involvement into their identity during an opportune moment in its formative stages. As Flanagan et al. (1997) observed, organized groups that provide youth with experience in service to the community connect them "to the broader polity and, in that process [help them] develop an understanding of themselves as civic actors" (p. 3).

An alternate interpretation, however, might be that the youth who participate in such groups and activities already possess fundamentally different attitudes and motivations than non-participants. Thus, it may be that the participation experience itself is less important than individual personality characteristics in fostering adult participation. At least one study (McAdam, 1988), however, which made use of a carefully selected comparison sample of nonparticipants, clearly illustrates the powerful and long-lasting experience of political participation on youth.

McAdam (1988) conducted a retrospective study of participants in the 1964 Freedom Summer project in the United States. In this initiative, college students primarily from colleges in the Northeastern U.S. spent a summer in Mississippi registering Black voters and educating Black school children. Twenty-five years later, participants were distinguishable from nonparticipants (who had been selected to participate but were unable to do so) in political outlooks, political behavior, voluntary joining of civic groups, and career choices. Participants held more liberal views, were more active in conventional and unconventional political behaviors, belonged to more voluntary groups, and had more frequently chosen careers in the education and service.

Significance for Communities and Democratic Society

Youth participation has significant benefits not only for the youth him/herself, but also for the communities in which they participate. As Weithorn (1998) notes,

> Adults may be surprised by how much they can learn from young people. Free from many of the concerns that often constrict adults' thinking and creativity, children and adolescents may bring fresh perspectives to situations…The partnerships between young people and adults forged to solve problems of mutual concern can promote closeness and enrich the relationships between adults and young people. (p. 8)

Moreover, children's participation in a civil society also has long-term significance for their community, nation, and world because of the need to socialize the knowledge, skills, values, and attitudes that are fundamental to sustaining a democracy (Flekkoy & Kaufman, 1997; Melton, 1998; Weithorn, 1998).

CONCLUSION

Few would question the idea that a healthy democracy requires citizens who are attentive, know how to participate in all levels of society, and actively engage in their communities. By these standards, many countries, including the United States, have reason to be concerned about the health of their democracies. Civic awareness among youth includes knowledge about the system but often only superficial understanding of how it works. In the area of civic and community values, majorities of students report respect for the rights of others, in a variety of settings, but students do not indicate an interest in participating in conventional political activities when they become adults. With regard to active community participation among youth (a good indicator of participation as an adult) most students do not report community engagement, and in some countries the percentage of youth who participate is at extremely low levels. Finally, in the area of opportunities for civic engagement, again students frequently report limited opportunities, and even those who do actively engage in community projects report feeling that they were not taken seriously and/or that their work was not valued by adults.

We need much further study of all the issues raised by the extension of participation rights to the younger members of our societies. To meet the obligations undertaken in acceptance of the CRC, we need to understand how to create conditions which will genuinely provide young people with the interest, motivation, and necessary information to productively participate in their societies. The work is necessary not only to fulfill our legal obligations but also to advance the vitality of our democracies. It is now clear that participation by youth is important for young people themselves, for their communities, and also for the larger democracies in which they live.

REFERENCES

Ben-Arieh, A., Kaufman, N.H., Andrews, A., Goerge, R., Lee, B., & Aber, L. (2001). *Measuring and monitoring children's well-being*. New York: Kluwer Academic Press.

Damon, W. (1998). Political development for a democratic future. *Journal of Social Issues*, 54, 621–627.

Eccles, J.S., & Barber, B. (1999). Student council, volunteering, basketball, or marching band: What kind of extracurricular involvement matters? *Journal of Adolescent Research*, 14, 10–34.

Eckman, T. (1999). Political participation of youth in Sweden. In B. Riepl and H. Wintersberger (Eds.), *Political participation of youth below voting age* (pp. 163–197). Vienna: European Centre.

Flanagan, C., & Gallay, L.S. (1995). Reframing the meaning of "political" in research with adolescents. *Perspectives on Political Science*, 24, 34–41.

Flekkøy, M.G., & Kaufman, N.H. (1997). *The participation rights of the child: Rights and responsibilities in family and society*. London: Jessica Kingsley Publishers.

Fletcher, A.C., Elder, G.H., Mekos, D. (2000). Parental influence on adolescent involvement in community activates. *Journal of Research on Adolescence*, 10, 29–48.

Glanville, J.L. (1999). Political socialization or selection? Adolescent extracurricular participation and political activity in early adulthood. *Social Science Quarterly*, 80, 279–290.

Green, D. (1999). Political participation of youth in the United Kingdom. In B. Riepl and H. Wintersberger (Eds.), *Political participation of youth below voting age* (pp. 199–223).

Ladewig, H., & Thomas, J.K. (1987). Assessing the impact of 4-H on former members. (Research Report.) College Station: Texas A & M University.

Lamborn, S.D., Brown, B.B., Mounts, N.S., & Steinberg, L. (1992). Putting school in perspective: The influence of family, peers, extracurricular participation, and part-time work on academic engagement. In F.M. Newman (Ed.), *Student engagement and achievement in American secondary schools* (pp. 153–191). New York: Teachers College Press.

Melton, G.B., Limber, S.P., & Teague, T.L. (1999). Changing schools for changing families. In R.C. Pianta & M.J. Cox (Eds.), *The transition to kindergarten*. Baltimore: Brookes.

Putnam, R.D., (1995). Bowling alone: America's declining social capital. *Journal of Democracy*, 6, 65–78.

Riepl, B. (1999). Political Participation of Youth in Austria. In Riepl & Wintersberger, H. (Eds.), *Political participation of youth below voting age* (pp. 23–61). Vienna: European Centre.

Sax, L.J., Astin, A.W., Korn, W.S., & Mahoney, K.M. (1999). *The American freshman: National norms for Fall 1999*. Los Angeles: Higher Education Research Institute, UCLA.

Sax, L.J., Lindholm, J.A., Astin, A.W., Korn, W.S., & Mahoney, K.M. (2001). *The American freshman: National norms for Fall 2001*. Los Angeles: American Council on Education.

Torney, J.V., Oppenheim, A.N., & Farnen, R.F. (1975). *Civic education in ten countries: An empirical study*. New York: John Wiley & Sons.

Torney-Purta, J., Schwille, J., & Amadeo, J. (1999b). Mapping the distinctive and common features of civic education in twenty-four countries. In J. Torney-Purta, J. Schwille, & J. Amadeo (Eds.), *Civic education across countries: Twenty-four national case studies from the IEA Civic Education Project*. Delft, Netherlands: Eburon Publishers.

Weithorn, L.A. (1998). Youth participation in family and community decision making. *Family Futures*, 2(1), 6–9.
Youniss, J., McLellan, J.A., Su, Y., & Yates, M. (1999). The role of community service in identity development: normative, unconventional, and deviant orientations. *Journal of Adolescent Research*, 14, 248–261.

CHAPTER 7

The Effects of Political and Economic Transformations on Children

The Environment

LOUISE CHAWLA

THE IMPACT OF CHANGES IN THE GLOBAL ENVIRONMENT ON CHILDREN'S LIVES

Since the beginning of the contemporary environmental movement in the 1970's, environmental reports have registered rising human populations, rising levels of consumption, and corresponding declines in ecosystem stability and biodiversity. *World Resources 2000/2001*, a report on a recent initiative to monitor global ecosystems by the United Nations Environment Programme, United Nations Development Programme, World Bank and World Resources Institute, revealed a perilous lack of knowledge about the thresholds that separate sustainable use from ecosystem collapse, even as it documented deteriorating productivity in the world's major forest, grassland, farmland, marine and freshwater ecosystems. When natural systems are degraded or destroyed, the poor, who are most likely to depend on local resources for their subsistence, suffer the most immediate effects.

Part of the problem is growing populations. According to estimates of the United Nations Population Division, the world's population crossed 6 billion in the year 2000, up from 1.7 billion in 1900, with a projected population between 8 to 11 billion by 2050. Nearly all of this growth—an estimated 98%—is occurring in the developing world (Swerdlow, 1998). These figures indicate that children and their families in the developing world will face increasingly severe competition for basic needs like food, fuel, fresh water, land, and shelter. Without a commitment to the responsible management of ecosystems, from local to national levels, the result is often a "PPE spiral" of interdependent poverty, population growth, and environmental stress, which threatens children's health and diminishes their life chances (UNICEF 1994).

The main cause of the assault on the natural environment has been increased consumption in the industrialized world. Between 1980 and 1997, the money spent on private consumption worldwide nearly tripled, with consumers in high-income countries, who represent about 16% of the world's population, accounting for 80% of the 1997 spending (World Bank 1999, cited in UNDP et al., 2000). The United States, the country with the highest per capita rate of consumption, transmits images of its lifestyle around the world by movies, videos, Internet, and satellite television, as the standard to which much of the world aspires. The latest statistics, however, show ever-widening gaps between rich and poor. *Human Development Report* 1997, which focuses on poverty reduction, shows that the poorest 20% of the world's people currently earn 1.1% of global income, down from 1.4% in 1991 and 2.3% in 1960, while the ratio of the income of the richest 20% to that of the poorest 20% has risen from 30 to 1 in 1960 to 78 to 1 in 1994 (UNDP 1997). Poor children grow up in a world of rising expectations and diminishing means of fulfillment. A new political will is imperative in order to reverse these trends through programs that simultaneously address environmental protection and poverty eradication. In this process, it is critical to learn how to incorporate children into these programs in ways that nurture their sense of hope and their skills for constructing a more viable world.

For rural children, the implication of these figures is that their families are more likely to be engaged in agricultural production or natural resource extraction for export to the global consumer market, rather than earning a subsistence living through small farms or fishing enterprises. As the geographer Cindi Katz (1986) has documented in the Sudan, with the introduction of rationalized agricultural development schemes for commodity production, children are likely to face a number of dilemmas. They are less likely to learn the more sustainable land use practices of their parents' or grandparents' generations; yet if they acquire traditional experience, they may never have land on which to apply it. Pressures for them to add to their family's cash economy may prevent their attending school; yet if they manage to go to school, they may be prepared for an industrial economy that will deliver few jobs. As children are incorporated into industrial agriculture, they lose the freedom to play as they work, as they could often do during traditional activities like herding, foraging, or trapping. Considering the importance of play as a way of assimilating experience and acquiring social and physical skills, these changing patterns of work, play, and learning deserve attention. Educational schemes to develop a viable agricultural economy or preserve sustainable systems of resource extraction need to be identified and evaluated as an alternative to these changes, and the best models need to be promoted (Espinosa, 1994; Horst, Morna, & Jonah, 1995; Nabhan, 1998).

As subsistence agriculture and fishing economies collapse, a related global environmental trend is urbanization. Although rates of urbanization vary in different parts of the world, families around the world continue to move away from the countryside into cities large and small (Satterthwaite, 1996). The United Nations Centre for Human Settlements (1996) estimates that within the opening two decades of the twenty-first century, more than half of humanity will come to live in urban areas. Within urban areas, some children may be involved in small-scale agriculture (Mlozi, 1995); but ultimately this transition signifies that most families no longer have any direct connection with the land that sustains them. Instead, children's experience is often restricted by fears of traffic, crime, and other hazards (Bartlett, de la Barra, Hart, Missair, & Satttherthwaite, 1999). The implication of this change on children's environmental learning and attitudes is poorly understood. Research indicates that environmental sensitivity, defined as an interest in the natural environment and disposition to act responsibly to protect it, is associated with positive childhood experiences of the natural world and adult role models of environmental interest and care. Therefore, different means need to be assessed to make areas of "nearby nature" accessible to urban children and their families in ways that promote positive environmental attitudes (Chawla, 1998).

In both urban and rural areas, children are often at severe risk from environmental hazards. Satterthwaite, Hart, Levy, Mitlin, Ross, Smit, and Stephens (1996) estimate that more than half of the world's children face risks to their health and often their lives within their homes, surroundings, and places of work and play; yet reports on global environmental degradation rarely draw links to consequences in the form of child mortality, malnutrition, and stunted development. Advocates for children and for the environment need to make these links and find common cause.

The most recent reports of growing environmental damage and growing gaps between rich and poor demonstrate that the world's leaders have not yet committed themselves to a new course of sustainable development that meets human needs within ecosystem limits. If international agreements on the environment win effective commitment, then the role of children will be central. The concept of sustainable development implies an investment in children as our bridge to the future. In the most widely quoted definition, sustainability requires that the present generation manage the environment in such a way that it meets its needs without compromising the ability of future generations to meet their needs (WCED 1987). In *Agenda 21*, the Programme of Action agreed upon by most of the world's nations at the United Nations Conference on Environment and Development, children and youth are identified as major actors whose interests must be "taken fully into account in the participatory process for sustainable development and environmental improvement" (United Nations 1992, Section 25.13b). This principle is reemphasized in the Programme of Action from the Second United Nations Summit on Human Settlements. As the Preamble to *The Habitat Agenda* states:

> The needs of children and youth, particularly with regard to their living environment, have to be taken fully into account. Special attention needs to be paid to the participatory processes dealing with the shaping of cities, towns, and neighborhoods;

this is in order to secure the living conditions of children and of youth and to make use of their insight, creativity and thoughts on the environment. (UNCHS 1996, paragraph 13)

This principle of child and youth participation is expected to be reaffirmed at the "Rio+10" Conference to be held in Johannesburg in September 2002. If implemented, it will require a profound transformation in development policies and in the operations of child-oriented organizations. Despite this growing international rhetoric about participation, there has been little systematic research to evaluate different forms of participatory practices and their effects on children, families, communities, and institutions (Chawla, 2001).

VARIATIONS BY AGE, CLASS, AND GENDER

The preceding changes represent a broad overview of global environmental trends. How are these changes manifested on regional and local levels, and how do they affect children according to age, class, and gender, as these characteristics are mediated by culture? Drawing on existing, though limited, research, some areas for attention can be suggested.

Statistics that indicate growing income gaps between rich and poor suggest radically different environments for children of different classes. Well-to-do parents can often purchase residences at a distance from "hot spots" for pollution, crime, drugs, crowding, noise, ugly surroundings, and disease. In some countries, including the United States, this physical separation amounts to a form of "geographic apartheid" in which rich and poor no longer inhabit the same spatial worlds (Massey & Denton, 1994). At the least, children of the better off are protected from homelessness and the stresses of insecure tenure and housing. At the most privileged, children of well-to-do families enjoy opportunities for travel and integration into the global culture of entertainment and communication. In the former Soviet Union, the egalitarian principles of communism involved state housing for all in "classless" neighborhoods, but as post-Communist states are integrated into the market economy, economic and geographic division are reemerging (UNICEF 1997).

Children of all classes, however, are vulnerable to what have been termed "new deprivations": a diminishing fabric of social support within the family and community; decreasing opportunities for socialization; lack of opportunities to demonstrate self-worth in the broader sphere; a sense of marginalization and uncertainty about the future (Blanc, 1994). Although these deprivations may be social, they are partly manifested through a lack of safe, accessible meeting places, community open spaces, and other places for work and play. As Stephens (1995) notes, concomitant with these changes exists a widespread discussion about "the disappearance of childhood" that applies to diverse cultures and classes. Although documenting the multiple risks which children of the poor face remains important, it is also vital to show that changes in the structure of everyday life, and their underlying social, economic, and political causes affect children of all classes.

Research results of the Growing Up in Cities Project (Chawla, 2002) indicate that social integration is a core element of children's own assessments of community quality. In this eight-nation study, children expressed the most positive attachment to where they lived in a slum on the periphery of Bangalore, in one of the poorest districts of Buenos Aires, and in old working-class and mixed income neighborhoods of Trondheim and Warsaw. They expressed high levels of alienation in a Johannesburg squatter camp, a suburb of Melbourne, an inner-city area of Northampton, and an immigrant community of Oakland, California. What distinguished positive and negative environments, in the children's assessments, were closely linked physical and social factors. Places where children wanted to continue to live were characterized by friendly inhabitants who welcomed and valued young people, safety and consequent freedom of movement, peer gathering places, a variety of activity settings to observe or join, a cohesive community identify, and a local tradition of self-help (which required general security of tenure). Children disliked areas where they felt unwelcome, harassed and stigmatized, and where there was violence, high rates of crime, heavy traffic, uncollected trash and litter, a lack of gathering places and interesting activity settings, a lack of provision for basic needs, and a general sense of political powerlessness.

In this study's most extreme case of social and geographic barriers, low-income immigrant children in Oakland showed almost no knowledge of their city beyond their immediate housing site and school, where they stayed confined by psychological fences constructed of fear and crime (Salvadori, 2002). Similarly, Buss (1995), studying 9 to 11 year olds in five areas of Los Angeles, found that commercial shops and malls were among the few places where they felt safe. The consequences of this constriction and commercialization of the geography of children's lives in the industrialized world, and the extent to which similar trends are shaping the developing world, need to be better understood. How do these changes relate, for example, to the skills that children learn, or don't learn, and to their sense of identity and sense of public life and responsibility? How can development policies protect supportive communities where they already exist for children?

All of these changes in children's lives need to be disaggregated by age, gender, and culture. The environment is a critical arena for developing competence, but the skills that children need to master vary with age, and are variously constructed according to gender and culture. Studies in a number of cultures show that in general boys have more privileges to roam and explore than girls, whereas girls have smaller ranges that confine them closer to home. Recent research in the industrialized world, however, shows that parents are reacting to rising fears of crime by becoming as protective of their boys as they have traditionally been with their girls (Valentine, 1997).

Not coincidentally, the children in the Growing Up in Cities Project, who ranged from age 10 to 15, stressed their desire for safe, friendly, multi-generational public places and places where they could gather with friends, and showed keen awareness of whether or not their neighborhoods were stigmatized by their larger societies. As pre-adolescents and young adolescents, they were at an age when they were expected to be engaged in defining new identities in the world beyond the family. At younger ages, the environment's provision of opportunities to develop other forms of physical and social skills may take priority, such as opportunities for wayfinding, cooperative and imaginative social games, games of physical dexterity, cultural creativity, and knowledge about built and natural environments (Chawla, 1992).

These results from the Growing Up in Cities Project point to the need to create quality of life indicators from children's own perspectives, and suggest that the current emphasis on quantitative physical indicators such as mortality rates, cash income, provision of water and sewer systems, and school attendance needs to be balanced by including social and even spiritual dimensions of children's environmental experience as well, such as those that relate to children's sense of social integration, self-esteem, self-efficacy, and relationship to the built environment of their culture and the natural environment that sustains them. These complementary life quality indicators will require participatory research in which children play an active role in defining the necessary questions and methods. In child research—as well as in the sphere of sustainable development—new processes need to be explored and promoted in which children will play a collaborative part in identifying their own concerns and priorities for improving their lives, and in putting good ideas into practice.

REFERENCES

Bartlett, S., de la Barra, X., Hart, R., Missair, A., & Satterthwaite, D. (1999). *Cities for Children*. New York/London: UNICEF/Earthscan Publications.
Blanc, C. (Ed.) (1994). *Urban children in distress*. Yverdon: Gordon & Breach.
Buss, S. (1995). Urban Los Angeles from young people's angle of vision. *Children's Environments*, 12(3): 340–351.
Chawla, L. (1992). Childhood place attachments. In I. Altman and S. Low (Eds.), *Place attachment*. New York: Plenum Press, 63–86.
Chawla, L. (1998). Significant life experiences revisited. *Journal of Environmental Education*, 29(3): 11–21.
Chawla, L., (Ed.) (2001). Children's participation—evaluating effectiveness. *PLA Notes 42*. London: International Institute for Environment and Development.
Chawla, L., (Ed.) (2002). *Growing up in an urbanising world*. Paris/London: UNESCO/Earthscan Publications.
Espinosa, M.F. (1994). The first summit of children and youth of the Ecuadorian Amazon. *Children's Environments*, 12(2): 192–196.
Horst, S., Morna, C.L. & Jonah, D.O. (1995). Educating our children to be farmers. *Children's Environments Quarterly*, 3(4): 43–51.
Katz, C. (1986). Children and the environment: Work, play and learning in rural Sudan. *Children's Environments Quarterly*, 3(4): 43–51.
Massey, D.S., & Denton, N.A. (1994). *American apartheid*. Cambridge, Mass: Harvard University Press.
Mlozi, M.R.S. (1995). Child labor in urban agriculture. *Children's Environments Quarterly,* 12(2): 197–208.
Nabhan, G.P. (1998). Handing down ecological knowledge. *Orion Afield*, 2(4): 28–31.

Salvadori, I. (2002). Between fences. In L. Chawla (Ed.), *Growing Up in an urbanising world.* Paris/London: UNESCO/Earthscan Publications, 183–200.

Satterthwaite, D. (1996). *The scale and nature of urban change in the South.* London: International Institute for Environment and Development.

Satterthwaite, D., Hart, R. Levy, C., Mitlin, D., Ross, D., Smit, J., & Stephens, C. (1996). *The environment for children,* New York: UNICEF; London: Earthscan Publications.

Stephens, S. (Ed.) (1995). *Children and the Politics of Culture.* Princeton: Princeton University Press.

Swerdlow, J. (1998). Population. *National Geographic,* October: 4–5.

United Nations. (1992). *Agenda 21,* New York: United Nations.

UNCHS (United Nations Centre for Human Settlements). (1996). *An Urbanizing World.* New York: Oxford University Press.

UNCHS (United Nations Centre for Human Settlements). (1997). *The Istanbul Declaration and the Habitat Agenda.* Nairobi: UNCHS.

UNDP (United Nations Development Programme). (1997). *Human Development Report 1997.* Oxford: Oxford University Press.

UNDP (United Nations Development Programme), UNEP (United Nations Environment Programme), World Bank and World Resources Institute (2000). *World Resources 2000/2001.* Washington, DC: World Resources Institute.

UNICEF (1994). *State of the world's children 1994.* Oxford: Oxford University Press.

UNICEF (1997). *Children at risk in central and East Europe.* Florence: UNICEF International Child Development Centre.

Valentine, G. (1997). Gender, children, and cultures of parenting. In R. Camstra (Ed.), *Growing up in a changing urban landscape.* Assen: Van Gorcum.

WCED (World Commission on Environment and Development) (1987). *Our common future.* Oxford: Oxford University Press.

World Bank (1999). *World development indicators 1999.* Washington, DC: World Bank.

CHAPTER 8

Children and the Media

BRIAN WILCOX

Describing the role of media in the lives of children around the globe is a daunting task. First, media diversity is increasing rapidly. The most recent entry is the personal computer and the Internet, but other media are appearing or changing shape as well. Access to the various media, mass and otherwise, also varies substantially from country to country and region to region.

Despite the proliferation of media, this analysis of media trends affecting the lives of children will focus almost exclusively of television. The reason should be obvious: television as a truly mass media reaches more children and, according to research, has a greater impact on the lives of these children and their families and communities than any other medium. It is also the most intensively studied medium, although significant gaps in our knowledge concerning the social effects of exposure to certain types of television content still exist. Other media have been scrutinized by researchers, including music (Christenson & Roberts, 1998) and video games (Federman, Carbone, Chen, & Munn, 1996), but these bodies of work remain fragmented and somewhat inconclusive.

Unfortunately, few studies exist in which the entirety of children's media "diet" is studied. One recent exception is an analysis of children's media use conducted in the United States by Roberts, Foehr, Rideout, and Brodie (1999), which included television, movies, videos, video games, books, magazines, computer games, internet chat rooms and web sites, and music. This nationally representative survey of American youth found that children and adolescents in the United States are immersed in media. They live in homes that are replete with media devices—on average, three television sets, two VCRs, two CD players, three radios, three tape players, a computer, and a video game system. Average media exposure for young children (ages 2–4) is quite high—over four hours per day, and media exposure increases to just over 8 hours per day for 12–13 year-olds before dropping off somewhat during the teen years. Television remains the dominant media for most children, although listening to music becomes an important activity for teens. One of the more startling findings from this study concerns the degree to which children's media use occurs in contexts where adults are absent. Even television viewing, which is more likely to take place in the presence of adults than other media use, often occurs in private: "Almost 15% of the youngest and a full third of the oldest youngsters watch television 'mainly alone'" (Roberts et al., 1999, pp. 81). Surprisingly, a majority of American youth has a television in their bedroom, and over a quarter of 2 to 4-year-olds have television sets in their bedrooms. This "privatization" of media use, in which much media exposure takes place outside of adult presence or supervision, should receive greater attention by researchers and child advocates.

In this brief analysis, I will attempt to address three issues. First, I will describe the television landscape confronting children around the world. This section will look at the penetration of television and related technologies around the globe and examine trends in television programming for children in a variety of countries and regions. Second, I will briefly describe the major concerns arising from children's television viewing, with particular attention to the issue of media violence. Finally, I will look at some approaches being taken in an attempt to address some of these concerns.

THE TELEVISION LANDSCAPE

Television is increasingly ubiquitous. A recent study supported by UNICEF found that seven out of ten households around the world have televisions (Lamb, 1997). While television's penetration into the homes and lives of children is widespread, it is also variable. Table 1 (based on Lamb, 1997) provides data on the number of television sets, the number of broadcast channels, and the number of satellite/cable/pay television channels in a sample of countries. Given the rapid developments taking place in the telecommunications field, especially in the satellite television arena, these numbers significantly underestimate the global reach of television in 2001.

While it is clear that many children around the world do not currently have access to television, with the exception of the poorest and most remote villages in Latin America, sub-Saharan Africa, and Asia, most of the population in the developing world should have some access to television within a decade or two. Television ownership is being spurred in part by rapid global growth in the cable and satellite television industry along with national efforts to develop satellite and cable communications infrastructure. Already, over 20% of the world's households have cable or satellite connections.

Numerous studies indicate that children spend a good deal of time watching television. Studies in the U.S. find that television viewing occupies much of a child's free time, averaging over 3 hours per day (Huston, Donnerstein, Fairchild, Feshbach, Katz, Murray, Rubenstein, Wilcox, & Zuckerman, 1992; Roberts et al., 1999). Viewing increases from the early childhood years through middle childhood, and then drops somewhat during adolescence. A recent UNESCO study finds television viewing by children to be commonplace and extensive in countries throughout Asia, Latin America, Europe, and Africa

Table 1 Television's global penetration (* = data unavailable)

Country	TV sets/1000 residents (est.)	# of broadcast channels	# of satellite/pay/cable channels
Armenia	10	1	0
Brazil	209	92	253
Cambodia	8	2	0
Columbia	118	5	0
Costa Rica	142	10	46
Croatia	353	5	0
Dominican Republic	90	10	40
Estonia	367	3	50
Georgia	*	2	0
Guatemala	53	7	0
India	40	19	17
Jamaica	142	2	0
Nicaragua	67	6	183
Russian Federation	377	11	0
South Africa	101	3	5
Thailand	117	2	8
United States	817	345	387
Zimbabwe	27	2	0

(Groebel, 1998). Clearly, television is an important presence in the lives of many children.

The spread of television around the globe has raised many concerns, some of particular relevance to children and youth, but one common concern relates to the threat to national cultures raised by the perceived preponderance of foreign programming aired around the globe. In particular, many are worried about the export of U.S. culture via U.S. television programming, given the enormous amount of programming produced in the United States. The most interesting television trend in recent years, however, seems to run counter to this fear. Local or regional programming in national languages is growing extremely rapidly. Despite the extended reach of programming from the United States, the United Kingdom, Canada, France, and Australia sent out via cable and satellite, in most countries, national broadcasters account for the greatest share of the television audience. In South Africa, for example, the three national channels account for over 80% of the viewers.

At the same time, when one looks at animated programming—the category that accounts for the largest amount of programming specifically intended for children—this general concern is borne out. Indeed, the five aforementioned countries are responsible for the majority of children's programming around the world, especially for animated programs. And children are watching foreign-produced programs. In South Africa, American sitcoms and music programs are the programs most frequently viewed by youth (Bulbulia, 1998).

This same viewing pattern holds for many of the Asian countries, with Thailand and a few others being the major exceptions (Goonasekera, 1998). Unfortunately, there are few studies available which give any details on the television viewing preferences and practices of children outside of a handful of western industrialized nations.

The technology by which television is delivered to children is changing rapidly around the world. Cable and satellite delivery of programming is growing at a very rapid pace, and the competition provided by these sources is changing the type of programming provided by traditional broadcast stations. Digital television is just beginning to appear, and while it may be decades before this new technology is widely adopted beyond the borders of the wealthiest countries, it has the potential to radically transform this medium. Additionally, the mid-1990s saw a wave of mergers among media giants, and forecasters predict that these mergers will influence what is seen on television around the globe (Baker & Dessart, 1998). Predicting the future in this industry is nearly impossible, given the rate of change in both technology and commerce.

CHILDREN'S PROGRAMMING: THE PERVASIVE THREAT OF VIOLENCE

Three issues tend to dominate policy discussions related to children's television programming: the need for educational programming, the threat of over-commercialization of children's television, and the potential harmful effects of violent programming and sexually explicit content (Kunkel & Wilcox, 2001; Wilcox & Kunkel, 1996). Of all the issues related to children's television, none has drawn more public or scholarly attention than the issue of violence. Concern over children's exposure to violence in television programming dates to the origins of televisions, and has been expressed in virtually every nation (Groebel, 2001).

While researchers do not unanimously support the contention that television violence represents a threat to the development and well-being of children, the vast majority of scholars do contend that exposure to media violence has the potential to harm children in several ways. Recent reviews of the media violence research have concluded that there are three primary types of effects of viewing violent television programming (Donnerstein, Slaby, & Eron, 1994; Wilson, Kunkel, Linz, Potter, Donnerstein, Smith, Blumenthal, & Berry, 1997). First, ample evidence supports the contention that children can and do learn aggressive behaviors and attitudes from viewing violence on television. Heavy viewers of television violence are more likely to see violence as a reasonable means for settling disputes, for example. Second, those who view relatively high levels of televised violence develop an increased and exaggerated fear of becoming a victim of violence. Gerbner has called this the "mean world" effect. Finally, viewers of television violence have shown a tendency to become desensitized to violence.

It is important to recognize that not all violent content leads to negative effects on viewer's attitudes, affect, and behaviors. Wilson and her colleagues at the University of California at Santa Barbara have summarized eleven contextual factors which influence the type of effect any particular portrayal of violence will have on viewers in relationship to the three primary types of effects described above. A review of each of these factors is beyond the scope of this analysis, but a summary of these relationships is depicted in Table 2.

Based on their review of this research, the Santa Barbara researchers created a composite index describing the characteristics of programs placing young viewers at greatest risk from the harmful effects of media violence. This composite includes five factors: "(1) whether the perpetrator is *attractive*, (2) whether the violence is *justified*, (3) whether the violence is *rewarded or punished* immediately after it occurs, (4) whether *harm and pain* is shown, and (5) whether the portrayal is likely to be perceived as *realistic*" (Wilson et al., 1998, p. 129). Using this composite index, the researchers assessed the extent to which high-risk programs—those containing all five of these factors— appeared in an extensive random sample of programming drawn from U.S. broadcast and cable sources. They found that of all television programs containing any violence, nearly 20 % were classified as high-risk programs. More importantly, fully half of these high-risk portrayals appeared in programs targeted to young children, and nearly all of these (92%) appeared in animated programs intended for children. Cartoons designed for young children, it appears, frequently contain portrayals of violence in which an attractive perpetrator—often the hero—engages in violence that is portrayed as justified, is rarely punished, and results in minimal harmful consequences for the victim.

Table 2 The relationships between program contextual factors and viewing effects (from Wilson et al., 1997) ($+++$=positive association; $---$=negative association)

| Contextual Factors | Outcomes of Media Violence | | |
	Learning Aggression	Fear	Desensitization
Attractive perpetrator	$+++$		
Attractive target		$+++$	
Justified violence	$+++$		
Unjustified violence	$---$	$+++$	
Presence of weapons	$+++$		
Extensive/graphic violence	$+++$	$+++$	$+++$
Realistic violence	$+++$	$+++$	
Rewarded violence	$+++$	$+++$	
Punished violence	$---$	$---$	
Pain/harm cues	$---$		
Humor	$+++$		$+++$

It is not uncommon to hear critics dismiss concerns about cartoon violence. Adult viewers are able to distinguish fantasy violence from real violence, but young children are frequently incapable of making this distinction. Unlike adults and older children, young children, especially those under seven years of age, are frequently incapable of "discounting" cartoon violence in their minds.

While this research reported on violence in programming in the U.S., it has broader ramifications due to the wide distribution of animated children's programming produced in the U.S. Some nations have regulatory structures that require that programs likely to be viewed by children be edited to remove much violent content, but other countries exert little control over television content, relying on voluntary efforts and parental oversight to protect the interests of children. In the U.S. at least, industry self-regulation with respect to television violence has shown little promise as an effective strategy in reducing exposure to violent programming (Kunkel, Farinola, Cope, Donnerstein, Biely, & Zwarun, 1998).

RESPONDING TO THE CHALLENGE

For the most part, individual nations have attempted to address the issue of media violence, along with concerns about sexual content, the paucity of educational programming, and over-commercialization, in their own ways. The "solutions" undertaken reflect the unique legal and regulatory structures in each country, the organization of the television industry (public ownership, private ownership, mixed ownership), and the manner in which the problems have been defined by the public. Countries in which the government has strong regulatory authority and total or partial ownership of the broadcasting infrastructure (e.g., Australia, Denmark, Thailand) tend to have greater restrictions in place with respect to content that is deemed harmful to children than countries where private ownership and non-regulatory philosophies prevail (e.g., Brazil, Germany, United States).

The changing nature of the television medium, both in terms of ownership and delivery technology, is challenging existing regulatory methods. One response to the challenges raised by the globalization of the television industry was made at the World Summit on Television and Children, held in March of 1995 in Melbourne. The head of children's programming for the BBC proposed a "Children's Television Charter" which could be adopted by organizations around the world and used as a set of principles to guide efforts to improve the quality of children's television. The Children's Television Charter has since been used as a template by organizers in Africa and Asia to develop regional resolutions, and also served as the focal point for discussions at the Second World Congress on Television and Children held in London in March of 1998. While the charter and the documents based on it address several of the concerns related to children's television, national and regional efforts stemming from the enactment of these documents have focused primarily on violence (Lisosky, 1998).

The economic forces allied against a global children's television policy are formidable. The industry grows larger and its power more concentrated every year. Yet change is possible. Several nations, including the U.S., have passed policies intended to respond to the needs of children *vis à vis* television. As nations grapple with the problems created by the rapid changes in information technology and associated industries, it is essential that advocates work to assure that the concerns of children remain on the political agenda. Decades of research tell us that media, generally, and television, specifically, play a very significant role in the lives of young people. All television is educational television; we would do well to attend more carefully to what it teaches our children.

REFERENCES

Baker, W.F., & Dessart, G. (1998). *Down the tube: An inside account of the failure of American television.* New York: Basic Books.

Bulbulia, N. (1998). An overview of children's broadcasting in South Africa. In U. Carlsson & C. Von Feilitzen (Eds.), *Children and media violence* (pp. 231–328). Goteborg, Sweden: Nordicom—The UNESCO International Clearinghouse on Children and Violence on the Screen.

Christenson, P.G., & Roberts, D.F. (1998). *It's not only rock and roll: Popular music in the lives of adolescents.* Cresskill, NJ: Hampton Press.

Donnerstein, E., Slaby, R.G., & Eron, L.D. (1994). The mass media and youth aggression. In L.D. Eron, J.H. Gentry, & P. Schlegel (Eds.), *Reason to hope: A psychosocial perspective on violence and youth* (pp. 251–280). Washington, DC: American Psychological Association.

Federman, J., Carbone, S., Chen, H., & Munn, W. (1996). *The social effects of electronic interactive games: An annotated bibliography.* Studio City, CA: Mediascope.

Goonasekera, A. (1998). Children's voice in the media: A study of children's television pro-grammes in Asia. In U. Carlsson & C. Von Feilitzen (Eds.), *Children and media violence* (pp. 203–214). Goteborg, Sweden: Nordicom—The UNESCO International Clearinghouse on Children and Violence on the Screen.

Groebel, J. (1998). The UNESCO global study on media violence. In U. Carlsson & C. Von Feilitzen (Eds.), *Children and media violence* (pp. 181–199). Goteborg, Sweden: Nordicom—The UNESCO International Clearinghouse on Children and Violence on the Screen.

Groebel, J. (2001). Media violence in cross-cultural perspective: A global study on children's media behavior and some educational implications. In D.G. Singer & J.L. Singer (Eds.), *Handbook of children and the media* (pp. 255–268). Thousand Oaks, CA: Sage.

Huston, A.C., Donnerstein, E., Fairchild, H., Feshbach, N.D., Katz, P.A., Murray, J.P., Rubinstein, E.A., Wilcox, B.L., & Zuckerman, D. (1992). *Big world, small screen: The role of television in American society.* Lincoln, NE: University of Nebraska Press.

Kunkel, D., Farinola, W.J.M., Cope, K.M., Donnerstein, E., Biely, E., & Zwarun, L. (1998, September). *Rating the ratings one year out: An assessment of the television industry's use of v-chip ratings.* Menlo Park, CA: Henry J. Kaiser Family Foundation.

Kunkel, D., & Wilcox, B.L. (2001). Children and media policy. In D.G. Singer & J.L. Singer (Eds.), *Handbook of children and the media* (pp. 589–604). Thousand Oaks, CA: Sage.

Lamb, R. (1997, February). *The bigger picture: Audio-visual survey and recommendations.* NY: United Nations Children's Fund.

Lisosky, J.M. (1998). The Children's Television Charter: Assessing the feasibility of a global con-sensus for television policy. In U. Carlsson & C. Von Feilitzen (Eds.), *Children and media violence* (pp. 359–363). Goteborg, Sweden: Nordicom—The UNESCO International Clearinghouse on Children and Violence on the Screen.

Roberts, D.F., Foehr, U.G., Rideout, V.J., & Brodie, M. (1999). *Kids and media @ the new millenium.* Menlo Park, CA: The Henry J. Kaiser Family Foundation.

Wilcox, B.L., & Kunkel, D. (1996). Taking television seriously: Children and television policy. In E.F. Zigler, S.L. Kagan, & N.W. Hall (Eds.), *Children, families, and government: Preparing for the 21st century* (pp. 333–354). New York: Cambridge University Press.

Wilson, B.J., Kunkel, D., Linz, D., Potter, W.J., Donnerstein, E., Smith, S.L., Blumenthal, E., & Berry, M. (1997). Violence in television programming overall: University of California, Santa Barbara Study. *National television violence study (Vol. 1)* (pp. 1–172). Thousand Oaks, CA: Sage.

Wilson, B.J., Kunkel, D., Linz, D., Potter, W.J., Donnerstein, E., Smith, S.L., Blumenthal, E., & Berry, M. (1998). Violence in television programming overall: University of California, Santa Barbara Study. *National television violence study (Vol. 2)* (pp. 3–180). Thousand Oaks, CA: Sage.

CHAPTER 9

Developmental–Ecological Considerations

Ross Thompson

As the chapters of this volume describe, global political, economic, and cultural transformations can affect the everyday lives of children in many ways. Economic transitions may increase or decrease unemployment, affecting family well-being and youth entry into the labor market. Children's access to transnational communications systems (such as the Internet, satellite and cable broadcasting, and even fax technology) can alter how they regard themselves and their communities within a worldwide context. Democratic reform can influence civics education in the schools, and the new literary, numerical, technological, and linguistic requirements for success in the new world order can further affect education. The national economic restructuring sometimes required by international lending institutions can affect health care, education, and social welfare programs. For some children and families, residential relocation is one of the significant consequences of the transitions provoked by globalization, with implications for the networks of social support upon which they commonly rely. Perhaps most significantly, periods of political and economic transition influence children's hopes for the future, their expectations for success in the adult world, and their estimates of what skills are required to live well as adults.

Understanding how these transitions affect children's everyday experience is a challenge to developmental scientists for several reasons. First, the term "children" denotes a very heterogeneous population, ranging in age from infancy to adolescence. Within this population, children vary significantly with age in: (a) how they are affected by changes in their social ecologies, (b) their understanding of these changes, and (c) their capacities to respond adaptively. Each of these developmentally variable characteristics mediates the impact of political and economic changes on children's development. For example, economic transitions can affect young children because of the family stress and child care conditions associated with parental unemployment, but for an adolescent they can have profoundly different implications, such as educational attainment and entry into the adult world of work. Thus, discussing the impact of globalization on "children" is unduly generalized without greater specificity of the ages of the children. The impact of globalization depends on children's developmental capacities.

Another challenge to developmental scientists is that socioeconomic and community conditions of children's everyday lives mediate the impact of political and economic transitions (Cochran, Larner, Riley, Gunnarsson, & Henderson, 1990; Thompson, 1995). Globalization differently affects children and youth to the extent that they have access to the Internet and cable broadcasting, live in families vulnerable to fluctuations in the economy, attend high-quality schools, and can participate in the consumer culture. Children's religious and ethnic status also mediates the effects of globalization, especially when political regimes in transition permit previously suppressed ethnic conflict to re-emerge, or find new ways of constructively addressing religious and ethnic differences. The socioeconomic and demographic influences that affect children's everyday lives mediate the effects of globalization; thus, these effects are not homogeneous.

Finally, understanding how political and economic transformations affect children's everyday lives is challenging not only because this understanding requires new ways of conceptualizing the effect of social change on children and youth (see Bronfenbrenner & Crouter, 1983; Elder, 1974), but also because the political, economic, and cultural changes of globalization are multifaceted and multilayered. These changes originate in international economic, communications, and political systems, for example, but are interpreted in light of indigenous cultural beliefs, history, and traditions. Global changes have direct effects on the proximal social systems in which children participate—family, school, neighborhood, religious community—but are also indirectly influential through the national treaty obligations, economic restructuring, and popular culture that transcend but infuse these local ecologies. Global change can influence virtually all levels of the social ecology, from the microsystems of child care centers to the macrosystems of national juvenile justice policies, but children and youths' understanding and response to these cultural transformations also significantly influence the impact they have. Conceiving the impact of global change on children's everyday experience stretches simple, conventional portrayals of the social processes affecting human development.

Understanding the impact of political and economic changes on the everyday lives of children is thus easy in theory, but difficult in practice. To comprehend this impact, this task must be approached from multiple perspectives, each with different conceptual and empirical implications for understanding the effect of social change on children and youth (see Thompson & Melton, 2000). Each perspective alone offers a valuable but limited view of the influence of globalization on children, but taken together, they can provide a more provocative and inclusive portrayal. This essay briefly considers three perspectives which aid in understanding the effect of these changes on children and youth (see Thompson & Melton, 2000). The first considers the impact on children of changes in their immediate social ecologies resulting from political or economic transitions. The second examines the cultural values concerning children, their mediation of changes associated with globalization, and the effect of these changes on cultural values. Finally, the third perspective focuses on children's interpretations of their everyday life experience in a changing world.

CHANGES IN CHILDREN'S SOCIAL ECOLOGIES

Developmental scientists commonly portray a child's social world as a series of concentric circles, with each circle representing a progressively broader level of the social ecology enveloping the child (for two examples, see Bronfenbrenner, 1979 and Lerner, 1991). The most immediate circle surrounding the child represents, of course, the family. The family ecology is complex (it can incorporate the parents' marital relationship, sibling relationships, and/or extended family support), and is important because it is the child's most important social setting and because it often mediates the impact of broader ecological influences. Especially when children are young, for example, the influences of the economy, community, and popular culture are developmentally influential primarily as they influence the family.

Broader social ecologies (represented by wider concentric circles) include (a) the neighborhood and community, encompassing schools, child care centers, religious organizations, workplace settings, health care agencies, voluntary community organizations, and other local agencies that affect children and families, (b) societal institutions, including print and electronic media, financial institutions, the justice system, policies of government agencies, and other institutions whose practices can directly or indirectly affect children, and (c) cultural values, beliefs, traditions, and history (including beliefs about children, as well as values related to modernism and nationalism) that constitute an interpretive framework of understanding for members of society. In addition, some ecological theorists describe the formal or informal connections that exist between different levels of the social ecology, such as events that bring families and schools together (e.g., parent–teacher conferences) or that mediate between families and workplace practices (e.g., after-school care agencies) (see Bronfenbrenner, 1979).

These developmental–ecological topography models offer a valuable avenue to understanding the effects of globalization on child development by focusing on the direct or indirect effect of global changes on children's immediate social ecologies. From this perspective, therefore, one might pose questions like the following (see also Larson, in press). Are the social benefits typically provided by government agencies to families with children, such as health care and education, significantly affected by changes in national economies? How are economic transitions affecting family life, especially through their impact on parental employment, youth job opportunities, or the need for cheap (child) labor? Have there been legal reforms in juvenile justice owing to international political agreements, such as the values articulated in the UN Convention on the Rights of the Child (see Andrews & Kaufman, 1999)? To what extent are Western humanistic and scientific values becoming incorporated into local educational reform? Are traditional values and beliefs becoming diminished in perceived importance as a result? How do broader economic and political changes affect neighborhood quality, especially the perceived safety of neighborhoods as settings for child development?

Such questions emphasize the opportunities and risks to children and youth arising from the changes in their social ecologies arising from globalization. Such questions can be empirically studied in several ways, each of which might be considered a "child impact analysis" of the effects of globalization on development (Thompson & Melton, 2000). These methods include demographic data concerning changes in school enrollment, family income and poverty (especially child poverty rates), health care statistics (including immunizations and child hospitalizations), and public expenditures on children that indicate the performance of social ecologies and institutions that affect children in the context of social change. Relevant data also include child social indicators (e.g., educational attainment, youth criminality, adolescent pregnancy, child literacy) that offer descriptions of the effect of these changes in social ecologies on children and youth.

However, a cautious interpretation of these large-scale survey data is important for several reasons. Social indicators can offer, at best, only a very indirect glimpse into the conditions affecting children's well-being and must be supplemented by other sources of information, such as those described below, that offer more incisive portrayals of children's everyday experience. Moreover, the reliability of these large-scale statistics can be questionable, especially for societies in transition, and they provide only lagging indicators that track, often at considerable delay, the changes that occur in children's social ecologies. Finally, because they are general indicators of social change, data such as these poorly document the mediational influences (e.g., of child age, ethnicity) that may be important for understanding the effects of globalization on children. For these reasons, additional conceptual and empirical perspectives are necessary.

CULTURAL APPROPRIATION OF GLOBAL INFLUENCES

Cultures, like children, are not passive recipients of outside stimulation. Although "globalization" is often discussed as if transnational economic, political, and cultural trends impose uniform demands on specific societies, each culture interprets and appropriates worldwide influences in unique ways, based on indigenous traditions, values, and social history. This interpretation and appropriation explains why, for example, some nations welcome the growing influence of multinational corporations as an avenue to economic prosperity, while other nations reject this influence because of nationalistic or fundamentalist reaction. Likewise, the influence of globalization on child and youth development depends on indigenous beliefs about children, the nature of their growth, and the roles of parents and others in their development.

children and youth compare the characteristics of global popular culture with the more indigenous or traditional elements of their own culture? How do the steps toward democratic reform evident worldwide affect how children and adolescents think about their own current and future roles as citizens?

Children's constructions of the social changes they experience can be studied in several ways. Interviews, focus group discussions, and peer-report methods can be useful depending on the age of the child. Often interview methods are most useful when they are supplemented by other approaches. The neighborhood walk strategy, pioneered by Bryant (1985), uses a shared stroll around the child's neighborhood as the structure for an interview about the child's everyday experiences, using familiar locations and landmarks as the basis for inquiries about events of significance to the child. Time-use studies can also be a useful supplement to interviews, with the interview questions scaffolded around the child's (or a parent's) previously collected account of the activities, events, and partners that characterized the child's daily activities for a week. Photographs and pictures, hypothetical stories, and actual news accounts can also be useful supplements to interviews to elicit the child's awareness of local and national events associated with global change. Finally, interviews with parents and other caregivers can be useful sources of information about children's constructions of their life experiences, especially when children are young and may have difficulty articulating aspects of their everyday responses to events. In these cases, carefully structured interview questions can take advantage of an adult's intimate, longstanding understanding of the child.

CONCLUSION

A developmental–ecological orientation to studying the impact of globalization on the everyday lives of children is essential. A developmental approach orients inquiry to the different influences of political, cultural, and economic transitions on children of different ages, these children's different capacities for understanding the changes they experience, and their different capabilities of responding constructively to them. An ecological approach orients inquiry of the direct and indirect effects various ecological systems have on children and youth, cultural beliefs' mediation of the social impact of global forces on children, and significant human development as a social construction. Taken together, a developmental–ecological orientation underscores the complex ways that children and youth are affected by social change.

Such a view is consistent with Bronfenbrenner's (1986) portrayal of the chronosystem, which he defined as the dynamic interaction between developmental changes in the individual and changes (and continuities) over time in the social ecology. As Bronfenbrenner described it, the chronosystem illustrates the mutual influence of changes in individuals and changes in their contexts (e.g., transitions in child-care arrangements, schools, or neighborhoods). One implication of his analysis is that periods of rapid social change make the outcome of developmental transitions less certain and predictable. During these periods, economic upheaval, political changes, technological advances, or other societal transitions alter the social processes traditionally supporting predictable transitions in child and youth development (e.g., educational preparation of children for citizenship; entry level avenues to adolescent workforce participation), which means that the current era of globalization offers developmental scientists a unique opportunity to explore the shaping and reshaping of development by broader global currents. This opportunity is well worth seizing.

REFERENCES

Andrews, A.B., & Kaufman, N.H. (Eds.) (1999). *Implementing the UN Convention on the Rights of the Child: A standard of living adequate for development.* Westport, CT: Praeger.

Arnett, J. (2000, April). The globalization of adolescence, for better or worse. In J. Arnett (Chair), *The globalization of adolescence, symposium conducted at the annual meeting of the Society for Research on Adolescence*, Chicago, IL.

Bronfenbrenner, U. (1979). *The ecology of human development.* Cambridge: Harvard University Press.

Bronfenbrenner, U. (1986). Ecology of the family as a context for human development: Research perspectives. *Developmental Psychology, 22,* 723–742.

Bronfenbrenner, U., & Crouter, A.C. (1983). The evolution of environmental models in developmental research. In P. H. Mussen (Ed.), *Handbook of child psychology* (4th Ed.), 1, History, theory, and methods (W. Kessen, Vol. Ed.); pp. 357–414. New York: Wiley.

Bryant, B.K. (1985). The neighborhood walk: Sources of support in middle childhood. *Monographs of the Society for Research in Child Development, 50*(3, Serial No. 210).

Cochran, M., Larner, M., Riley, D., Gunnarsson, L., & Henderson, C.R. (Eds.) (1990). *Extending families: The social networks of parents and their children.* New York: Cambridge University Press.

Diversi, M. (2000, April). Street kids in Nikes: In search of humanization through the culture of consumption. In J. Arnett (Chair), The globalization of adolescence, symposium conducted at the annual meeting of the Society for Research on Adolescence, Chicago, IL.

Elder, G.H., Jr. (1974). *Children of the Great Depression.* Chicago: University of Chicago Press.

Larson, R. (in press). Macro societal trends and the changing experiences of adolescence. *Journal of Research on Adolescence* (Special Issue on Adolescence in the 21st Century), in press.

Lerner, R.M. (1991). Changing organism-context relations as the basic process of development: A developmental contextual perspective. *Developmental Psychology, 27,* 27–32.

Rogoff, B. (1990). *Apprenticeship in thinking: Cognitive development in social context.* New York: Oxford University Press.

Schlegel, A. (2000, April). The global spread of adolescent culture. In J. Arnett (Chair), The globalization of adolescence, symposium conducted at the annual meeting of the Society for Research on Adolescence, Chicago, IL.

Thompson, R.A. (1995). *Preventing child maltreatment through social support: A critical analysis.* Thousand Oaks, CA: Sage.

Thompson, R.A., & Melton, G.B. (2000). Changing societies, changing childhood: Studying the impact of globalization on child and youth development. Manuscript submitted for publication, University of Nebraska, Lincoln, NE.

Vygotsky, L.S. (1978). *Mind in society: The development of higher psychological processes.* Cambridge, MA: Harvard University Press.

Vygotsky, L.S. (1987). *Thinking and speech.* N. Minick (Trans.). New York: Plenum.

Wertsch, J.V. (1985). *Vygotsky and the social formation of mind.* Cambridge, MA: Harvard University Press.

PART III

Applying the Lens of Global Change to the Actual Lives of Children

Analyzing the Impact of Global Change on the Actual Lives of Children

CHAPTER 10

The Transition to "Democracy" in Latin America
Challenges and Implications

ELAINE C. LACY

In discussions with residents of Mexico City just before the presidential elections of summer 2000 (which resulted in the end of the Partido Revolucionario Institucional's (PRI) roughly seventy-year monopoly on power), I was struck by the recurrence of two themes: a lack of confidence in the ability of any political party to provide true democratic government, and the higher priority given to a need for economic over political reform. Today virtually all of Latin America's thirty-three countries are governed by democratically elected officials. However, citizens throughout the region have voiced sentiments similar to those of the Mexicans with whom I spoke, raising questions regarding the ability of these regimes, many of which are new, to adequately respond to the needs of their citizenry, and the future of those regimes that are not able to do so. This chapter will examine the nature of "democracy" in Latin America and the challenges these new governments face, and will assess the implications of the new political and economic reality on the region's residents. Given the number and diversity of countries in Latin America, I will attempt only to identify and discuss broad patterns and trends.

Most Latin American nations became independent republics in the early nineteenth century, and since that time the majority has endured swings in the political pendulum between autocratic rule and more "democratic" forms of government. During the latest round of authoritarian rule, which occurred during the height of the Cold War, elected civilians ruled only four mainland countries. However, for a variety of reasons, the situation has been reversed.[1] The regional tendency was rule by middle-class military leaders and technocrats who engaged in repressive tactics and governed in the interests of the upper classes. These dictators usually presented their forced intervention into

---

[1] The countries included Mexico, Costa Rica, Venezuela, and Colombia.

politics as necessary in order to halt Leftist (or "communist") activities in the country, to bring about economic recovery, or to restore law and order. Virtually all declared the return to democracy as their goal, once political and/or economic problems had been solved. Rather than restoring economic well-being, however, the policies adopted by the military regimes led to worsening conditions, and their massive external borrowing resulted in a foreign debt crisis by the early 1980s when Mexico, Brazil, Argentina, and other Latin American countries were forced to reschedule their debt.

Between 1978 and 1990, fifteen Latin American countries moved toward elected civilian rule. The transition occurred in an episodic fashion as result of massive demonstrations against political and economic conditions, economic crises, labor strikes, war losses, and/or international pressure. Furthermore, with the end of the Cold War the United States no longer felt compelled to prop up authoritarian regimes because of their anti-communist stance. Few of these new governments had democratic traditions to fall back on, and some, including El Salvador, Nicaragua, and Bolivia, had virtually no history of democracy. Many observers hoped that a return to democratic rule in the region would result in more equitable distribution of resources, more effective and responsive political institutions, and improvement in human and civil rights. Unfortunately, these changes have not occurred. Inequity and poverty rates increased in the 1980s and 1990s, mainly as result of the neoliberal economic policies adopted first by a number of the military governments, and later, by the new democratic leaders. The process through which neoliberal reform programs were adopted underscores the vulnerability of regional economies to global economic forces.

In the 1930s, most Latin American countries moved away from the export-led growth model that had been in place since before independence and adopted an inward-oriented economic paradigm, relying on import substitution industrialization (ISI) and broad governmental protections to reduce a growing economic disparity with the industrialized world. However, largely because of structural weaknesses in the ISI paradigm, regional economies grew increasingly dependent on international investment and loans, which after the 1970s became much more mobile and accessible. This dependence on foreign capital exacerbated the vulnerability of Latin American economies, and when the debt crises of the early 1980s struck, international financial institutions, including the International Monetary Fund (IMF) and the World Bank, made adoption of structural adjustment programs a requirement for international loans. Governments throughout the region had little choice but to adopt "neoliberal" economic reform programs, which include the removal of barriers to international trade, privatization of industries, relatively unhindered foreign investment, an end to government subsidies, and curtailment of social spending (on education, health care, and other services), in an attempt to end the immediate crises and to generate long-term economic growth.

The dramatic economic restructuring associated with neoliberal forms has resulted in greater access to international capital, lower inflation, increased exports, and a somewhat higher growth rate (3% per year for the region in the 1990s, as opposed to 1.9% in the 1980s). Still, the growth rate does not approach the 6% regional rate of the 1960s and 1970s, nor does it meet the 3.4% that the World Bank deems the minimum for reducing poverty (Hakim, 1999/2000). Additionally, practices such as the lowering of tariffs, closing or modernizing of industrial plants, reduction of benefits for workers, privatizing of state-owned firms, restructuring of labor markets, reduction of the minimum wage, decreasing of social spending, and curtailment of government subsidies have resulted in business failures, rampant unemployment, a weakened labor force, and increased poverty. Leaders refer to such economic and social dislocations as temporary, but the fact is that neoliberal programs emphasize economic reforms only, generally ignoring social needs or political reform.

Neoliberal reforms have further exacerbated economic inequities: some countries in the region have the highest income disparity in the world (Inter-American Development Bank (IDB)). In 1995 the wealthiest one percent of the region's population earned 417 times more than the poorest one percent, while in 1970 it had earned 363 times more. In Chile, the one country in the region that has implemented a variety of social programs to address economic disparity, national wealth is still controlled by the upper 20% of the population. In the first half of the 1990s, the number in extreme poverty increased by 1.5 million and those deemed moderately poor grew by 5 million people (Karl, 2000). At the same time, the number of people in the "informal economy" grew dramatically. Furthermore, the volatility of international capital has contributed to an overall economic downturn in Latin America in the 1990s, worsening the plight of the majority. According to the World Bank, the number of people living on less than US$1 per day increased from 63.7 million in 1987 to 78.2 million in 1998 (World Development Report 2000/2001, Table 1.1). As conditions deteriorate in the region, concerns increase that, in adopting free market programs, leaders lose the ability to devise policies that would benefit lower socioeconomic groups. As one analyst put it, neoliberal policies in Latin America have "ripped the heart out of democratization, turning what could have been a flowering of political and social participation into a brand of 'low-intensity democracy'" (Green, 1995, p. 164).

Another characteristic of Latin America's new democracies is their failure to provide effective and responsive political institutions, leading some to label them "authoritarian democracies" or "elite democracies". The nature of the current crop of "democratic" regimes has generated a debate regarding the definition of democracy. There is general agreement, at least in regards to Latin America, that the "minimalist" definition proposed by Robert Dahl (1961, 1971) applies: a democracy will include broad participation in regularly scheduled, competitive elections, and citizens are protected by civil and political liberties. The degree of adherence to these requirements varies greatly in the region, however. Most observers recognize that while it may occur in the future, "liberal" democracy, which incorporates a broad range of egalitarian principles, is generally absent in Latin America today.[2] The majority of states in the

---

[2] Unless otherwise noted, generalizations regarding the nature and status of democracy in Latin America were drawn from sources listed in the attached bibliography. The number of publications on the topic has mushroomed since the early 1990s and is too extensive for mention in the text.

region transitioned from dictatorships to civilian rule without changing some of their authoritarian and oligarchic underpinnings and behaviors. While some have described the "illiberal" nature of the new democracies as a legacy of former military dictatorships (see Petras, 1997; Zakaria, 1997), a broader historical perspective demonstrates that the pattern is far more longstanding. In the transition to democracy, few countries have undertaken constitutional reform or improved basic governmental institutions, which would facilitate effective democratic rule. Presidentialism, or strong-man rule, is widespread in the region, and dilutes democracy in part because these "new caudillos", like the military leaders before them, weaken and discredit basic democratic institutions including judicial systems, legislatures, and political parties.

Even though most of the region's constitutions deny consecutive presidential terms, Carlos Menem in Argentina, Alberto Fujimori in Peru, Fernando Henrique Cardoso in Brazil, Perez Balladares in Panama, and Hugo Chavez in Venezuela have circumvented this stipulation to win consecutive terms, or have attempted to do so. Fujimori and Chavez have shut down Congress, rewritten constitutions to enhance their own power, and used the military rather than democratic institutions to govern. Fujimori agreed not to complete his third term in office in September 2000 only after his security chief, Vladimiro Montesinos Torres, was videotaped bribing an opposition congressman to support Fujimori in the disputed election.[3] The strongman behavior of Fujimori and Chavez led one analyst to comment in mid-2000, "These two countries are leading the way to hybrid regimes that are formally democratic but where wide powers are progressively concentrated in one authoritarian and neopopulist leader" (Petrash in LaFranchi, May 2000). Bolivia's Hugo Banzer, elected in December 1999, earlier ruled the country as dictator. Guatemala's Alvaro Arz, known for controlling the country's press, reportedly models his government after that of Mexico's PRI, which monopolized Mexican politics throughout much of the twentieth century.

Among the reasons these strongmen are elected and re-elected is their populist posturing. They promise to reverse the ill effects of neoliberal reforms and to take a hard line against terrorism, corruption, rising crime rates, drug trafficking, and other social and economic problems, which have become pandemic. Some of the region's new leaders have also presented themselves as nationalists, ready to rescue national identity in the face of increasing globalization. Chavez, who has presented himself as the new Simón Bolívar—South America's liberator—was apparently re-elected in 2000 by the lower classes (which make up a majority of the population), based to a large extent on his promise to focus on jobs, personal safety, and an end to political corruption.

The failure of democratic regimes to modify old institutional structures has also impeded democratic reform and has often meant little change from past repression, corruption, and a resulting lack of trust in government. Institutional

---

[3] In September 2000 Fujimori, bowing to pressure, announced that new elections would be held in spring 2001. He indicated, however, that he hopes to be a presidential candidate again in the future.

weakness is particularly evident in Venezuela, Colombia, Argentina, Peru, and virtually all of Central America. A paucity of responsive and responsible political parties, poorly designed electoral systems, corrupt and/or ineffective judiciaries, failure of the rule of law, brutal police and security forces and continued autonomy of the armed forces exemplify this failure. An early 2000 IDB report says that only Africa ranks lower than Latin America in failure of rule of law and increased corruption. The same report states that the number of murders in the region, which were the highest in the world in the 1970s, have risen, now approaching rates roughly 40 times that of the developed world. Some of this behavior is tied to longstanding cultural practices, as is seen in the case of Brazil: with the transition to democracy in the late 1980s, the country's new political openness led to a return to the traditional political practices of favoritism, bribery, and clientelism both at the regional and national levels. The political parties that emerged in this milieu are corrupt, parochial, and personalistic (See Kingstone & Power, 2000). The failure of the new regimes in this regard is seen by some as a threat to their longevity. In an early 2000 opinion poll of 17 countries in the region, only 37% of respondents expressed satisfaction with the way democracy worked in their countries, a number similar to a 1997 poll. As was true in 1997, satisfaction was higher in countries enjoying relative peace and prosperity, such as Uruguay and Costa Rica. One in four Brazilians indicated that they might prefer authoritarian government to the current regime ("Yours Discontently", 2000).

The formal democracies have also failed to address human and civil rights abuses in Latin America. Amnesty International reports that in 1999, the armed forces were involved in atrocities against the civilian population in Colombia, Ecuador and Mexico. In the Mexican state of Chiapas, Catholic Church officials issued a report to the United Nations High Commissioner on Human Rights accusing the Mexican military of atrocities in its six-year-old war against the mostly indigenous Zapatistas (America, 1999). Reports of torture, killings, disproportionate use of force, and arbitrary detentions by police and security forces in 1999 came from 23 countries in the region, including Ecuador, Jamaica, Brazil, El Salvador, Venezuela, Bolivia, Haiti, and Nicaragua. The most common victims include indigenous groups, peasants, journalists, human rights and land reform activists, prisoners, members of trade unions, and even minors. Arbitrary arrests and detention without due process were reported in eight countries (Amnesty International Report, 2000).

While the involvement of some of the region's armed forces in human rights violations is a concern to human rights activists, their high political profile in a number of countries has raised fears that the armed forces would politically intervene once again, given the volatility of regional economic conditions. In the late 1980s and early 1990s, military revolts against constitutional governments occurred in Argentina, Ecuador, Guatemala, Panama, and Venezuela. A high level of military involvement in politics is evident today in Chile, Guatemala, Ecuador, Paraguay, Venezuela, and Peru. In 1999, Ecuadorian military officers (like Chavez in Venezuela) evoked the name of Simón Bolívar as they forcibly replaced one President with another. In May of 2000 army officers attempted a coup in Paraguay, and some observers also fear a military revolt in Venezuela because of Chavez' populist tactics and anti-military posturing. Those who led the Ecuadorian coup are in prison, but have vowed to take power through fair elections upon release (again, as did Venezuela's Chavez) (LaFranchi, 2000).

An active civil society is generally considered crucial to guaranteeing human and civil rights and to democratic reform in general.[4] In Latin America, contrary to expectations, a strong civil society did not accompany the return of democratic rule. Among the reasons: the negotiated nature of the transition to more democratic rule; a legacy of fear and mistrust of government; the "top-down nature of the democratization process"; and the impact of neoliberal reforms.[5] The number of regional non-government organizations (NGOs) declined after democratization (although foreign NGOs are increasingly active in the region, as described below) in part because many were "captured by the state during the democratic transition" (Gwynne, 2000, p. 25). With the end of authoritarian rule, social activism became less political and often proved too weak to oppose elite democracies (Grugel, 2000). Neoliberalism has also altered the nature of social activism, since by exacerbating social and economic inequality it has limited the areas of common concern (Roberts, 1997). As a result, civil society is more fragmented and thus weakened. Levels of social and political activism also vary within the region depending on degrees of literacy, local political culture (for example, the extent of disillusionment with democracy) and the local social and political context. In the 1990s civil society was more inclusive and active in countries with higher literacy rates, such as Chile, Argentina, Costa Rica, and Uruguay.

Elsewhere, this fragmentation has been evident. Indigenous and peasant groups, rural women's organizations, Black communities, religious organizations and other groups agitate separately, for the most part, for land reform, improved social and economic benefits, bilingual education, an end to genocidal violence, political representation, an end to corruption, and other causes. Some alliances have occurred, however. In Mexico, Brazil, Bolivia, Colombia, and Paraguay, what were once peasant movements increasingly include educated citizens who have knowledge of issues both national and international, and who know that they must work together with urban groups. Such alliances resulted in general strikes in Ecuador, Brazil and Bolivia in 1996 and 1997, and have meant that the Zapatista rebellion in Mexico has found support throughout the country. In addition, the majority of these groups' leaders are young, between twenty and thirty years of age (Petras, 1998).

Some observers pin their hopes for a more active civil society on religious groups. Protestant organizations are making inroads among the lower and

[4] This statement rests on the notion of civil society as reflecting notions of inclusion, the importance of local pressure or interest groups for development and democratization, and the concept of social mobilization and activism whereby "'ordinary' people make demands on the state and manage to resist state pressures" (Grugel, 2000, pp. 88).
[5] Patricio Silva (2000) argues that "the increasing impact of the process of globalization in the national economic and political agendas has ... discouraged many people about the real possibilities they have to influence decision-making in their countries" (see pp. 51–61).

middle classes, and are beginning to seek access to political power (Bastian, 1998). One scholar argues that Protestant activism in Latin America will play a role in building democratic infrastructures similar to the role Alexis de Tocqueville assigned Protestants in the nineteenth century United States (Ireland, 1999). In Mexico, the Catholic Church supports civic culture, and has consistently voiced opposition to neoliberal policies and corruption (Camp, 1999). In Brazil, an activist group established by the Brazilian Bishops' Conference was among the backers of country-wide public demonstrations against poverty and exclusion in September 2000. The primary target of these anti-poverty demonstrators was the IMF (*Latinnews*, 2000).

CONCLUSION

In the mid-1990s, the primary concern of analysts examining the transition to democratic governance in Latin America was whether the new regimes would endure. Five years later most are relatively certain that, having weathered severe crises in recent years, most governments in the region will continue to act as formal if not liberal democracies, at least for the time being. The question now is whether regional leaders can or will address the myriad of social, political and economic problems that have resulted from their failure to restructure political institutions and their reliance on neoliberalism, and whether democracy will be broadened to include people of all socioeconomic sectors. The structure of the global economy and the regional economies' continued dependence on foreign capital and markets mean that neoliberal economic policies are here to stay, at least for the foreseeable future. Furthermore, just as was the case in the early twentieth century, Latin America is currently subject to neocolonialism, which results in limited autonomy for the state. Regional governments are subject to international forces and their responses are limited.

Not all countries in the region have reached the same stage of democratization, and to date most have not achieved a state of real democracy at all. Social and economic inequality, continued repression, authoritarian-style leadership, failure of the judiciary and rule of law, and continuing military prerogatives indicate that what has happened in many countries is no more than a transition from military to civilian rule. The shift to neoliberal economic policies has limited the ability of the civilian regimes to address economic and social ills created by the free market reforms. As stipulated by the rules of the new global order, leaders must respond to the needs of the international community before they respond to the needs of their own citizenry.

To date, democratic regimes have reacted in different ways to the challenge. Many have declared the social and economic results of neoliberal policies temporary, and promise to carry out needed reforms of social and political institutions when macroeconomic conditions improve. Some, like Chile, have initiated limited social programs such as broadened education and job training (Gwynne, 2000). Others, eager to advance economic development at any cost, have promoted the idea that consumerism is synonymous with liberty. As Larraín (2000) has noted, "the former values of equality, state-sponsored welfare, fairness and general austerity ... are now replaced by individual success, conspicuous consumption and privatized welfare. The point now is no longer justice, full employment or industrial development but rather to become winner nations comparable to the Asian tigers" (p. 196).

The search for alternatives to regional problems has required paradigmatic shifts. A number of Leftist parties in the region are engaged in revising their ideological and political positions and are proposing solutions to the economic problems associated with neoliberalism similar to those adopted in parts of Europe. Most of these proposals are variations on the social democratic theme, and involve a greater role for the state in distribution of economic benefits while maintaining free market competition (Roberts, 1997). As LaFranchi (1999) recently observed, such programs are called "cambio lite" in Argentina and "socialismo descafeinado" in Chile. These socialists and social democratic programs have been presented as a "third way".

Still, while the shortcomings of Latin American democracies are obvious, none of the countries has returned to strict authoritarian rule, in part because of new regional and international economic and political constraints. Trading blocs such as Mercosur and NAFTA, the IMF, the IDB, and other organizations have stipulated democratic government as a prerequisite for membership or loans. Some observers have expressed faith in the efforts of international agencies to build democracy in the region. A determination to "shore up the region's fragile democracies" emerged from the Summit of the Americas in April 1998, resulting in agreements among regional leaders to set up a training center for the region's judges and prosecutors and endorsement of the Inter-American Human Rights Commission's efforts to monitor individual freedoms.[6] The U.S. Agency for International Development (USAID) became the primary funding agency for support of democracy in Latin America after the Summit of the Americas in 1994. A cooperative effort was launched that year to address the most pressing needs in the region, including democratic governance. USAID works with the OAS, the IDB, the World Bank, and the Working Group on Democracy in Latin America in democratization efforts, which include not only providing development assistance but strengthening judicial systems, encouraging civil society, and providing training and support for new local officials (USAID Congressional Presentation, 1998). European Union countries supply over half of all aid flowing into Latin America, and increasingly this aid is channeled through European NGOs to encourage democracy in the region. Up until the 1990s, European NGOs concentrated on economic and developmental issues, but since that time they have shifted their focus to include the objectives of developing citizenship and civil society to promote democratization (Grugel, 2000).

---

[6] The IDB and World Bank offered loans totaling US$8.2 billion for such education between 1998 and 2001 (*The Economist*, 1998).

Will "democracy", in whatever form, last in Latin America? Yes, at least in the foreseeable future. Current economic policies benefit the wealthy and international sectors, and despite efforts on the part of the Left and civil society in general, the corporate culture of those groups portends their willingness to maintain the status quo as long as their demands are occasionally met (Weyland, 1998). Still, some analysts view ongoing inequality as the most serious threat to democratic reform, in that it reduces aspirations and undermines rules and institutions. As Tocqueville put it, the real threat to democracy is not sudden authoritarian takeover but a gradual decline in its quality. As long as a majority of people in the region rank improved economic conditions above democratic reform, as did those Mexicans in summer 2000, real democracy will remain elusive.

REFERENCES

America (U.S.) (1999). (18 December), 181(20), 5.

Amnesty International Report (2000). On the web at http://www.web.amnesty.org/web/ar2000web.nsf/

Andrews, G.R., & Chapman, H. (Eds.) (1995). *The social construction of democracy, 1870–1990.* New York: New York University Press.

Barahona de Brito, A. (1997). *Human rights and democratization in Latin America: Uruguay and Chile.* New York: Oxford University Press.

Bartell, E., & Payne, L. (Eds.) (1995). *Business and democracy in Latin America.* Pittsburgh: University of Pittsburgh Press.

Bastian, J. (1998). The New Religious Map of Latin America: Causes and Social Effects. *Cross-Currents,* 48(3), 330–347.

Bauzon, K.E. (1993). *Development and democratization in the Third world: Myths, hopes and realities.* Washington, D.C.: Crane Russak.

Camp, R.A. (1996). *Democracy in Latin America: Patterns and cycles.* Wilmington, DE: SR Books.

Camp, R.A. (1999). Democracy through Mexican lenses. *The Washington Quarterly,* 22(3), 229–39.

Carranza, M. E. (1997). Transitions to electoral regimes and the future of civil-military relations in Argentina and Brazil. *Latin American Perspectives* 24(3), 7–28.

Cleary, E.L. (1997). *The struggle for human rights in Latin America.* Westport, Conn.: Praeger.

Dahl, R.A. (1961). *Who governs? Democracy and power in an American city.* New Haven: Yale University Press.

Dahl, R.A. (1971). *Polyarchy: Participation and opposition.* New Haven: Yale University Press.

Diamond, L., Linz, J.J., & Lipset, S.M. (Eds.) (1989) *Democracy in developing countries.* Four volumes. Boulder: Lynne Rienner.

Domínguez, J. I. (1998). *Democratic politics in Latin America and the Caribbean.* Baltimore: The Johns Hopkins University Press.

Dussell, I., Finocchio, S., & Gojman, S. (1997). *Haciendo Memoria En El Paos de Nimca Mas.* Buenos Aires: Editorial Universitaria de Buenos Aires.

The Economist (1998). 347(April 25) 37.

Gardella, J.C. (Ed.) (1996). *Derechos Humanos y Ciencias Sociales: Problematicas a Fin de Siglo.* Rosario, Argentina: Homo Sapiens.

Green, David (1995). Silent revolution: the rise of market economics in Latin America. As cited in R.N. Gwynne & C. Kay (Eds.), *Latin America transformed: Globalization and modernity,* 25. New York: Oxford University Press.

Griffith, I.L., & Sedoc-Dahlberg, B. (Eds.) (1997). *Democracy and human rights in the Caribbean.* Boulder, Colo.: Westview.

Grugel, J. (2000). Romancing civil society: European NGOs in Latin America. *Journal of Interamerican Studies and World Affairs,* 42(2), 87–107.

Gwynne, R.N. (2000). Globalization, Neoliberalism and Economic change in South America and Mexico. In R.N. Gwynne & C. Kay (Eds.), *Latin America transformed: globalization and modernity* (pp. 69–98). New York: Oxford University Press.

Gwynne, R.N., & Kay, C. (2000). Latin America transformed: changing paradigms, debates and alternatives. In R.N. Gwynne & C. Kay (Eds.), *Latin America transformed: Globalization and modernity* (pp. 2–30). New York: Oxford University Press.

Hakim, P. (1999/2000). Is Latin America doomed to failure? *Foreign Policy,* 117, 104–113.

Hall, J. (1995). Search of civil society. In John Hall (Ed.), *Civil society: Theory, history, and comparison* (pp. 1–31). Cambridge: Polity Press.

Inter-American Development Bank (2000). *Development beyond economics.* Washington, D.C.: IDB.

Ireland, R. (1999). Popular religions and the building of democracy in Latin America: saving the Tocquevillian parallel. *Journal of Interamerican Studies and World Affairs,* 41(4), 111–136.

Jelin, E., & Hershberg, E. (Eds.) (1996). *Constructing democracy: Human rights, citizenship, and society in Latin America.* Boulder, Colo.: Westview.

Karl, T.L. (2000). Economic inequality and democratic instability. *Journal of Democracy,* 11(1), 149–156.

Kingstone, P.R. & Power, T.J. (Eds.) (2000). *Democratic Brazil: Actors, institutions, and processes.* Pittsburgh: University of Pittsburgh Press.

LaFranchi, H. (2000). Learning democracy in Caracas. *Christian Science Monitor,* 23 May.

LaFranchi, H. (2000). Stirring in South America's barracks. *Christian Science Monitor,* 1 June.

LaFranchi, H. (1999). Latin America tiptoes to the left. *Christian Science Monitor,* 22 October.

Larraìn, J. (2000). Modernity and identity: Cultural change in Latin America. In R. N. Gwynne & C. Kay (Eds.), *Latin America transformed: Globalization and modernity* (pp. 182–202). New York: Oxford University Press.

Latinnews, September 12, 2000

Linz, J.J., & Stepan, A. (Eds.) (1995). *Problems of democratic transition and consolidation: Southern Europe, South America, and post-Communist Europe.* Baltimore: The Johns Hopkins University Press.

Mainwaring, S., & Valenzuela, A. (Eds.) (1998). *Politics, society and democracy: Latin America, essays in Honor of Juan J. Linz.* Boulder: Westview Press.

Mainwaring, S., & Shugart, M.S. (1997). *Presidentialism and democracy in Latin America.* Cambridge: Cambridge University Press.

Morales, I., de los Reyes, G., & Rich, P. (Eds.) (1999). *Civil Society and democratization.* Annals of the Academy of Political and Social Science.

Nef, J. (1995). Demilitarization and democratic transition in Latin America. In S. Halebsky & R.L. Harris (Eds.), *Capital, power and inequality in Latin America.* Boulder: Westview Press.

Petras, J. (1997). Alternatives to neoliberalism in Latin America. *Latin American Perspectives,* 24(1), 80–91.

Petras, J. (1998). Learning from Latin America's rural poor. *Tikkun,* 13(2), 15–19.

Riley, M. (1999). Latin America's tide of semidemocracy. *World and I,* 14(12), 60–62.

Roberts, K.M. (1997). Rethinking economic alternatives: left parties and the articulation of popular demands in Chile and Peru. In D.A. Chalmers et al. (Eds.), *The new politics of inequality in Latin America: Rethinking participation and representation.* New York: Oxford University Press.

Silva, P. (2000). The new political order in Latin America: towards technocratic democracies? In R.N. Gwynne & C. Kay (Eds.), *Latin America transformed: Globalization and modernity* (pp. 52–65). New York: Oxford University Press.

Smith, W.C., Acuna, C.H., & Gamarr, E.A. (Eds.) (1994) *Democracy, markets, and structural reform in Latin America: Argentina, Bolivia, Brazil, Chile, and Mexico.* Transaction.

Taylor, R. (2000). Fading neoliberalism. *World Press Review,* 47(1), 18.

Tulchin, J. (Ed.) (1995). *The consolidation of democracy in Latin America.* New York: Lynne Rienner Publishers.

Veltmeyer, H., Petras, J.F., & Vieux, S. (Eds.) (1997). *Neoliberalism and Class Conflict in Latin America: A comparative perspective on the political economy of structural adjustment.* Hampshire: MacMillan Press Ltd.

Weyland, K. (1998). Swallowing the bitter pill: sources of popular support for neoliberal reform in Latin America. *Comparative Political Studies,* 31(10), 569–589.

World Bank (2000). *World Development Report 2000/2001: Attacking Poverty.* New York: Oxford University Press.

Yours discontentedly, Latin America. (2000, 13 May). *The Economist,* 34–35.

Zakaria, F. (1997). The rise of illiberal democracy. *Foreign Affairs,* 76, November/December, 22–43.

CHAPTER 11

Promises Kept, Promises Broken

Recent Political and Economic Trends Affecting Children and Youth in Brazil[1]

Irene Rizzini and Gary Barker

INTRODUCTION

The irresistible global changes described in Chapter One are the broader context for countries that are experiencing change in their own specific way. The global changes might provide new challenges as varied as setting a higher bar for young people's search for a decent paying job or for meeting new standards for the treatment of children. The global changes may provide new opportunities or may provide new problems for a country experiencing more than its fair share of domestic problems.

The interconnections between national and international changes in Brazil are quite varied. The common factor is the sheer rate of change at both levels. Sometimes international change has had a direct bearing on local changes as in Brazil's willingness to use international standards on children's rights to develop a new legislative framework for national protections for children, including child labor eradication. Sometimes globalization simply exacerbates national challenges. Brazil's struggle to increase the educational level of young people, only half of whom enter high school, becomes more critical as freer international trade increases the rewards to countries with a highly trained

[1] We wish to thank the following organizations and individuals for information and data supplied for this paper: Save the Children, Recife, Brazil, Per Miljeteig (Childwatch International Research Network, Oslo), Jussara de Goias (Instituto Nacional de Estudos Socio-Economicos, Brasilia), Jorge Barros (Childhope, Rio de Janeiro), Comissao Nacional da Marcha Global pela Erradicao do Trabalho Infantil (Sao Paolo), Adelaide Consoni (IPA-International Play Association, Sao Paolo), and Carlos Eduardo Sartor, for his guidance and the document elaborated by him for CESPI/USU.

work force. And sometimes international patterns find a parallel in national trends as in the increasing or continuing inequality of income.

Perhaps the most salient consequence of global changes for Brazil is that the country has to face up to the consequences of globalization at the same time that it is facing huge domestic challenges, many of which have a dramatic impact on children. This chapter describes some of those challenges that particularly affect children. Overall, as we will argue in this chapter, some undeniable advances and improvements have been made at the policy level on behalf of low-income children in Brazil. At other levels, however, actions have not followed the promises.

BRAZIL IN TRANSITION

In the last 50 years, Brazil has experienced impressive economic growth and major structural transformation; however, this economic growth has for the most part exacerbated rather than improved social inequities, and contributed to increased concentration of wealth and land ownership in the hands of a relatively small number of people. Brazil currently has the dubious distinction of having one of the world's worst income distributions.

After rapid economic growth in the 1960s and 1970s, the 1980's were marked by recession, widespread economic instability, high external debt, high unemployment, and staggering inflation, which in 1989–1990 reached more than a hundred per cent per month. This hyperinflation further increased income inequalities in Brazil and made life harder for most people. The middle and upper classes had their income indexed for inflation, but low-income families saw their real income fall.

These economic trends have to be understood in the context of the political situation. Brazil was run by a military dictatorship that assumed power in 1964 and ruled for more than 20 years. This authoritarian regime killed, repressed or simply "disappeared" many members of the opposition, including student activists, members of civil society, and academics.

During the period of the military dictatorship, the social and economic problems in Brazil—particularly land and income distribution—worsened rather than improved, contrary to the so-called "Brazilian economic miracle" that was widely promoted (Schilling, 1994). The country also underwent rapid urbanization. The lack of effective land reform created a situation of abandonment and increasing poverty in rural areas, and brought thousands of low-income families to marginalized areas of Brazil's cities—families with few prospects for meaningful employment. The lack of social support for these families resulted in homeless or street families, or people ended up working in marginalized and unsafe conditions, such as garbage dumps or waste recycling. Others got involved in drug trafficking groups as a way to guarantee their survival.

By the early 1980s, it became increasingly difficult for the military government to control the political and economic situation in the country. After significant social mobilization, the government finally agreed to hand over rule to a civilian president elected by Congress in 1985. Direct presidential elections resumed in 1989. Even after this return to democratic rule, however, political upheaval continued. Brazil's first directly elected president following military rule was impeached and resigned over corruption charges in 1992.

Brazil's current president, Fernando Henrique Cardoso, was re-elected (and originally came to power) for his role in stabilizing Brazil's hyperinflation. In 1994, under Cardoso's leadership, the Brazilian government adopted an economic and monetary policy that has until recently succeeded in controlling inflation, but has caused some prices to stabilize at a level beyond the reach of much of the population. Various events at the international level have led to financial instability and slower economic growth, particularly in 2000 and 2001.

After a number of years of rising expectations in the 1990s, Brazilians in general do not have much reason to celebrate; in fact most Brazilian families feel the results of the neoliberal economic policies in their daily lives. According to a recent analysis of structural adjustment policies in Latin America in the 1990s, such policies are not working and economic stability has not been achieved. Indeed, instead of stability, real wages have fallen: "in some countries, the minimum wage lost up to 75% of its purchasing power" ("Neoliberalismo criticado," 1999). In addition, the Brazilian currency, the real, lost approximately half of its value against the U.S. dollar between 1998–2001. Recently, the real has been unstable against the U.S. dollar, varying between R$2.5 to US$1 up to R$2.8 to US$1.

According to Celso Furtado, renowned Brazilian economist and former planning minister, what the Brazilian government proposed to do—that is carry out structural adjustment and promote development—is an impossible task. For him, "Brazil is on a path to rising social tension" due to unemployment, the failure of the state, and threats to democracy ("Furtado alerta," 1999).

During the last few years, a period of intense economic turmoil, the Brazilian government demonstrated rhetorical commitment to the poor, but in practice the models of development adopted in the country have done relatively little to address income inequalities and social exclusion. According to World Bank data, Brazil has the worst income distribution among more than 60 countries for which data is available. As of 1989, the richest 10% of the population controlled 51.3% of total income, while the poorest 20% of the population had access to just 2.1% of total income (World Bank, 1997). Recent figures show that "while 9% of the Brazilians live with less than US$1 a day, 46.7% of the national income are in the hands of 10% of the population" ("Brasileiro elege," 2001). Indeed, recent macroeconomic analyses of the Brazil economy suggest that skewed income distribution continues to be one of, if not the, major impediment to social development in Brazil.

As a region, Latin America has the worst income distribution in the world. While Latin America has experienced significant modernization and economic growth in the past two decades, this growth has not—contrary to many neoliberal economic theories—led to more equitable income distribution ("Distribuicao de renda," 1998).

Despite its immense natural wealth and capital development, which places it among the world's ten largest economies, Brazil is still considered a developing country. However, this tremendous wealth sharply contrasts with the level of poverty experienced by the majority of its population of approximately 160 million. Recent figures suggest that over 40% of the entire population lives in a situation of extreme poverty.

It is difficult to evaluate completely the situation of poverty of Brazil; figures presented by the government and other sources are sometimes incomplete, distorted, and exaggerated. Nonetheless, census data probably gives the clearest idea of the level of poverty faced by a large portion of the population. Census data from 1995 found that 23.6% of the population has a monthly family income of less than one half of the minimum wage (which in 1999 represented about US$70), and 19% of the population has a monthly family income between US$70 and US$140 (Brazilian Institute of Geography and Statistics (IBGE)/UNICEF, 1997).

Demographically, Brazil is a young country with 38.8% of its population under age 18. Unfortunately, poverty in Brazil falls disproportionately on its children and youth: about half of its young people live in poverty. According to official figures, approximately 75% of children ages 0 to 14 live in families with a monthly per capita income of up to two minimum salaries (Table 1). While somewhat imprecise, this data reflects the situation of poverty and income inequality that affects all regions of Brazil (Ribeiro & Sabóia, 1994; IBGE/UNICEF, 1997; Bercovich, Dellasoppa, & Arriaga, 1998; IBGE, 2001).

The size of Brazil's child and adolescent population, and the number of poor children and youth, present tremendous challenges for the social services sector, the most important being the public education system. Nearly 50% of Brazil's population is under the age of 25. The public education system in Brazil can best be represented as a bottleneck, with nearly universal enrollment at the primary level decreasing to dramatically reduced enrollment at the secondary and tertiary level. The school enrollment rate in Brazil falls sharply

Table 1 Families with children ages 0 to 14

Groups of family income per capita in minimum salaries	
Total	100
	20.066.95
Up to 1/2	27.7%
More than 1/2 to 1	25.5%
More than 1 to 2	21.9%
More than 2 to 3	8.0%
More than 3 to 5	6.0%
More than 5	5.4%

Source: Síntese de indicadores sociais 2000/IBGE. Departamento de População e Indicadores Sociais [synthesis of social indicators. Department of Population and Social Indicators. Brazilian Institute of Geography and Statistics]. Rio de Janeiro: IBGE, 2001.

from 95.7% at ages 7–14 (the primary level, and the level at which education is compulsory) to 78.5% at ages 15–17 (the secondary level) (IBGE, 2001).

One of the main reasons for high rates of school drop-out and retention in Brazil, in addition to the lack of adequate education infrastructure, is the need for children and youth to work. Household survey data from 1990 find that 50% of youth ages 15–17 and 17.2% of 10–14 year-olds were working. In urban and rural areas in Brazil many low-income children are frequently compelled to forgo school attendance to support themselves and their families. Data from National Research per Household Sample (IBGE/PNAD, 1995) indicated that 3.6% of children aged 5 to 9 were working an average of 16.2 hours a week.

It should also be mentioned, however, that the number of working children in Brazil is decreasing, albeit slowly. Household survey (PNAD) data showed that in 1998 7.7 million children ages 5–17 worked, down from 9.7 million in 1992, a 20% reduction. The total percentage of children ages 5–17 working decreased from 22 to 17 in this period. At least part of this decrease is probably due to governmental actions in the last ten years related to child labor eradication, including wage supports to families with working children, income supports to low-income families in general, and modest but real increases in school enrollment in Brazil.

Within the issue of low -income children and youth in Brazil, the common image and focus of considerable attention has been that of street children. In the late 1980s, UNICEF and some international advocacy organizations estimated that as many as 7 million children and youth spent most of their time and/or slept on the streets in Brazil, a number that is now recognized as an overstatement (Barker & Knaul, 1991). In the past few years, however, a number of censuses and studies in some Brazilian cities have provided what seems to be a more reasonable estimate of the number of children and youth in this situation. A study in Sao Paulo found that 4,520 children and youth circulated in the streets during the day, but only 895 slept on the streets at night ("Pesquisa muda," 1995). In Salvador, Bahia, a study found 15,743 children and youth working in the streets and 468 living in the streets ("Projeto Axe," 1993). In Fortaleza, research found 184 children and youth living in the streets out of 5,962 children and youth working in the street (Secretaria de Ação Social, 1994). The consensus that is now emerging is that the number of children and youth living in the streets is not nearly as large as once estimated, and is the "tip of the iceberg" of low-income children, the majority of whom continue to live with their families but often in difficult situations that compromise their development (Rizzini, Barker, & Cassaniga, 1998).

In sum, while it is impossible to adequately describe the complexities of Brazil's recent social, economic, and political history in a few pages, it is important to highlight that Brazil represents a country of extremes and disparities, with income and technological and social advances unequally distributed by social class and by geographic region. For example, Brazil's northeast region continues to be the poorest area of the country, and the region where birthrates remain high. The rest of the country has experienced declines in birthrates, with fertility rates nearly on par with industrialized regions. Finally, the country's historical disparity of income distribution is likely only to worsen given the current global economic crisis—a situation with direct implications for children's well-being.

A BRIEF HISTORY OF CHILDREN'S POLICY IN BRAZIL, THE RETURN TO DEMOCRACY, AND A NEW FRAMEWORK FOR CHILDREN'S RIGHTS

Before discussing in detail the current state of children in Brazil, it is important to present a brief historical overview of child policy. A review of the history of social policies in Brazil focusing on children in poor families finds that since the beginning of the century, children wandering and/or working on the streets were systematically placed in large, closed-door institutions, many of which followed a prison-like model, with the justification that it was for their own protection in the case of young children and for re-education in the case of teenagers. For most of the twentieth century, the government's attitude toward poor children has been ambivalent: the policies adopted voiced a concern with protecting children and youth while at the same time seeking to protect society from the potential *danger* of so-called antisocial children and youth. There were few major policy initiatives that sought to promote economic development that would allow low income families to support their children with dignity. Instead, the tendency has been to implement compensatory, remedial, or dependence-creating policies and programs that often separate children and adolescents from their families and communities.

While the practice of housing children in large institutions has become less common in recent years, up until the 1980s thousands of Brazilian children passed their childhoods in closed institutions which were often distant from urban areas. The majority of these children were neither orphaned nor abandoned. Instead they nearly always came from low-income families who thought that their children could be better cared for in state institutions. Other families sought to relieve the burden of caring for one more child, in the absence of other forms of support from the state. After being interned, children generally lost contact with their families and communities of origin; as time passed such ties were gradually lost. Thus, it is appropriate that such children came to be called children of the state (Rizzini, 1997). Until recently, generations of children passed their infancies in such situations, sometimes with irreversible damage to their development. They were frequently labeled as abandoned minors or delinquents in spite of the fact that they generally had families and most had never committed any infraction of the law.

In addition, from the beginning of the century until 1989, the Minors' Codes adopted in Brazil offered little variation in the way that the children of the poor were treated, particularly those who were found on the streets and were seen as a threat to society. Violence and maltreatment on the part of police and the institutions (where they where placed without a hearing) and a general disregard for their rights were the general rule. The state could summarily withdraw guardianship without either proper notification or participation of children or their families. Furthermore, criteria for withdrawal of guardianship were often subjective and discretionary. Poor children who were on the streets or without the immediate protection of a guardian were considered delinquents unless proven otherwise.

In the 1970s and 1980s, with tremendous migration from the poorest areas of the Northeast to the major cities in the Southeast, and an increase in urban poor, the number of children found wandering, working and, in some cases, living on the streets became more visible. The social mobilization that resulted from this phenomenon led to accusations against the government, for failing to develop adequate public policies to address poverty in the country.

Starting in the mid-1980s, a number of non-governmental organizations (NGOs), university-based researchers, advocates, and grassroots movements, including some that were linked to the Catholic Church, together with some progressive factions within the government, began collaborating to improve children's policies and programs. Media reports on the often abysmal conditions in existing children's institutions and the treatment of homeless children by police, plus advocacy efforts by NGOs, resulted in a considerable national outcry on behalf of the "street children" and low-income children in general.

Brazil's Children's Act (known officially as the Statute on the Child and the Adolescent) was born out of this national movement. One of the results of this advocacy and social mobilization movement on behalf of poor children was a debate within the context of the Federal Constitution, approved in 1988, which contained for the first time in Brazilian history an article specifically pertaining to children's rights. Article 227 incorporates and extends the basic content of the International Convention on the Rights of the Child:

> It is the duty of the family, the society, and the State to guarantee to the child and adolescent, with absolute priority, the right to life, health, nutrition, education, leisure, professional training, culture, dignity, respect, liberty, and community and family living, as well as protecting them from discrimination, exploitation, cruelty, and oppression.

Inspired in part by the UN Convention on the Rights of the Child (CRC), the Statute went through numerous revisions during the 1980s, and with constant organization, advocacy, and public pronouncements by broad sectors of Brazilian society, eventually became law in its current form in October 1990. The statute, in terms of its level of detail and scope in the protection and promotion of children's rights and participation, and its decentralized nature, is considered a model for Latin America.

Following the general tenor of the CRC, the new act guarantees children and adolescents a number of basic rights: immunity from criminal prosecution for children under age 18; freedom of movement and expression; and the right to participate in family and community life; among others. Perhaps more important in the Brazil context, however, is that the Statute called for a fundamental re-ordering of the way society viewed children. Until then, the concept of childhood was not associated with rights. The Statute introduced the notion that children were entitled to all human rights and, furthermore, entitled to additional rights and protection because of their special stage in development.

For implementation, the Statute stipulates the formation of two specific bodies which constitute democratic tools to defend children's rights. The Children's Rights Councils, established at the municipal, state, and federal levels, are responsible for coordinating and setting policies for children and for coordinating governmental and non-governmental efforts on behalf of children. Guardianship Councils are municipal-level councils responsible for responding to individual cases of children in conditions of need or risk and for ensuring that children receive the best possible assistance.

The Statute soon became well known as progressive; yet real implementation has been very slow in coming. The institutional infrastructure itself is far from complete. By 1997, only about 55% of Brazil's approximately 5500 municipalities had created a Municipal Children's Rights Council, and many of these are only partially implemented. Guardianship Councils, the direct links to children and youth, have even further to go; in 1997, there were only about 2050 initiated (Brazilian Institute for Municipal Administration (IBAM), 1998). Moreover, even when these newer institutions are established, they face inertia already mentioned: while new policies are in place at the local level, it is frequently the same actors who are responsible for children's policy, actors who often continue to operate with a "business-as-usual" attitude (Klees, Rizzini, & Dewees, 1999).

The implementation of the Statute has been uneven, reflecting the vast regional differences in public administration and levels of public resources. Given the relative lack of experience in the kind of local policymaking and participation set forth in the Statute, it has become clear that it requires changes in local culture as much as it does changes in policy. Furthermore, it is important to keep in mind that the Children's Act and the social movements associated with it imply changes in a sector—children's policy and the juvenile court system—that have historically been among the most conservative in Brazil. Finally, it is important to highlight that the Children's Act was only possible within the context of redemocratization of the country. The social activism and participation of civil society in pressuring the military dictatorship to relinquish power created the same broad social movement that led to the statute.

RECENT TRENDS AND TRANSFORMATIONS AFFECTING CHILDREN AND YOUTH

The following themes represent a combination of general macro-level social trends related to children in Brazil, as well as areas in which emerging research is providing new information on the situation of children.

As pointed out previously, Brazil has seen important social movements on behalf of children in the last 20 years. Nevertheless, there are still many challenges to be faced so that all children benefit from equal opportunities as stated in national and international legislation.

The Paradigm Shift in Children's Rights and
Societal Attitudes Toward Children

The Children's Act and the related social movement have led to a real change in societal perceptions of children and general and widespread recognition of children as subjects of rights. There is a greater awareness of the needs of low-income children in Brazil, and more services and protection available to them than before the Statute. In only a few years, the term "minor" and its negative implications have effectively been eliminated from the juvenile justice system.

There has also been greater concern and attention on the part of broad sectors of society in terms of children in situations of risk, including children and youth living on the streets, and those exploited through prostitution and involved in illegal activities, such as drug trafficking. Rather than seeing children as the cause of these problems, there has been a marked awareness that children are the victims in such activities, and that children's participation in such activities is largely a form of survival.

It is also clear that there has been a significant change in attitudes—on the part of families of working children, national and local policymakers, unions, and employers—toward child labor. In less than ten years, Brazil has moved from fairly widespread acceptance of child labor to nearly universal condemnation of child labor. Until the early 1990s, some governmental programs for children in Brazil advocated work as a way to educate low-income children with the general belief that working was better than being on the streets. National and local efforts to eradicate child labor represent one of the most impressive social mobilization efforts in recent years.

Decentralization of Policymaking and the
Important Role of Civil Society

The end of military rule in the 1980s and the new constitution have led to a greater allocation or delegation of policymaking to states and municipalities. Decentralization has allowed some municipalities and states to develop some innovative policies and programs on behalf of children, although other states and municipalities have lacked resources, political will or policy expertise to develop such initiatives.

Since the return to democratic rule in 1985, civil society has had a stronger role both in policymaking and service delivery. NGOs are more involved in social service delivery of all kinds, in particular services for low-income children and youth. New, community-based programs for children have arisen, some representing private-public partnerships. These new programs have sought to provide developmentally appropriate services and activities—including tutoring, cultural and recreational activities, and vocational training—to all children and youth in the community. In Ceará, for example, these programs have been targeting low-income communities that research found were pushing large numbers of children to the street (Rizzini, Barker, & Cassaniga, 1998).

In addition, NGOs working on behalf of children continue to serve as vocal advocates on behalf of children. While some of these NGOs have adversarial relationships with policymakers, evidence exists of increasing collaboration between governmental bodies and NGOs, including governmental funding of services via NGOs. NGOs have also promoted a growing awareness of the importance of preparing children and youth to be current and future citizens. For the most part, the increasing role of civil society and the decentralization of policymaking have had a positive impact on children in Brazil.

Another trend and change related to civil society that should be mentioned is the growth in corporate donations to NGOs. In the last ten years, private sector funding to NGOs, many of those assisting children, has grown dramatically. With the decline in international funding to NGOs and social projects in Brazil, the private sector is becoming an even more important partner to NGOs working with children.

Continuing and Increasing Social Segregation and a New Focus on Racial Inequalities

Reviewing trends in recent years, one could reasonably argue that in spite of the Statute and a return to democratic rule, the worlds and realities of poor children and their middle and upper class counterparts are further apart than ever before. Children from various social classes in Brazil rarely meet. A common feature of Brazil's major cities is strictly segregated and divided cities with separate residential areas, recreational areas, and commercial areas for the middle class and wealthy and for low-income groups. Even when (or particularly when) low-income urban areas (favelas) are geographically next to wealthier areas, there is considerable segregation between wealthy and middle class children and poor ones. In terms of children's everyday lives, they simply do not have the chance to meet and interact with children from other social classes.

Rio de Janeiro represents a good example of this division. In the wealthiest part of the city, families live in gated condominiums in which mini-cities are built. Residents of these complexes for all practical purposes do not need to leave their complex to obtain goods and services they need. In this situation, children live in supposed safe "paradises" with all the facilities they need. They often socialize only with peers from the same social class who share their same worldview.

Recently, one of Brazil's national television networks presented a special segment on children living in such complexes. Two children living in these buildings, ages 14 and 15, were filmed on what was their first visit to downtown Rio de Janeiro—a distance just 30 kilometers from their homes. For the first time in their lives, they used public transportation. The interviews focused on the children's first contact with an unknown universe. They were shocked to see street children, who until then they had only seen on television. In striking contrast, the children who had never been to downtown Rio had traveled to Disneyland in the U.S. twice.

The consequences of this trend have not yet been identified, but they are visible in terms of hostility between children of different social classes, and a large scale flight of the middle and upper classes from services and spaces where low-income children may also be present. For example, most middle and upper class children and their families are afraid to use public transportation or visit many public spaces in Brazil's cities because of the perceived threat of violence from "delinquent" youth and adults. While attitudes have changed at the policy level, many middle and upper income families continue to believe that low-income children are dangerous and they seek to keep their children apart.

The trend toward privatization of the health and education sectors has also meant increasing social segregation. Middle income families have sought to opt out of the public health and education systems in large numbers, seeking private schools and private health plans for their children. This desertion of the public health and education systems has led to poorer quality services for low-income children in public schools and public health facilities. This trend has direct implications for child labor; low-income children have access to a precarious education system that has little to attract their interest, thus making work seem even more attractive for them and their families.

Within the issue of social segregation, we also find racial inequality. Racial inequality is not a new phenomenon in Brazil, but it is gaining increasing attention. Brazil's history is characterized both by considerable racial mixing and intermarriage, and by the subjugation and exploitation of indigenous populations and of African slaves transported to Brazil during the colonial era to serve the plantation economy. More recently (starting at the beginning of the twentieth century), Brazil experienced various waves of migration from Eastern Europe, Italy, Lebanon, Japan, and elsewhere—ranging from middle class, educated immigrants to working class and low-income immigrants (Ribeiro, 1995). While poverty is slightly less segregated by race in Brazil than in the U.S., involuntary African immigrants and enslaved or exploited indigenous populations have fared much worse on various social indicators than have immigrants of European and Asian descent.

Recent data found that among young people ages 15–24 in Brazil, 51.9% classified themselves as white and 47.6% classified themselves as black or mixed race (which includes any possible combination of indigenous, European and/or African descent). However, a few statistics on educational enrollment and infant mortality serve to demonstrate the extent of racial inequality. Fifty-five percent of enrolled students ages 15–24 are white, while only 44.2% are black or mixed race. Among students who are classified as low-income, however, 69.2% are black or mixed raced, compared to 30.6% who are white. As of 1995, 14.3% of white youth ages 15–24 were enrolled in higher education, compared to only 3.1% of black or mixed race youth (Sabóia, 1998). In addition, the under-five infant mortality rates of black and mixed race infants in

Brazil are two-thirds higher than the rates for white children of the same age (Folha de Sao Paulo, 1998).

In recent years, increasing numbers of NGOs and researchers have been examining race in Brazil. Particularly among Brazilians of African descent, a number of NGOs, including some working with children and youth, have looked for ways to call attention to the role of African culture in Brazil and its importance in the lives of children and youth. For the most part, though, race and ethnicity are issues that deserve greater attention.

Recent Trends in Education and Schooling

Current statistics on educational attainment demonstrate the challenges facing low-income youth. In recent years, particularly during the Cardoso Administration, the Brazilian government has made improvements in educational enrollment at both the primary and secondary levels through a combination of educational reforms: greater local control over education, educational infrastructure, teacher training, scholarships for low-income families to send their children to school (with the idea that the scholarship would offset the loss in income from the child's work), and increases in teacher salaries. Nonetheless, for the most part, the resulting improvements have been in quantity of children enrolled rather than in quality of education.

Public education continues to poorly prepare children and youth to take on the increasingly complicated tasks associated with the modernizing economy. With the return to democracy—and the provisions of the Children's Act calling for children's active participation in their own learning—the public education system does not for the most part prepare children to be citizens in a modern democracy. Public education generally follows traditional, authoritarian, and rote learning methodologies which teach children to memorize rather than to think independently and creatively.

In addition, in recent years a number of researchers have started calling attention to gender differences in education in Brazil, where girls are faring better than boys. Figures from 1995 found that 95.3% of young women ages 15–24 were literate compared to 90.6% of boys, and that 42.8% of girls in this age range were enrolled in school compared to 38.9% of boys. Boys are also more likely to have repeated a grade and to be behind in school, although repetition and low school attainment and enrollment are major problems for both girls and boys (Saboia, 1998). The most frequent explanation given in Brazil for boys' lower school enrollment and achievement is that boys, particularly low-income boys, more frequently begin working outside the home at earlier ages. Saboia (1998) suggests that it is relatively easier for girls to combine their household chores with school, as compared to boys whose work outside the home may interfere with school. Few researchers or policymakers, however, have examined this trend.

A challenge to greater educational enrollment at the secondary level is the need for children from many low-income families to work. Statistics on youth

Table 2 Discrepancy between age and
formal education

Percentage of discrepancy for children 7 to 14,
by age:

7 years	16.6%
8	33.8%
9	45.2%
10	49.8%
11	55.7%
12	62.2%
13	66.8%
14	72.7%

Source: Síntese de indicadores sociais 2000/IBGE.
Departamento de População e Indicadores Sociais
[synthesis of social indicators. Department of
Population and Social Indicators. Brazilian Institute of
Geography and Statistics]. Rio de Janeiro: IBGE, 2001.

employment demonstrate the double bind that many low-income youth in
Brazil face: their families expect them to begin working when young; usually
the work available to youth is low-paying and unstable, with few rights guaranteed, if any work is available at all. As of 1995, 65.2% of all 15–24 year
olds in Brazil worked (Arias, 1998). In spite of the relatively large number
of adolescents working, it is important to point out that during the years of
1992–1995—which were characterized by relative economic stability and
growth in Brazil—only 31% of working youth ages 15–24 worked in jobs that
would be considered stable and had their full rights guaranteed (they had their
carteira assinada, or official work card signed, meaning that they were eligible
for benefits and had their rights guaranteed according to Brazilian labor laws).

One of the main consequences of the high drop-out rates of is the tremendous discrepancy between age and formal education. For example, when children reach the age of 14, almost 73% of them are already behind (see Table 2
for more discrepancies).

Recent Trends in Child Labor

The factors that lead children to work are diverse, and include social, psychological, and cultural factors. However, family income and poverty deserve
special attention. According to official data, 3.9 million children aged 5 to 14
work (IBGE/PNAD, 1995). In 1999, 2.4% of children ages 5 to 9 worked, mostly
in traditional, family agricultural occupations (IBGE, 2001).

In the age range of 10–16, the percentage of children working rises to 19.7,
representing approximately 5 million children, with the average work load being
over 26 hours per week. The main occupation remains in agricultural/livestock
farming, followed by commerce, industry and services. Many working children
are involved in street vending or itinerant work, including washing clothes or

guarding/washing cars. Many working children receive no fixed wage; 56.6% live on tips or commission. Among those child laborers with a salary, 88.8% earn minimum wage or less.

The Brazilian constitution of 1988 stipulated that children had to be at least 14 to be able to work, with children ages 12–14 eligible to work as apprentices. In 1999, the minimum working age was raised to 16 (Brasil, 1988). Thus, Brazil has laws on the books that prohibit children from working. Nonetheless, the realities of the lives of millions of low-income children and adolescents attest to wholesale violations of children's rights. A study commissioned by UNICEF in Brazil concluded that:

> An analysis of data from the first half of the 1990s shows that large numbers of children and adolescents continue to participate in the work place. In other words, the relevant legislation on child work continues to be ignored, leaving the country far from complying with Convention 138 and recommendation 146 of the ILO, and Brazil's own Children's Act. (Saboia, 1996, p. 17)

As previously mentioned, the Brazilian government—with considerable UNICEF and ILO support—has enacted a number of policy and program initiatives that are slowly reducing child labor in the country. Intense social mobilization with the participation of different groups on municipal, state, and national levels has placed eradication of child labor into the political agenda. Most notably, the federal government has initiated relatively low cost interventions that have the potential to reach large numbers of children and families, as in case of the Bolsa-Escola (an income support program for low income families) program, which is expected to reach 866,000 children nationally by the year 2002. The future, however, is uncertain given the changes in state and national leadership.

Recent Trends in Family Life

There has been a marked increase in the proportion and number of women-headed households, and in the number of children living in these households, according to the 1990 census. Women-headed households represented 20% of all households in Brazil, with higher percentages in low-income, urban areas (Bruce, Lloyd, Leonard, Engle, & Duffy, 1995). Between 1980 and 1991, the number of children and adolescents ages 0–17 living in women-headed households increased from 4.8 million to 7.8 million (IBGE, 1994). Women-headed households are more likely to face poverty, with 60% of female-headed households having a monthly income of one-half or less of the monthly minimum wage in 1989 (Ribeiro & Sabóia, 1994). Currently, 26% of the households are headed by women (IBGE, 2001).

Instability of employment—for women and men—and the lack of viable employment in the industrial sector for many working class and low-income men, have no doubt contributed to stress in male-female relations and to the growing rate of marital dissolution. Many low income men have abandoned their families, become abusive, or turned to alcohol when they have been unable to fulfill the role of provider in Brazil's unstable economy. For many low-income adolescent males and boys, the absence of fathers and other positive male role models in the home or in the extended kinship network has apparently led to stress for some young men—an issue that has gained recent attention (Barker & Loewenstein, 1997).

While systematic data is limited, the conclusion that emerges is that a growing number of families are women-headed and that a growing number of children have limited or no contact with their fathers and little financial or emotional support from them. One study from southern Brazil found that father participation and fathers' residence with the mother and child was related to a father's income. Barros (cited in Engle, 1994) concluded that men with higher and more stable incomes were more likely to be involved with their children than men with lower and less stable incomes. This conclusion is similar to research studying low-income fathers elsewhere in the Americas, suggesting that when fathers are unable to fulfill the role of provider they are less likely to be involved in other ways in their children's lives (and/or that mothers are less likely to facilitate or encourage this involvement). However, little research to date has focused on the impact on children of this apparent decreasing contact and support from their fathers.

While more research is needed to document trends in Brazilian families, increased rates of work outside the home by women and relatively limited involvement by fathers results in children having less interaction and perhaps less guidance from parents. These trends seem to be similar to those found in other parts of the world, and seem to affect children of all social classes, although the situation is exacerbated by poverty.

Middle class families are often able to pay for alternative child care arrangement—day care centers, nannies, etc.—while low-income families may rely on extended kinship network or have no alternative care arrangements. The tendency seems to be that the children of the poor continue to be expected to care for themselves—and even to contribute to the family income—while middle class children may be left alone within the relatively protected spaces of homes and gated apartment complexes.

A recent study by CESPI and PROMUNDO in two low income communities in Rio de Janeiro concluded that informal child care arrangements or children simply being left alone were much more common than children having access to structured and organized day care or early child education programs. Several recent studies have suggested that early childhood education programs reach only a minority of low-income children in Brazil (Rizzini, Barker et al., 2001).

Increasing Urban Violence

There has been growing attention to the issue of violence as a social problem facing low-income children. Increased violence in urban areas has brought attention to youth violence, but scholars have identified the historical context of a "culture of violence" in Brazil, rooted in the country's colonial history of subjugation and slavery and the deep social divisions mentioned previously (Rizzini, 1994). Violence is no doubt deeply connected to the enduring class structure. There is a culture of impunity and collusion for extrajudicial uses of violence by the state and by members of the privileged classes, while at the same time there is a widespread practice of imprisoning low-income alleged criminals without due process (Bercovich, Dellasoppa, & Arriaga, 1998). Partly as a result of its historical class structure and partly as a result of twenty years of authoritarian military rule, Brazil also lacks widespread, credible, functioning structures for the resolution of conflicts and for criminal justice. Popular or extrajudicial justice continues to be commonplace, both among low-income populations who exact vengeance or carry out extrajudicial justice in their communities, or through vigilante justice and "extermination" groups who represent the ruling class and use extrajudicial violence against low income individuals.

Homicides and other forms of violence increased substantially in the past decade. Brazil currently has the second highest homicide rate in the world after Colombia, with homicides increasing from a rate of 11.2 per 100,000 in 1980 to 23.8 per 100,000 in 1995 (Bercovich, Dellasoppa, & Arriaga, 1998). Research also confirms that these homicides are not randomly distributed among the population but are concentrated by geographic area, gender, age and social class. Low-income, young men ages 15–24 are the most common victims of homicides in Brazil. From 1980–91, the death rate for all age ranges declined in Brazil, with the exception of adolescent males 15–19 and young men ages 20–34, for whom death rates increased during the period (Yunes & Rajs, 1994).

Currently there are about 13,500 deaths from external causes including accidents and suicides, per year in Brazil among adolescent males ages 15–19; of these, about one fourth (3,200) are homicides by firearm (Szwarcwald & Leal, 1998). These deaths are concentrated in low-income urban areas in the Southeast regions of the country (Rio de Janeiro and Sao Paulo states), with Rio de Janeiro responsible for 30% of all deaths by firearms among the age range 15–24 (while it represents only about 5% of the total population of Brazil). In Rio de Janeiro in 1995, there were an alarming 183.6 deaths per 10,000 population among adolescent males ages 15–19. While some of these young men are involved in commandos (armed, drug trafficking groups) or other forms of violence, and are killed by other young men, it would be grossly unfair to portray this situation as simply being intra-group violence. Many of these young men are victims of violence by police, vigilante groups or hired security personnel. Between 1988 and 1990, Brazil's Federal Police confirmed that 4,611 youth and children were murdered, mainly at the hands of police and vigilante groups (CEAP, 1993).

A few studies on other forms of violence have found high rates of victimization of various forms of violence by adolescents. A survey with 1,034 adolescents (average age 15.6) in low income areas in Rio de Janeiro, found that 63% said they had been victims of assault or robbery, 30% had been involved in street fights, and 3% had been imprisoned by police without clear cause (Ruzany et al., 1996). Additional data from Rio de Janeiro finds that the number of children and youth who are victims of homicide is increasing. In the first semester of 1998, 247 children and youth were killed. From 1991 to 1998, 2996 youth ages 15–17 were killed by firearms, a rate that makes juvenile homicide higher in Rio de Janeiro than in New York City and Colombia.

Few researchers or policymakers have considered how a culture of violence shapes the way that children and youth view their world. Brazil currently has a generation of low-income, urban-based children who have witnessed violence in alarming numbers, and middle class children whose families construct protective barriers around them in response to violence (which middle class families tend to blame on low-income youth).

In terms of its implications for child labor, the rates of violence in low-income urban areas (including the participation of youth in drug trafficking groups) has led some families to believe that working is a "safe" or at least "safer" activity than playing. Many low-income, urban families believe that if they keep their children occupied (including in the workplace), they are less likely to become involved in delinquency.

Violence also occurs in the home. Limited research in various settings in Rio de Janeiro finds that an alarming percentage of children and adolescents suffer violence in their homes. In a recent survey of adolescents ages 13–18 carried out by CESPI and PROMUNDO in one low income setting in Western Rio de Janeiro, 21% of young people reported being victims of violence in their homes at least once (Rizzini, Barker et al., 2001).

Conclusions: Promises Kept, Promises Broken

With so many children and adolescents living in situations of poverty in Brazil, what can realistically be done to improve their life conditions and enhance their opportunities in an age of globalization? In recent years, much of the attention has focused on universal public education. In recent years, the government has made improvements in educational enrollment at both the primary and secondary levels through a combination of educational reforms. As a result, primary education enrollment rates have increased. However, what happens after primary school? As of 1999, Brazil had over 31 million people between the ages of 15–24. Combining the age range of adolescents and youth (ages 10–24), this cohort totals, numerically and proportionally, the largest youth population in the country's history and the largest "youth boom" that Brazil may ever face. The public secondary education infrastructure has not been able to offer spaces to the youth cohort. The primary education system has been able to offer nearly full coverage to the younger age cohort, in part because it is smaller. This current "youth boom" also represents a tremendous challenge for labor policy with unprecedented numbers of young people in the job market when employment in the formal sector has been decreasing.

But simply enrolling children in school, particularly in overcrowded classrooms with poorly paid and poorly trained teachers, is clearly insufficient. The public education system does not for the most part prepare children and youth to be citizens in a modern democracy. Some studies have also found that for many low-income children, while school continues to be valued, it is seen as irrelevant for their immediate needs and realities (CESPI/USU, 1998).

What alternatives then, are available? The technical solutions tried by the government, while important, have largely been limited in impact. The cornerstone of the government's child labor eradication program has been scholarships to low-income families, in the form of a monthly subsidy so that their children stay in school. In rural areas, public-private partnerships have started rural boarding schools providing schooling as well as skills in agro-business and agricultural production.

Thousands of governmental and non-governmental initiatives also seek to offer activities and vocational training for children and youth outside of school. A 1997 review of several major governmental youth initiatives found the following numbers of youth participating in these initiatives: 32,000 youth being reached in school-based substance abuse education; 160,000 youth participating in "official" technical training schools; 9,150 youth participating in governmental-sponsored literacy campaigns; 23,800 youth in 17 states participating in new government-sponsored vocational training programs; and 78,000 youth participating in government-funded community-based sports activities (Berquó, Camarano, Cannon, Castro, & Correa, 1997).

These initiatives have been important in assisting some low-income children, and in preparing some of them for an increasingly technologically-based labor market. However, these policies and programs do not address the underlying income inequalities in the country. The social organization of the economy and of households in Brazil is based on the widespread availability of cheap, unskilled labor, particularly low-paid domestic and service labor. While middle class families are able to support their children for years as they prepare themselves for a modernizing economy, the children of the poor continue to work at early ages with little questioning of this reality. Indeed, most middle class households depend on this low-paid labor to maintain their lifestyles. Until there is greater questioning of social inequities in Brazil, governmental solutions will only touch the surface of the problem.

The trends examined in this paper affect low-income children and youth and middle-income children and youth in very different ways. As Brazil's economy has stagnated in the last few years, and already precarious government services have been, the gap between poor and middle/upper class children has widened. Children and youth are also affected by the increasing participation of women in the workforce; the longer work day; and the heightened role of television and peers as socializing agents. And while violence disproportionately affects low-income children and youth in Brazil, the presence and fear of violence is often the chief worry of parents of all income groups in Brazil.

While we have often emphasized the problems and challenges that face Brazilian families, no progress has been made. In particular, the Children's Act has been a watershed of societal and judicial change, making children and youth subjects of rights rather than simply wards or dependents of the state. While much remains to be done to fully implement the statute, it provides an important tool for policymakers, researchers, and advocates. Furthermore, the civic and social groups that spearheaded the Children's Act continue to be powerful advocates for policies, legislation, local advocacy, and program development in favor of children.

The efforts to remove children from hazardous work and work in general in Brazil has been cited by UNICEF and the ILO as exemplary. Investments in the social area by the private sector, and the professionalization of a philanthropic sector, are also positive trends. The current administration has demonstrated concern for child well-being, through school reform measures, minimum wage programs for low-income families, and serious commitments and budgetary allocations in the area of child labor. A national initiative in the area of early childhood development is another positive sign of concern and incorporation at the national policy level of children's rights issues.

But if these trends are positive, much remains to be done. Income inequalities, school enrollment rates that are lower than many of its neighboring (and poorer) countries, and alarming levels of violence against children and youth (both in and outside the home) are jarring examples of promises unkept.

Other trends cited here represent major social transformations connected to global changes but with specific local manifestations. The impact of these changes on children and youth is still unclear, but previous systems of support for children (particularly the family and extended kinship networks) are under stress, and that traditional supports are changing. What will this mean in the long run for the daily lives of children and youth and for their futures? These fundamental questions remain for research, policy and program development. We need additional insights from families, children and youth themselves on what these trends mean for their lives and how they are coping now.

More research is needed in Brazil on a number of social issues—violence, racial segregation, education, social segregation—and their impact on generations of low-income children and youth. Very little attention is being paid to the apparently widening social division between middle and upper class children and those in the lower class. There is also a need for additional research on how families are coping with economic instability, and how they are finding ways to care for their children. There is also a need to integrate diverse research, disseminate research conclusions, and integrate research policy and program development.

There is also tremendous need to raise public awareness about globalization. The government as well as NGOs need to promote greater involvement and participation in improving the situation of families. They also need to work towards the creation of educated and empowered citizens who can make Brazil a truly modern democracy capable of enhancing the potential within the globalization challenge.

REFERENCES

Barker, G., Knaul, F. (1991). *Exploited entrepreneurs: street and working children in developing countries*. New York: Childhope/USA. Working paper No. 1.

Barker, G., Loewenstein, I. (1997). Where the boys are: Attitudes related to masculinity, fatherhood, and violence toward women among low-income adolescent and young adult males in Rio de Janeiro, Brazil. *Youth & Society,* 29/2, 166–196.

Bercovich, A., Dellasoppa, E., Arriaga, E. (1998) "J'adjuste, mais je ne corrige pas": Jovens, violência e demografia no Brasil. Algumas reflexões a partir dos indicadores de violência. In Comissão Nacional de População e Desenvolvimento (CNPD), Ed., *Jovens acontecendo na trilha das políticas públicas.* [Youth in the path of public policy]. Brasília: CNPD. 293–359.

Berquó, E., Camarano, A., Cannon, L., Castro, M. Correa, S. (1997). Os jovens no Brasil: Diagnostico nacional. *Reunião regional na America Latina sobre saude sexual e reprodutiva dos adolescentes,* Costa Rica, December 1997.

Brasil (1988). *Constituição do Brasil* Brasília: 8 de outubro.

Brasileiro elege social prioridade. (2001, September 16). *Jornal do Brasil.* Rio de Janeiro.

Bruce, J., Lloyd., C., Leonard, A., Engle, P. & Duffy, N. (1995). *Families in focus: New perspectives on mothers, fathers and children.* Population Council, New York.

CEAP—Center of Marginalized Populations (1993). Rio de Janeiro: CEAP.

CESPI/USU (Belem, R. et al.) (1998). Adolescentes em Conflito com a Lei: o caso do Rio de Janeiro. Relatório final de pesquisa. Rio de Janeiro: Coordenação de Estudos e Pesquisas sobre a Infância (CESPI/USU)/Juizado da Infância e Juventude—Núcleo de Psicologia.

Distribuição de renda piora. Dados do Informe Anual sobre o Progresso Econômico e Social (BID). (1998, November 16). *Jornal do Brasil.* Rio de Janeiro.

Engle, P. (1994). *Men in families: Report of a consultation on the role of males and fathers in achieving gender equality.* New York: UNICEF.

Folha de São Paulo (1998). *Raça* São Paulo: Datafolha, 16 November.

Furtado alerta para tensão social. (1999, September 9). *Jornal do Brasil.* Rio de Janeiro.

IBGE/PNAD (1995). National Household Survey.

IBGE (1996) [Brazilian Institute of Geographic and Statistics]. Mapa do mercado de trabalho no Brasil Rio de Janeiro: IBGE, n.1.

IBGE/UNICEF (1997). Indicadores sobre crianças e adolescentes: Brasil, 1991–96. Brasilia, Rio de Janeiro.

IBAM [Brazilian Institute for Municipal Administration] (1997/1998). Os Conselhos de Direitos da Criança e do Adolescente e os Conselhos Tutelares no Brasil: dados da pesquisa nacional. Rio de Janeiro: IBAM.

IBGE (2001). Síntese de indicadores sociais 2000. Rio de Janeiro: IBGE.

Pesquisa muda tese sobre meninos de rua (1995, May 17). *Jornal do Brasil.* Rio de Janeiro.

Klees, S., Rizzini, I., & Dewees, A. (1999). A new paradigm for social change: social movements and the transformation of policy for street and working children in Brazil. In R. Mickelson (Ed.), *Children on the streets of the Americas. Globalization, homelessness and education in Brazil, Cuba, and the United States.* London/New York: Routledge (forthcoming).

Miséria fotografada e cadastrada: meninos de rua do Rio ganham uma carteira de identificação do Juizado de menores. (1998, September 11). *O Globo,* Rio de Janeiro.

Neoliberalismo é criticado. (1999, September 12). *Jornal do Brasil.* Rio de Janeiro.

Pesquisa Nacional de Domicilios (1988). Vol. 12. Rio de Janeiro, Brazil: Instituto Brasileiro de Geografia e Estadisticas (IBGE).

Projeto Axé (1993). Meninos que vivem nas ruas de Salvador: mapeamento e contagem [Children living in the streets of Salvador: mapping and counting]. Slavador (mimeo).

Ribeiro, D. (1995). O povo brasileiro: A formação e o sentido do Brasil. São Paulo: Companhia das Letras.

Ribeiro, R.M., Sabóia, A.L. (1994). Children in Brazil: Legislation and citizenship. In I. Rizzini, (Ed.), *Children in Brazil today: A challenge for the third millennium.* Rio de Janeiro: Editora Universitária Santa Úrsula.

Rizzini, I. (1994). Children in the city of violence: The case of Brazil. In K. Rupesinghe & M. Rubio (Eds.), *The culture of violence* (257–291). New York: United Nations University Press.

Rizzini, I. (1997). *Philanthropy and repression: children in the construction of Brazil's national identity.* Trondheim: Urban Childhood Conference.

Rizzini, I. (1998). Poor children in Latin America: a case example of social inequality, ABA Center on Children & the Law. Loyola University Chicago School of Law: *Children's Legal Rights Journal*, Vol 18, Number 1, winter.

Rizzini, I., Rizzini, I., & Borges, F.R. (1998). Children's strength is not in their work. In C. Salazar & W.A. Glasinovich (Eds.), *Child work and education: five cases in Latin America*. Brookfield, Florence: Ashgate, UNICEF.

Rizzini, I., Barker, G., & Cassaniga, N. (1998). From street children to all children: improving the opportunities of low income urban children and youth in Brazil. Youth in Cities: Successful mediators of Normative Development. The Johann Jacobs Foundation Conference, Germany.

Rizzini, I., Barker, G. et al. (2001). Children, youth and their developmental supports. Strengthening family and community supports for children and youth in Rio de Janeiro. Rio de Janeiro: CESPI/USU/Instituto Promundo.

Ruzany, M. Peres et al. (1996). Urban violence and social participation: A profile of adolescents in Rio de Janeiro. Rio de Janeiro: Adolescent Health Unit, State University of Rio de Janeiro. [Draft study report; unpublished.]

Sabóia, A.L. (1998). Situação educacional dos jovens. In Comissão Nacional de População e Desenvolvimento (CNPD), Ed., Jovens acontecendo na trilha das políticas públicas. Brasília: CNPD. 507–517.

Sabóia, J. (1996). Trabalho infanto-juvenil no Brasil dos anos 90. Brasilia: UNICEF. Cadernos de Políticas Sociais, n. 3.

Schilling, P.R. (1994). Brasil: a pior distribuição de renda do planeta—os excluídos. São Paulo: CEDI/Koinonia.

Secretaria de Ação Social (1994). Report on census of street and working children. Fortaleza/Ceará: Secretaria Estadual de Ação Social (State Social Action Secretary].

Szwarcwald, C. & Leal, M. (1998). Sobrevivência ameaçada dos jovens brasileiros: A dimensão da mortalidade por armas de fogo. In Comissão Nacional de População e Desenvolvimento (CNPD), Ed., Jovens acontecendo na trilha das políticas públicas. Brasília: CNPD. 363–384.

Yunes, J., & Rajs, D. (1994). Tendencia de la mortalidad por causas violentas en la poblacion general y entre los adolescentes y jovenes en la region de las Americas. Caderno de Saúde Publica, Rio de Janeiro 10(Supl. 1). 88–125.

World Bank (1997). *World Development Report 1997: The state of a changing world*. New York: Oxford University Press.

CHAPTER 12

The Effects of Structural Adjustment Programs on the Lives of Children in Jamaica

SIAN WILLIAMS

Children are amongst those who have been structurally adjusted. The losers were clear. They were seen in the increased numbers of homeless and mentally ill searching routinely through the garbage containers, they were absorbed among the numbers of youth recruited into criminal posses, they were included among the fixed income pensioners whose private poverty could not be relieved by food stamps, and they were numbered among those who stood grimly in visa lines. (Anderson & Witter, 1991)

The Jamaican government secured "structural adjustment" loans (SALs I-III) from the World Bank between 1982 and 1985. However, the term structural adjustment came to be used to refer to the set of policy conditions imposed by lending agencies (The International Money Fund (IMF), World Bank, U.S. Agency for International Development (USAID)) as conditions for balance of payment support from 1977 onwards, and to their consequences until 1995, when Jamaica withdrew from the IMF. Whether the SAL enterprise was conceptualized as a continuation of colonial/imperialistic goals pursued by countries to extract resources from Jamaica and retain control or as a necessary process which unfortunately had negative side effects for vulnerable groups, isolating the impact of SALs from the effects of government policies and other internal factors, or from the world recession which started in the mid 1970s after the oil crisis has been very difficult (Williams, 1994).

During the 1980s, government expenditure on social welfare declined and no safety net was or has been established for the very poor. By 1999, public finance had become severely constrained as debt servicing accounted for over 60% of total public expenditure.

Jamaica is a country of 2.6 million people. The wealthiest fifth of its citizens consume seven times as much as its poorest (Government of Jamaica/ UNICEF, 1995a). Twenty percent of households across the country, or one family in five, fall below the poverty line. Urbanization and emigration have had profound effects on families. Half of the country's resident population lives in the metropolitan Kingston area, but at least twice the total resident population live in foreign states. Longstanding networks of rural extended family supports have been drastically stretched, stressed, or broken. "Barrel children" (children dependent on income from one or both parents abroad) have become a new constituency of children in need (Brown, 1997).

Thirty-seven percent of the population are estimated to be children under the age of 18 and 50% are under 25 years old (Planning Institute of Jamaica, 1996). This chapter explores the transformation in their living conditions and outlooks.

LOSS OF FAMILY INCOME, LOSS IN PROVISION OF PUBLIC SOCIAL SERVICES

> To the living standards of those whose only income is labour income, the devastation of public social services was probably as detrimental as the decline in real wages. The recovery and maintenance of those services are the single most important short run measure to ameliorate their living standard. (King, 1993)

Jamaica is accumulating a huge social debt to the people affected by over twenty years of SALs related policy, debt measured by the amount of resources that would now be required to overcome poverty and the unequal impact of adjustment. This debt is owed to "the lower income groups who have borne the brunt of the adjustment through informalisation of work, the increase in unemployment and underemployment, the development and expansion of criminal underground economy, the spread of poverty" (Henry, 1993). Recent escalation of economic crisis, in the financial sector in particular, has provoked the private sector to denounce the government's macro economic policies which have hitherto protected them. This criticism has elicited a sharp response from the Minister for Finance, asking the private sector to carry their share. The fostering of private sector growth in bauxite, tourism, manufacturing, and in service industries negatively affected the very poor, working poor, and small businesses. These trends increase the harm: (1) the development of growth "enclaves" which demanded skills not present in the urban working class; (2) the acceleration of rural urban drift; and (3) the reduction in education spending and the introduction of "cost sharing" with parents of children in secondary education, making it difficult for parents to keep their children enrolled in schools, colleges, or vocational training for their periods of entitlement.

The crisis that affects education starkly reflects the loss of a public service to the poor (World Bank, 1999). Because of the past legacy of an elitist education system, public resources have not been allocated equitably. There are higher levels of spending in secondary high schools attended by high achieving students (the great majority of whom are in the upper consumption quintiles of the population), a relatively limited supply of places in Grades 10 and 11 which restricts access of the poor to upper secondary education, and a high level of public spending on tertiary education (relative to its low enrollment and low participation by the poor in tertiary education). In a context of dwindling resources to the education sector as a whole, a marked disparity exists in the resource levels of the secondary high school and the all age schools for the poor—seven times the per capita grant. Moving quality education, not only beyond the reach of the poor but also of those who are in a position to pay for it, reflects a growing crisis in education. For the rich, the developing private sector provision of "extra lessons" lengthens the school day for students at both primary and secondary levels, and goes some way to providing coverage of the curriculum; but for the poor, the short school day (less than 5 hours of teaching contact time) and the short school year disadvantage children from the outset. Total household expenditure on education accounted for 6% of GDP in 1998, an extremely high level of spending in comparison with other countries in the region (between 2% and 3% on average elsewhere). However, for the poorest quintile of the population, total household expenditure on education accounted for 17%. Undeniably, the private cost of education (lunch, books, transportation, uniforms, shoes) falls disproportionately on the poor. These figures for both richest and poorest quintiles in the population also reflect the very high value Jamaicans attach to education, and the willingness to pay for quality improvements if they could save on paying for extra lessons. The inability of the poor to pay the direct cost of schooling has been cited as a major reason for the higher non-attendance and dropout rates, as well as lower educational attainment among the poor.

INTERGENERATIONAL POVERTY, IMPACT ON CHILDREN

Since 1977, Jamaica has failed to sustain priority attention to break the intergenerational reproduction of poverty and social dislocation, passed down from parents to children. The efforts to create children's policy in Jamaica have provided a framework for sustaining priority attention; however, policy is developed separate from the critical understanding needed of the difficult relationship between the necessary conditions for the productive transformation of Jamaica, and the necessary conditions for human development.

> Many of the social problems in Jamaica are preventable and rooted in the neglect of children, starting during the earliest years of their life. The causes of poverty can be traced back to a mix of sociological, economic and political factors operating at the macro level which impact negatively on children's development, but it is the dynamics of these disruptive processes and how they handicap children and their families which need to be analysed and understood, for effective planning and action for human development. (Newman, Williams, & Sabatini, 1995)

In 1995, UNICEF developed a global model (adapted from "Adjustment with a Human Face" UNICEF, 1987) encompassing the more recently advanced principles of "Development with a Human Face". The model distinguishes between the social "flow variables" which respond quickly to changes in economic conditions (household cash income, government policies affecting expenditure and distribution and relative prices of goods, parents' time for childcare and child education) and the social "stock variables" which respond very slowly (household assets, values, attitudes and practices at community and household level, parenting skill and parents' education).

> This capital stock can actually cushion the effect of short-term recessions, but it does respond to prolonged economic crises, and has tremendous long-lasting implications for social and economic development. Social outcome indicators are evident in Jamaica: functional illiteracy, lack of socialisation and self esteem, lack of life skills and productive skills in youth, migration and brain drain. The ultimate manifestation of the damages done by persistent economic crises is the observed deterioration of the social capital, as shown by the disintegration of solidarity within society, disruption of social cohesion and general insecurity. The consequence is a reduced financial, physical and human capital available for economic growth. (Newman, Williams, & Sabatini, 1995)

Among the population as a whole, fewer children failed to thrive (using indicators of nutrition and health status); for the poorest children, rates of malnutrition, low weight, stunting and abuse have doubled. The UNICEF/ Government of Jamaica (GOJ) Country Programme (1997–2001) found that four out of every ten children under the age of 14 years living in extreme poverty in a population where 40% are under 14 years of age.

Performance and attainment at pre primary, primary, and secondary levels, and in access to training, vocational and micro enterprise possibilities reflect the economic fragility of the lives of the very poor in Jamaica. Despite widespread pre schooling (85% of children 3–6 years), about 20% of children in the first (poorest) quintile, and 14% in the second quintile do not have access compared to only 9% in the fifth (richest) quintile (World Bank, 1999). Quality of provisions in the community based basic schools is generally poor, and benefits of attendance appear to be greater in social rather than in emotional or cognitive development (Adams, 1994). At the primary level, despite high enrollment, attendance rates are estimated at 70% and are lowest in all age schools (for the least advantaged in the population), among those in the two poorest quintiles, among boys, and in rural areas. One third of students throughout the primary cycle need help with reading; the assumption appears to be that children on entry to primary schooling can make a smooth transition from patois to standard English. However, without special attention to listening and reading comprehension at early childhood and primary levels, standard English remains broadly inaccessible (Miller & Evans, 1997b). In the all age schools, 48% of students in grade 6 were revealed as functionally illiterate (defined as not reading with comprehension at a fourth grade level) and by grade 9, half of those attending still had not acquired functional literacy or numeracy. Half the children in the first quintile drop out after grade 9 in comparison with 71% of children in the fifth quintile who go on to complete grade 11 (World Bank, 1994). Indicators on educational attainment and quality clearly show that educational opportunity is not equal for the rich and for the poor. As education imparts productivity-enhancing skills and has a positive relationship with future lifetime earnings, the lower level of educational attainment and achievement among the poor is putting then in a seriously disadvantaged position for life.

Jamaica has had relative success in meeting survival goals, but sustaining these goals and addressing the problems in relation to protecting and promoting the interests of children remain a real challenge. UNICEF has identified the need to target geographic areas for poverty reduction and to provide support to communities which have a convergence of high rates of malnutrition, high infant mortality, poor water supply and sanitation, poor educational opportunities, and a large proportion of households below the poverty line.

FAMILY LIFE, GENDER ROLES, AND SURVIVAL STRATEGIES

Family structure in Jamaica is distinguished by the practice of mating outside conjugal unions, so children are born into a variety of family types and domestic situations. Children may move through several living arrangements, including resident-mother and visiting-father, common law union or a legal marriage, or find his or her situation "redefined to that of step-child in a household where the mother or father has a new resident partner. In other cases, the children of earlier unions may be shifted to live with grandmothers or other relatives" (GOJ/UNICEF, 1995a). However, the potentially disruptive effects of these changes can be counterbalanced by close association with a wider kin network, which can provide community for the child and assists with identity development and sense of self. However, this network can also open the door to exploitative relationships.

Child shifting is a particular phenomenon of poor families; children are often shifted to live with a grandmother or other relatives in order to avoid the stresses of a new step parenting relationship, to reduce the burdens of child care for single mothers, to facilitate migration, or to provide companionship or household labor for an older relative. As a child grows older the possibility of separation from both natural parents increases considerably. Fewer than 10% of children under three years live away from both natural parents, whereas almost one quarter of children 12–14 years fall into this category (GOJ/UNICEF, 1995b).

Research into gender socialization in low income communities in Jamaica reveals a growing pattern of female headed households (48% of households), and a growing number of children who make their living on the streets. These patterns differ from those in the wider region: female headship accounts for approximately 30% of households in North America and 15% in Latin America (20% in Brazil); at 48%, Jamaica has one of the highest incidences in the world. Children from female headed households are of policy concern in Jamaica because of the high incidence and the perceived vulnerability of households headed by women. However, research has shown that these children are no worse off than their counterparts in male headed households, both because of the expenditure behaviour of female headed households and because of the differential use of health care inputs (Handa, 1995). Children who work (approximately 4.6% of children between the ages of 6 and 16) are not typically abandoned or homeless. Unlike the pattern in Latin American, in

Jamaica, the children work to increase family income, the school system having failed to provide them with outcomes or routes which would improve their earning possibilities were they to complete the course of their educational entitlement.

> Child participation in paid work is visibly on the rise. The informal sector is currently the fastest growing area of child labour. This is largely because of the rapid growth of the informal sector which has spawned a number of enterprises that are unregistered and unfettered by regulations that govern working conditions in the formal sector. Children who work as household servants might be the most exploited children of all and the most difficult to protect. (Handa, 1995)

Traditional patterns of gender distinctions central to child rearing have been affected by forces in the wider economic and social spheres (Brown & Chevannes, 1995). These traditional patterns include preferences at birth, division of domestic chores, types of sanctioned leisure activities, preferred social values and skills, discipline practices and the exhibition of affection, emotion, and preparation for sexuality. The patterns are revealed in the protection of daughters for as long as possible from early sexuality and resulting pregnancy and the encouragement of boys to become independent and to acquire skills for economic survival. In the face of increased hardships and survival imperatives, these patterns have led to double standards for boys and girls: boys leave school younger and learn to survive on the street, bringing home what they can (and however they can) in terms of goods and income. Girls are expected to stay in or near home, learning survival skills under the supervision of women in their yard, and continue to go to school as an extension of the yard, as their education is seen as assisting later independence and delaying childbearing for as long as possible.

Greater economic marginalization is now shaping gender expectations: boys start out in grade one behind girls, and by secondary school, they are outnumbered by girls as formal education abandons those who are poor and provides no guarantee of upward mobility. This trend is less a result of intrinsic male demoralization and demotivation and more a result of the greater (or only) earning opportunities in informal and illicit sectors and the seeming potential for faster upward mobility. However, young males have become a high risk group in the society, facing high prospects of social immobility and poverty in the immediate future (Planning Institute of Jamaica, 1997).

Such contradictions and confusions are shaping children's lives. The traditional patterns have been undermined by economic forces in society and by parents' helplessness in face of the erosion of their authority. In a study of urban poverty and violence (Masser & Holland, 1995), Jamaica's murder rate was the highest in the region over the last two years. Members of warring communities prioritised community based activities with a particular emphasis on youth activities as the route to peace. Safe centers in which families could seek help to reduce violence and build interpersonal communication were identified as important initiatives. Of particular concern was the physical abuse of children, perceived to be widespread and a part of everyday life. The second priority was the provision of work and training opportunities. The survival strategies identified revealed a priority for the kind of projects, initiatives, and programs which build, or rather rebuild, social capital as an essential first step towards economic regeneration.

ALTERNATIVE SOCIETIES, CULTURAL NEEDS

Urban communities, in particular the politically controlled "garrison" communities, are moving beyond the reach of government policies, programs and initiatives, and children inevitably have become members of an alternative society in which the "Don" provides support for school fees and books, and welfare assistance to those greatest in need. Dons are perceived as providing strong leadership within communities, ensuring stability and paternalistically distributing jobs and money, as well as providing protection. Some are political party activists, others have created their own wealth and patronage base, often with drugs, working for politicians during election periods.

The failure of the government to articulate the interests of the poor, and to shape pro poor investment strategies to make them accessible to community groups, is resulting increasingly in marooned communities in urban garrisons and rural outposts. The impact of economic harshness on the culture can be felt in the music, the lifestyles, the "otherness" of values, attitudes, and social expectations that are developing away from the mainstream of society. For all community members including children, mobility has become restricted; child to child interactions are frequently constrained within the cramped conditions of the yard while overcrowding, with its early exposure of children to adult sex, can increase the incidence of teenage pregnancy.

In many areas dance halls, youth clubs, and sports facilities no longer function because of the levels of violence. Youth clubs are perceived as places in which peace and harmony can be built through learning self expression, meeting and socialising without arguments, staying off the streets, getting help with school work and developing an alternative vision. By comparison, the lack of youth facilities is perceived as depriving youth of developing a vision of how their lives might be, keeping them on the streets and exposed to trouble, encouraging them to carry weapons because of the likelihood of trouble and of meeting other youth "in war."

GLOBALIZATION AND THE DRAW OF NORTH AMERICA

Jamaica is now flooded with North American television, partly through cable and partly through the purchase of U.S. programs by the two local television stations. Tastes, fashions, and lifestyles from North America are given little resistance by the local media. Passion for basketball is replacing cricket and becoming, next to football, the sport for young, poor males; Kobe Bryant and Tim Duncan are more their idols than Courtney Walsh and Jimmy Adams. The look of a sophisticated African American takes precedence over images of black independence, resilience and self determination in Africa. The look is MTV and BET, not Nelson Mandela. Migration to England and low level employment was once the escape route from poverty; that access gone, the visa lines for the U.S. continue to grow.

EMERGENCE OF A CHILD RIGHTS AGENDA

In October 1996 Jamaica and sixteen other countries in the Caribbean region signed the Commitment to Action to improve national capacities to meet obligations to children, an outcome of the Caribbean Conference on the Rights of the Child. Six months later, the Kingston Accord committed governments across the region to specific strategies for implementation, and the Bridgetown Accord committed them specifically to the Plan of Action for Early Childhood Education, Care and Development in the Caribbean.

These initiatives were supported by UNICEF and were underpinned by CARICOM that secured timescales for implementation as part of a six year Human Resource Development Strategy, 1997–2003. The English speaking Caribbean countries share legislative and political characteristics, and while moves towards federation had a difficult and turbulent history, moves towards greater cooperation in trade and human resource development have been more successful. The development of children's policy and the political structures which have been established for implementation reflect UNICEF's priorities within Jamaica, within the wider Caribbean, and within the Latin American region as a whole.

The Belize CRC Conference recognized that national legislative reform is both a lengthy and costly exercise, and therefore recommended regional collaboration (Williams, 1997) in areas of research and drafting of legislation (all participating countries having evolved Westminster style democracies). Increasing regional collaboration would also involve learning from current national activities that could inform other countries' initiatives. A few such examples include: (1) defining child legal status (Montserrat, Dominica, Guyana, Turks, and Caicos); (2) licensing and standards for child care facilities (St. Lucia, Jamaica, Trinidad, and Tobago); (3) defining parent and state responsibilities for children (Trinidad and Tobago); and (4) developing national policy development/advocacy groups with all social partners (Jamaica, Belize, Trinidad and Tobago, Montserrat).

Ratification of the Convention on the Rights of the Child in Jamaica, and submission of both governmental (1993) and non governmental (1994) reports, have paved the way for the National Policy on Children: "We must care and guide them." The subtitle illustrates the emphasis on survival and protection. The Policy envisages a strengthening of partnerships with a well established church and NGO presence in services for the protection of children within a framework for continuing collaboration. Programmes for Children and Youth at Risk, and Decentralised Community Development for Children, are trying to make specific linkages with poverty alleviation programs in selected geographical areas of the country.

In the last twelve months, the ratification of Convention 182 concerning the prohibition and immediate action for the elimination of the worst forms of child labor (International Labour Organisation, 1999) has strengthened the protection agenda. By far the greatest impetus to the re-formulation of "care" and "protection" into a rights agenda was provided by the publication of the devastating second report of Human Rights Watch into the conditions in which children are held in police lock ups in spite of Jamaican laws which forbid such treatment. Some of the children (numbering just over 100 in total) had not been detained on suspicion of criminal activity but because they were deemed to be "in need of care and protection." Children are not let out of cells, have no education or exercise periods, no access to medical care or legal advice, and are at risk of adult victimisation. Reports of beatings, rapes and stabbings by older prisoners, and in one case rape by a police officer, were documented in full. No real progress had been made by the Jamaican government to improve conditions between the first report in 1994 and the second in 1999. The report on the incidence of sexual exploitation of children, and particularly commercial sexual exploitation, published later in the year and followed by a national consultation process in February 2000, served to increase the urgency for government direction in policy and legislation (Human Rights Watch, 1999).

In recent consultations in May 2000 on the draft Child Care and Protection Bill (1999), agencies involved in child protection and the promotion of child well being were united in their insistence that the proposed legislation should specifically address the CRC not only in the preamble to the draft Act but also in the way in which each section of the Act is drafted.

In order to strengthen national capacity in planning for children, the government has reorganised Children's Services into an executive agency, more able to function effectively and promptly on matters of child protection. The government is also undertaking a strategic review of the management of early childhood services to develop a regulatory system for what is primarily a private sector, community based activity. These are encouraging indications that policy and services for children are to be given higher profile. The organizational improvements will strengthen the capacity to make links between children's interests and those of the government's general policies and provisions, such as health care, maternity leave provisions, employment policies for fathers and mothers, housing development policies, Education for All, transportation policy and provision, poverty eradication/job creation programmes, environmental safety and sanitation requirements. Quality provisions, particularly in contexts of poverty, cannot be sustained without these policies of convergence aimed at strengthening whole communities.

REFERENCES

Adam, S. (1994). *Public Sector Expenditure Review and Examination of Ministry/Statutory Body Relationships, Education Sector*. World Bank, Kingston, Jamaica.

Anderson, P. & Witter, M. (1991). The distribution of the social cost of Jamaica's structural adjustment 1977–1989 (unpublished), University of the West Indies, Mona, Kingston.

Brown, J. (1997). *Fundamental change affecting children*, presentation, Chapin Hall for Children, Chicago, USA, November.

Brown, J. & Chevannes, B. (1995). *Gender Socialisation in the Caribbean*, Caribbean Child Development Centre with the Faculty of Social Sciences, UWI, Mona, Jamaica.

Government of Jamaica/UNICEF (1995a). *Situation Analysis of Children and Women in Jamaica*, Kingston, Jamaica.

Government of Jamaica/UNICEF (1995b). *Five Year National Plan of Action for the Survival, Protection and Development of Children 1996–2000*, Kingston, Jamaica.

Handa, S. (1995). Expenditure behaviour and children's welfare: An analysis of female headed households in Jamaica. *Journal of Development Economics, 50*, 165–187.

Henry, R. (1993). quoted in *UNECLAC—Achieving Social Justice, Equity and Development: A Review of the Status of Women of the Caribbean Subregion in Preparation for the Fourth World Conference on Women, 1995. Submitted to the Sixth Conference on the Integration of Women in Economic and Social Development of Latin America and the Caribbean*, Mar del plata, Argentina, September 25–29.

Human Rights Watch (1999). *Nobody's Children: Jamaican children in police detention and government institutions*, New York.

King, D. (1993). *Structural adjustment and the labour market in Jamaica*, Department of Economics, UWI, Mona, Jamaica.

Miller, E. & Evans, D. (1997b). *Concept paper: Correcting Underachievement and Reclaiming Excellence* (CURE), USAID Project, Mona, Jamaica: Education Research Centre, School of Education, University of the West Indies.

Moser, C. & Holland, J. (1995). *Urban poverty and violence in Jamaica*, Urban Development Division, World Bank.

Newman-Williams, M. & Sabatini, F. (1995). *The economics of child poverty in Jamaica*, UNICEF, Caribbean Area Office (CAO), Barbados Planning Institute of Jamaica (1996) Survey of Living Conditions, Kingston, Jamaica.

Planning Institute of Jamaica (1998). *Survey of Living Conditions*, Kingston, Jamaica.

Planning Institute of Jamaica/Statistical Institute of Jamaica (1997). *Jamaica Survey of Living Conditions, Report 1996*, PIOJ/STATIN, Kingston, Jamaica.

Williams, L. (1994). *Structural adjustment: Its implications for youth in Jamaica* (unpublished) School of Continuing Studies, UWI, Mona, Jamaica.

Williams, S. (1997). *From Belize to Barbados: Affording children their rights from birth. A regional assessment of early childhood policy and provisions in the Caribbean*, UNICEF CAO, Barbados.

Williams, S. (1999). *Sexual violence and exploitation of children in Latin America and the Caribbean: The Case of Jamaica*. Report prepared for the Inter American Children's Institute, Montevideo, Uruguay, Caribbean Child Development Centre, University of the West Indies, Mona, Kingston, Jamaica.

World Bank (1994). *Jamaica. A Strategy for Growth and Poverty Reduction, Country Economic Memorandum*. Washington: World Bank.

World Bank (1999). *Jamaica Secondary Education: Improving Quality and Extending Access*, Human Development Department, Caribbean Country Management Unit, Latin America and Caribbean Region, Washington D.C.

PART IV

Conclusions

Conclusions

NATALIE HEVENER KAUFMAN AND IRENE RIZZINI

As we begin this new century we are aware of political, social, and economic transformations that affect children's present and future, but the complexity and speed of these changes often elude our full comprehension. While many children benefit tremendously from technological and material progress, others suffer from increasing social and economic inequality.

On the positive side we have seen an increase in democratization, and at least initial steps, in many countries towards acceptance of the values of equality and basic human dignity. At the global level, a large number of treaties, UN resolutions, and declarations from international conferences reflect an emerging consensus on shared norms of human rights and specifically children's rights. The increased level of global consensus on children's rights, as reflected in the Convention on the Rights of the Child (CRC), has great potential for supporting the work of child advocates, including children and youth themselves. The CRC lays out clear state and local responsibilities for respecting the rights of the child and advancing child well-being. The Committee on the Rights of the Child, especially through its monitoring of state efforts to implement the CRC, can play an important role in stimulating domestic debate and fostering domestic as well as international work on behalf of children and youth.

Also on the positive side, technological and economic changes have led to the possibility of raising standards of living throughout the world. Yet as the economic condition of many families improves, the gap between the poor and well-off continues to grow both within and among countries. Economic changes often have complex effects. Transformations in global trade and financial activity have created, for example, a large new middle class in parts of India giving many more children, as they grow up, the chance for middle class jobs. Yet the majority of children in India face lives of poverty and in some countries very few families have access to the most rewarding parts of the global economy. It is hard to imagine how some countries, for example those in sub-Saharan Africa, will even begin the process of developing advanced economies. Rural–urban migrations continue apace in many countries, and while migration gives some parents new economic opportunities, it often places their children in massive slums where their basic health and safety are at daily risk.

While we see that many changes hold the potential for improving children's lives, we are often confounded by the obstacles preventing the fulfillment of that potential. In this volume we have raised questions about how these rapid global transformations affect children and what might be done to increase the likelihood that such changes will enhance their lives.

Of particular concern to the authors is the absence of children from the discussion of these issues. Children have not been included in descriptions of the effects of globalization, and children do not participate in the debates over preferred options for the future.

We want to bring children to our discussions not as passive victims, or simply as future adults, although understandings from these perspectives are necessary. We want to describe children primarily in their everyday lives, and to include in those descriptions children's view of their experiences. We also want to honor the diversity of children's experiences and to respect the wide variety of cultural values that affect how children are raised and how they experience their world. The rapid sharing of information across national borders and among divergent cultures may promote increased understanding and respect, but we need to remain sensitive to justifiable concerns about cultural imperialism.

We have learned that the transformations we have been studying massively affect children in key areas of their lives. The changes affect their parents' economic status and will affect the children's chances in job markets that demand new skills even for some low-paying jobs. The changes create fresh waves of migration sometimes of whole families, sometimes of fathers or mothers separately, as they seek employment far away from their children. While some migrations are by choice, some are forced by war and violence, leaving children not in a new country with new opportunities but in refugee camps or as nomads in dangerous war zones. In the cultural sphere, even children who stay at home are exposed via the Internet to influences from all over the world. These influences confront them with both the opportunities and the challenges of new ways of thinking about many aspects of themselves and the world they inhabit. In the political sphere, some countries are experiencing a greater transparency that includes more information about the condition of children, a change that may result in either cosmetic or substantive improvements in children's well-being.

As researchers who want both to describe the conditions of children and who wish to wrestle with ways to improve children's lives, we have been confronted with some basic questions that will continue to shape our work. How do we capture the changing complexity of the lives of different children in different places? How wide is the gap that separates good intentions as exemplified in national and international codes on children's safety, health, education, and basic economic condition and the reality of the lives children actually experience? How do these good intentions get translated into real change? How can the most vulnerable children get minimal protections in the face of political instability and violence? How can more children who grow up on "the wrong side of the tracks," especially in the vast urban slums of the world's largest cities be helped to participate in the economic mainstream? And finally, how in the light of the answers to these questions and the triumph in many people's minds of unregulated capitalism, can "the democratic will...be asserted over business and private power" (Giddens & Hutton, 2000, p. 50) to provide children with the childhoods that will prepare them for decent futures?

We conclude by restating our conviction about the importance of bringing children into these debates. It is easy to ignore those who are without power and legitimized voice. Yet when we do so we risk much. Thinking about how children are affected by massive changes in their societies focuses our attention on a key part of the human reality of those changes and gives us indications of how those changes will shape the rising generation. Those insights should be informed by the views of children and their parents. Listening to our children and respecting their views, considering their well being in the development of our policies and programs, is part of the obligation we accept in recognizing the dignity of the child. These essays present a new direction for the investigation of the enormous social, political, and economic changes that are taking place globally and locally, and offer researchers and policy makers possibilities for enhancing the potential for positive change in children's everyday lives.

REFERENCE

Giddens, A. & Hutton, W. (2000). In conversation. In W. Hutton & A. Gidding (Eds.) *Global capitalism*. New York: The New Press, p. 50.

Index